The Deeds of God through the Franks

A TRANSLATION OF GUIBERT DE NOGENT'S

Gesta Dei per Francos

Guibert of Nogent's account of the First Crusade is an important but difficult chronicle which will be welcomed in this first English translation. It is a valuable addition to Boydell & Brewer's repertoire of crusading material, and is an interesting text because it represents an attempt to produce a critical history from the eyewitness sources, the *Deeds of the Franks* and Fulker of Chartres' *History of the Expedition to Jerusalem*. In the process, it reveals considerable detail on Western attitudes to the First Crusade, and, through Guibert's own bias, on medieval *mentalités* in general.

In this translation, Professor Levine has rendered the difficult and idiosyncratic Latin prose and verse into idiomatic English prose, while preserving as far as possible the construction favoured by Guibert. In addition, he provides a brief introduction containing biographical and bibliographical information, as well as a summary of the translation.

Professor ROBERT LEVINE teaches in the Department of English, Boston University.

The Deeds of God
through the Franks

A TRANSLATION OF GUIBERT DE NOGENT'S

Gesta Dei per Francos

ROBERT LEVINE

THE BOYDELL PRESS

First published 1997
The Boydell Press, Woodbridge

Transferred to digital printing

ISBN 978-0-85115-693-4

The Boydell Press is an imprint of Boydell & Brewer Ltd
PO Box 9, Woodbridge, Suffolk IP12 3DF, UK
and of Boydell & Brewer Inc.
668 Mt Hope Avenue, Rochester, NY 14620, USA
website: www.boydellandbrewer.com

A CiP catalogue record for this book is available
from the British Library

This publication is printed on acid-free paper

CONTENTS

INTRODUCTION

The four-year period (1095–1099) between the call for a crusade by Pope Urban II at the Council of Claremont and the capture of Jerusalem produced a remarkable amount of historiography, both in Western Europe and in Asia Minor. Three accounts by western European eye-witnesses – an anonymous soldier or priest in Bohemund's army, Fulker of Chartres, and Raymond of Aguilers – provoked later twelfth-century Latin writers from various parts of what are now France, Germany, England, Italy, and the Near East, to take up the task of providing more accurate, more thorough, more interpretive, and better written versions of the events.

Very little is known about most of the earliest rewriters; Albert of Aix, Robert the Monk, and Raoul of Caen are little more than names, while Baldric of Dole is known to have occupied a significant ecclesiastical position, and to have composed other literary works. Guibert of Nogent, on the other hand, is better known than any other historian of the First Crusade, in spite of the fact that *The Deeds of God Through the Franks*, composed in the first decade of the twelfth century (1106–1109), did not circulate widely in the middle ages, and no writer of his own time mentions him. Guibert himself, in the course of the autobiographical work he composed in the second decade of the twelfth century (1114–1117), never mentions the *Deeds*, and it has never been translated into English.[1] What measure of fame he currently has is based mostly on his autobiography, the *Monodiae*, or *Memoirs*, an apparently more personal document, which has been translated into both French and English.[2]

---

[1] A translation into French was done more than 170 years ago by F. Guizot, in vol. 9 of his *Collection des mémoires relatifs à l'histoire de France*, Paris, 1825.

[2] John Benton, *Self and Society in Medieval France*, New York, 1970; Guibert de Nogent, *Autobiographie*, edited and translated by Edmond-René Labande, Paris, 1981; Paul J. Archambault, *A Monk's Confessions*, University Park, 1995. The *Monodiae*, however, was also not popular in its own time. No medieval writer mentions the work, and no manuscript has survived. See Labande's edition, pp. xxiii–xxviii, for a discussion of the editorial problems that stem from being compelled to work from BN f.l. Baluze 42. For recent discussion of Guibert, see M.D. Coupe, "The personality of Guibert de Nogent reconsidered," *Journal of Medieval History* IX, no. 4 (Dec. 1983), pp. 317–329, which supplies a summary and judgement of the work of J. Kantor, Benton, and others. See also Jacques Charaud, "La conception de l'histoire de Guibert de Nogent," *Cahiers de civilisation médiévale* VIII (1965), pp. 381–395, and Klaus Schreiner, "Discrimen veri ac falsi," *Archive für Kulturgeschichte* XLVIII (1966), pp. 1–51. Both Charaud and Schreiner are concerned to demonstrate the degree to which Guibert's vision of history is ruled by theology, and tropology in particular; both articles can be read as respectful corrections of Bernard Monod, "De la méthode historique chez Guibert de Nogent," *Revue historique* 84 (1904), pp. 51–70. Unfortunately, Laetitia Boehm's thesis, "Studien zur Geschichtsschreibung des ersten

1

Although the *Memoirs* contain a strong historical component – the third book, in particular, if used with discretion, offers rich material for a study of the civil disorder that took place in Laon between 1112 and 1114 – the first book has attracted the attention of most recent scholars and critics because it offers more autobiographical elements. However, Guibert did not include among those elements the exact date and place of his birth.[3] Scholarly discussion has narrowed the possible dates to 1053–1065, although the latest editor of the *Memoirs*, Edmonde Labande, categorically chooses 1055. Among the candidates for his birthplace are Clermont-en-Beauvaisis, Agnetz, Catenoy, Bourgin, and Autreville, all within a short distance of Beauvais. No record of his death, generally assumed to have occurred by 1125, has survived.

In spite of the lack of exactitude about places and dates, the *Memoirs* provide an extensive account of some of the ways religious, psychological, and spiritual problems combined in the mind of an aristocratic oblate, who became an aggressive Benedictine monk, fervently attached to his pious mother, fascinated and horrified by sexuality, enraged at the extent of contemporary ecclesiastical corruption, intensely alert to possible heresies, and generally impatient with all opinions not his own.[4] The personality that dominates the *Monodiae* had already permeated the earlier, historical text. As cantankerous as Carlyle, Guibert reveals in the *Deeds* the same qualities that Jonathan Kantor detected in the *Memoirs*:

> The tone of the memoirs is consistently condemning and not confiding; they were written not by one searching for the true faith but by one determined to condemn the faithless.[5]

Such a tone is clearly reflected in the *Deeds*, whose very title is designed to correct the title of the anonymous *Gesta Francorum*, generally considered to be the earliest chronicle, and possibly eye-witness account (in spite of the evidence that a "monkish scribe" had a hand in producing the text), of the First Crusade.[6] Throughout his rewriting (for the most part, amplifying) of the *Gesta Francorum*, Guibert insists upon the providential nature of the accomplishment; by replacing the genitive plural of Franks with the genitive singular of God, Guibert lays the

---

Kreuzzuges Guibert von Nogent", Munich, 1954, has remained unpublished. Georg Misch also makes an attempt to characterize Guibert, for the most part on the basis of Book One of the *Monodiae*, in *Geschichte der Autobiographie*, vol. 3, part two, first half, Frankfurt, 1959, pp. 108–162

3 Early in the *Memoirs* Guibert says that his father died eight months after his own birth; later he gives the time between his birth and his father's death as scarcely six months; in both instances he neglects to give the year.

4 Characteristics at work also in his other writings; see Guibert's *De pignoribus sanctorum* (Migne, PL 156.607–684) for an extended attack on those who believe in the wrong relics.

5 *Journal of Medieval History* 2 (1976), p. 299 (of pp. 281–303).

6 See Louis Bréhier's edition and translation, *Histoire anonyme de la première croisade*, Paris, 1924; for a later edition, see Rosalind Hill, *Gesta Francorum*, London, New York, 1962.

credit and responsibility for the deeds – done *through*, not *by* the French – where they properly belong.[7]

Guibert also sees to it that his characters explicitly articulate their awareness of providential responsibility; in Book Four, one of the major leaders of the Crusade, Bohemund, addresses his men:

> Bohemund said: "O finest knights, your frequent victories provide an explanation for your great boldness. Thus far you have fought for the faith against the infidel, and have emerged triumphant from every danger. Having already felt the abundant evidence of Christ's strength should give you pleasure, and should convince you beyond all doubt that in the most severe battles it is not you, but Christ, who has fought."

The *Gesta Francorum*, however, the text that Guibert sets out to correct, did not neglect the providential aspect of the First Crusade, although the surviving text contains no prologue making such an agenda blatantly explicit. Nevertheless, the anonymous author provides more than enough characters, direct discourse, and action to assure every reader that God looked favorably upon the Crusade. The warning given to Kherboga by his mother, for example,[8] indicates that even pagans were aware that God was on the side of the Christians; the appearance of the divine army, led by three long-dead saints,[9] is another example of divine support. Perhaps the most vivid example is the series of visits Saint Andrew pays to Peter Bartholomew,[10] urging him to dig up the Lance that pierced Christ's side.

Redirecting, or redistributing the credit for victory, then, was not a radical contribution by Guibert. A far more noticeable correction, however, was the result of Guibert's determination to correct the style of his source:

> A version of this same history, but woven out of excessively simple words, often violating grammatical rules, exists, and it may often bore the reader with the stale, flat quality of its language.

The result of his attempt to improve the quality of the *Gesta*'s language, however, is what has distressed some of the modern readers who have tried to deal with Guibert's strenuously elaborate diction,[11] itself a part of his general delight, perhaps obsession, with difficulty. The utter lack of references to Guibert by his contemporaries may indicate that earlier readers shared R.B.C. Huygens' recent judgement that it is marred by an "affected style and pretentious vocabulary."[12]

---

[7] Baldric of Dole and Robert the Monk also insistently added to the story of the First Crusade what Riley-Smith (pp. 135–153) calls "theological refinement."

[8] Bréhier, 119–125.

[9] Bréhier, 155.

[10] Bréhier, 133–135.

[11] For a preliminary study of Guibert's diction, see Eitan Burstein, "Quelques remarques à propos du vocabulaire de Guibert de Nogent," *Cahiers de civilisation médiévale* XXI (1978), pp. 247–263.

[12] *La tradition manuscrite de Guibert de Nogent*, The Hague, 1991, p. 20. Last year, however, in

Guibert seems to have anticipated such a response; at the beginning of Book Five of the *Gesta* he claims to be utterly unconcerned with his audience's interests and abilities:

> In addition to the spiritual reward this little work of mine may bring, my purpose in writing is to speak as I would wish someone else, writing the same story, would speak to me. For my mind loves what is somewhat obscure, and detests a raw, unpolished style. I savor those things which are able to exercise my mind more than those things which, too easily understood, are incapable of inscribing themselves upon a mind always avid for novelty. In everything that I have written and am writing, I have driven everyone from my mind, instead thinking only of what is good for myself, with no concern for pleasing anyone else. Beyond worrying about the opinions of others, calm or unconcerned about my own, I await the blows of whatever words may fall upon me.[13]

However, anyone who reads the conventionally obsequious opening of the dedicatory epistle to Bishop Lysiard would have difficulty accepting the claim that Guibert has no concern for pleasing anyone else:

> Some of my friends have often asked me why I do not sign this little work with my own name; until now I have refused, out of fear of sullying a pious history with the name of a hateful person. However, thinking that the story, splendid in itself, might become even more splendid if attached to the name of a famous man, I have decided to attach it to you. Thus I have placed a most pleasing lamp in front of the work of an obscure author. For, since your ancient lineage is accompanied by a knowledge of literature, an unusual serenity and moral probity, one may justly believe that God in his foresight wanted the dignity of the bishop's office to honor the gift of such reverence. By embracing your name, the little work that follows may flourish: crude in itself, it may be made agreeable by the love of the one to whom it is written, and made stronger by the authority of the office by which you stand above others.

We do not know whether Lysiard shared Guibert's fascination with what is difficult, but the failure of any other medieval writer to mention Guibert implies a negative reception in general for the *Gesta Dei*.

Not every modern reader, however, has been alienated by Guibert's posture. Labande expresses some enthusiasm for "la virtuosité du styliste,"[14] and declares

---

a note informing me of the impending publication of his edition of the *Gesta Dei*, Professor Huygens reported that he has changed his mind. The latest modern edition is more than 100 years old (*Recueil des Historiens des Croisades, Historiens Occidentaux* IV, Paris, 1879, pp. 115–263), and Professor Huygens, the latest reader of the eight surviving manuscripts of the *Gesta Dei per Francos*, finds the edition pretentious, orthographically aberrant, and of no philological value whatever.

[13] Guibert perhaps has some support for this preference: in Praeloq. 2.30 212A Rather of Verona quotes Ambrose on interpreting the difficulties of scripture: "*quod difficilius invenitur, dulcius tenetur.*"

[14] 339, n. 3.

that Guibert's various uses of literary devices "mériteraient une étude attentive." Acknowledging the fact that Guibert's language is somewhat "alambique" and "tarbiscoté," Labande had argued in an earlier article, although only on the basis of the historical material in the *Monodiae*, that Guibert deserved to be appreciated as an historian, with some "modern" qualities.[15] Going even further than Labande, Eitan Burstein admires "la richesse et la complexité" of Guibert's diction.[16] One might also point out that Guibert was not the first to compose a text of an historical nature in a self-consciously elaborate, difficult style. A century earlier Dudo of Saint Quentin had used such a style for his history of the Normans;[17] Saxo Grammaticus' *History of the Danes* indicates that the acrobatic style did not die out with Guibert.[18]

Translating into English the work of a deliberately difficult writer, whose declared aspiration is to be as hermetic as possible, might become a quixotic task, if Guibert's passion and energy had been focused only on providing a performance worthy of Martianus Capella.[19] The Abbot of Nogent, however, also provides additional material, excises or corrects stories that he considers inaccurate, or worse, and, as his corrective title indicates, alters the focus of the material. The results of Guibert's efforts certainly provide unusually rich material for those interested in medieval *mentalité*. In addition, since history was a branch of rhetoric during the middle ages (i.e., it was a part of literature),[20] those interested in intertextual aspects of medieval literature will find a treasure trove, particularly since Guibert eventually sets about correcting and improving *two* earlier texts.[21]

A clear example of what Guibert means by improvement occurs in his

---

[15] 1973, p. 613.

[16] p. 255.

[17] *De Moribus et Actis primorum Normanniae Ducum*, ed. Jules Lair, Caen, 1865.

[18] J. Olrik and H. Raeder (eds.), *Saxonis Gesta Danorum*, 1931, 1957, Hauniae, 2 vols. *The History of the Danes*, transl. Peter Fisher, ed. H.E. Davidson, Totowa, 1979, 1981, 2 vols.

[19] For the significance and influence of Martianus, see W.H. Stahl, R. Johnson, and E.L. Burge, *Martianus Capella and the Seven Liberal Arts*, New York, 1971; Danuta Shanzer, *A philosophical and literary commentary on Martianus Capella's* De Nuptiis Philologiae et Mercurri, *book one*, Berkeley, 1986.

[20] For a densely compacted discussion of this hypothesis, see Herbert Grundmann, *Geschichtsschreibung im Mittelalters*, Göttingen, 1965. For a more extensive, lavishly detailed discussion, see Bernard Guenée, *Histoire et culture historique dans l'occident médiéval*, Paris, 1980. In English, the argument was popularized by R.G. Collingwood, *The Idea of History*, Oxford, 1946; p. 258 gives a useful formulation.

[21] Aimon's early eleventh-century rewriting of both Gregory of Tours' sixth-century text and the eighth-century *Liber Historiae Francorum* is only roughly comparable, since he was much further removed in time from the authors whose work he was correcting. See Gregory of Tours, *Historiae Francorum*, edited by W. Arndt and Bruno Krusch, *Monumenta Germaniae Historica, Scriptores Rerum Merovingicarum*, vol. I, Hanover, 1885; Aimon, *De Gestis Francorum*, in *Recueil des historiens des Gaules et de la France*, ed. M. Bouquet, vol. III, 1869, pp. 20–143; Bruno Krusch, *Fredegarii et Aliorum Chronica; Monumenta Germaniae Historica*: Scriptorum Rerum Merovingicarum, Hanover, 1888.

amplification of the Crusaders' arrival at Jerusalem. Where the *Gesta Francorum* had provided:

> We, however, joyful and exultant, came to the city of Jerusalem . . .

Guibert composes a veritable cadenza on the arrival:

> Finally they reached the place which had provoked so many hardships for them, which had brought upon them so much thirst and hunger for such a long time, which had stripped them, kept them sleepless, cold, and ceaselessly frightened, the most intensely pleasurable place, which had been the goal of the wretchedness they had undergone, and which had lured them to seek death and wounds. To this place, I say, desired by so many thousands of thousands, which they had greeted with such sadness and in jubilation, they finally came, to Jerusalem.

Amplifications like this, magnifying the internal, psychological significance of the events, while simultaneously insisting upon the religious nature of the expedition, characterize Guibert's response to the *Gesta Francorum*. His desire to correct is complicated by the competitive urges that emerge when he faces the other apparently eye-witness account of the First Crusade that became available to him, Fulcher of Chartres' *Historia Hierosolymitana*.[22] Where he had offered gently corrective remarks about the crudeness of the *Gesta Francorum*, Guibert mounts a vitriolic attack on Fulker's pretentiousness:

> Since this same man produces swollen, foot-and-a-half words, pours forth the blaring colors of vapid rhetorical schemes,[23] I prefer to snatch the bare limbs of the deeds themselves, with whatever sack-cloth of eloquence I have, rather than cover them with learned weavings.[24]

However, to convince readers of his superiority Guibert knew that stylistic competence was necessary but not sufficient, particularly because both Fulker and the author of the *Gesta Francorum* had convinced most readers, including Guibert himself, that they were eye-witnesses of most of the events in their texts.[25] Guibert then had to deal with the commonplace assumption passed on by Isidore of Seville:

---

[22] Two editions are available: *Recueil des Historiens des Croisades, Historiens Occidentaux* III, Paris, 1866, pp. 319–585; *Fulcheri Carnotensis Historia Hierosolymitana*, ed. Heinrich Hagenmayer, Heidelberg, 1913.

[23] A judgement contained within the less sardonic assessment, almost nine hundred years later, by Ernest Baker, who called Fulcher, "a kindly old pedant," in the *Encyclopaedia Britannica*, 11th edition, Cambridge, 1910.

[24] Guibert's decision to insert verses of his own composition, in a variety of meters, some unusual, in his predominantly prose text, also seems to be an attempt to outdo Fulker, who had chosen to compose occasional verse for his predominantly prose text, although he limited himself to hexameters and elegaics.

[25] "Quod ego Fulcherus Carnotensis, cum ceteris iens peregrinis, postea, sicut oculis meis

Apud veteres enim nemo conscribebat historiam, nisi is qui interfuisset, et ea quae conscribenda essent vidisset.[26]

Among the ancients no one wrote history unless he had been present and had seen the things he was writing about.

To overcome his apparent disadvantage, Guibert offers a defense of his second-hand perspective several times in the course of his performance.

In the fifth book, immediately after acknowledging the fascination of what is difficult, Guibert provides two paragraphs on the difficulties of determining exactly what happened at Antioch. These paragraphs offer another opportunity to watch Guibert rework material from an earlier text. The author of the *Gesta Francorum* had invoked a variation of the topos of humility,[27] just before giving his account of how Antioch was betrayed by someone inside the city:

I am unable to narrate everything that we did before the city was captured, because no one who was in these parts, neither cleric nor laity, could write or narrate entirely what happened. But I shall tell a little.[28]

When Guibert takes his turn at the topos, he is clearly determined to outdo the author of the *Gesta Francorum*, both stylistically and in terms of the theory of historiography:

We judge that what happened at the siege of Antioch cannot possibly be told by anyone, because, among those who were there, no one can be found who could have observed everything that took place throughout the city, or who could understand the entire event in a way that would enable him to represent the sequence of actions as they took place.

At the beginning of the fourth book of the *Gesta Dei*, Guibert's defense of his absence is again intertextual, but openly polemic as well, as he declares the battle between modern Christian writing (saints lives and John 3.32) and ancient pagan authority (Horace, *Ars Poetica*, 180–181) no contest:

perspexi, diligenter et sollicite in memoriam posteris collegi" (RHC.HO III.327) The case for the *Gesta Francorum* as a text composed by an eye-witness is inferential only.

26 Isidore of Seville, *Etymologies*, I, XLI, ed. W.M Lindsay, Oxford, 1911. See also Bernard Guenée on the topos of the eye-witness, in *Histoire et culture historique dans l'occident médiéval*, Paris, 1980. For a paradigmatic example of the difficulties generated by trying to determine whether a medieval text of an historical nature is the product of an eyewitness, see Stubbs' argument (Rolls Series 38.1) that the *Itinerarium Regis Ricardi* is the product of an eye-witness of the Third Crusade, then Gaston Paris' argument that *L'Estoire de la guerre sainte*, Paris, 1897, is the eye-witness account that the author of the *Itinerarium* was translating, and then Hans Eberhard Mayer, *Das Itinerarium peregrinorum*, Stuttgart, 1962, for the argument that neither is an eye-witness account; see also the discussion in M.R. Morgan, *The Chronicle of Ernoul and the Continuations of William of Tyre*, Oxford, 1973, pp. 61ff.

27 See E.R. Curtius, *European Literature and the Latin Middle Ages*, New York, 1953, pp. 83–85.

28 Translation by Rosalind Hill, London, 1962, p. 44.

If anyone objects that I did not see, he cannot object on the grounds that I did not hear, because I believe that, in a way, hearing is almost as good as seeing. For although:

> Less vividly is the mind stirred by what finds entrance through the ears than by what is brought before the trusty eyes.[29]

Yet who is unaware that historians and those who wrote the lives of the saints wrote down not only what they had seen, but also those things they had drawn from what others had told them? If the truthful man, as it is written, reports "what he has seen and heard," then his tale may be accepted as true when he describes what he has not seen, but has been told by reliable speakers.

Guibert then goes on to challenge those who object to do the job better.

Correcting the *Gesta Francorum*, castigating Fulker, and challenging his other contemporaries, however, do not absorb all of Guibert's competitive urges. He also attacks both the Graeco-Roman and Jewish texts upon which he heavily depends.[30] His use of moderns to castigate the ancients begins in Book One:

> We wonder at Chaldean pride, Greek bitterness, the sordidness of the Egyptians, the instability of the Asiatics, as described by Trogus Pompeius and other fine writers. We judge that the early Roman institutions usefully served the common good and the spread of their power. And yet, if the essence of these things were laid bare, not only would their bravery be considered praiseworthy by wise men, but the relentless madness of fighting without good reason, only for the sake of ruling, would obviously deserve reproach. Let us look carefully, indeed let us come to our senses about the remains, I might have said dregs, of this time which we disdain, and we may find, as that foolish king said,[31] that our little finger is greater than the backs of our fathers, whom we praise excessively. If we look carefully at the wars of the pagans and the kingdoms they traveled through by great military effort, we shall conclude that none of their strength, their armies, by the grace of God, is comparable to ours.

Throughout the text Guibert relentlessly insists that the Crusaders outdo the ancient Jews; in the last book he attempts to strip them of every accomplishment:

> The Lord saves the tents of Judah in the beginning, since He, after having accomplished miracles for our fathers, also granted glory to our own times, so that modern men seem to have undergone pain and suffering greater than that of the Jews of old, who, in the company of their wives and sons, and with full bellies, were led by angels who made themselves visible to them.[32]

---

[29] Translated by H. Rushton Fairclough, *Horace*, London, 1966, p. 465.

[30] Guibert's behavior in this respect suggests that the anxiety of influence which Harold Bloom assigned primarily to the English Romantic poets existed earlier and more extensively (*Anxiety of Influence*, Oxford, 1973).

[31] III Reg. xii.10; II Par. x.10.

[32] Book VII, p. 239.

Partisan outbreaks like this fill the *Gesta Dei per Francos*, perhaps more clearly distinguishing it from the earlier accounts of the First Crusade than Guibert's more elaborate syntax and self-conscious diction.

His hatred of poor people also penetrates the text, often to bring into higher relief the behavior of aristocrats. In Book Two, for example, he offers a comic portrayal of poor, ignorant pilgrims:

> There you would have seen remarkable, even comical things: poor men, their cattle pulling a two-wheeled cart, armed as though they were horses, carrying their few possessions together with their small children in the wagon. The small children, whenever they came upon a castle or town on the way, asked whether this was the Jerusalem they were seeking.

In the seventh and last book, Guibert tells the story of the woman and the goose, again to ridicule the foolishness of the poor:

> A poor woman set out on the journey, when a goose, filled with I do not know what instructions, clearly exceeding the laws of her own dull nature, followed her. Lo, rumor, flying on Pegasean wings, filled the castles and cities with the news that even geese had been sent by God to liberate Jerusalem. Not only did they deny that this wretched woman was leading the goose, but they said that the goose led her. At Cambrai they assert that, with people standing on all sides, the woman walked through the middle of the church to the altar, and the goose followed behind, in her footsteps, with no one urging it on. Soon after, we have learned, the goose died in Lorraine; she certainly would have gone more directly to Jerusalem if, the day before she set out, she had made of herself a holiday meal for her mistress.

Poor people, however, are not merely comic, but dangerous, to themselves, as Guibert's version of the story of Peter the Hermit indicates, and to others, as Guibert's version of the death of Peter Bartholomew emphasizes.

The story of the goose, however, is a comic reflection of a persistently urgent problem on the First Crusade; Guibert addresses the problem of famine often, and expresses particularly warm sympathy towards aristocratic hunger:

> How many jaws and throats of noble men were eaten away by the roughness of this bread. How terribly were their fine stomachs revolted by the bitterness of the putrid liquid. Good God, we think that they must have suffered so, these men who remembered their high social position in their native land, where they had been accustomed to great ease and pleasure, and now could find no hope or solace in any external comfort, as they burned in the terrible heat. Here is what I and I alone think: never had so many noble men exposed their own bodies to so much suffering for a purely spiritual benefit.[33]

---

[33] Book VII.

Furthermore, he bends over backwards to defend aristocrats towards whom other historians of the First Crusade were far less sympathetic. Guibert's description of the Count of Normandy, for example, shows remarkable moral flexibility:

> It would hardly be right to remain silent about Robert, Count of Normandy, whose bodily indulgences, weakness of will, prodigality with money, gourmandising, indolence, and lechery were expiated by the perseverance and heroism that he vigorously displayed in the army of the Lord. His inborn compassion was naturally so great that he did not permit vengeance to be taken against those who had plotted to betray him and had been sentenced to death, and if something did happen to them, he wept for their misfortune. He was bold in battle, although adeptness at foul trickery, with which we know many men befouled themselves, should not be praised, unless provoked by unspeakable acts. For these and for similar things he should now be forgiven, since God has punished him in this world, where he now languishes in jail, deprived of all his honors.

His defense of Stephen of Blois also shows a remarkably complex tolerance and sensitivity towards aristocratic failure:

> At that time, Count Stephen of Blois, formerly a man of great discretion and wisdom, who had been chosen as leader by the entire army, said that he was suffering from a painful illness, and, before the army had broken into Antioch, Stephen made his way to a certain small town, which was called Alexandriola. When the city had been captured and was again under siege, and he learned that the Christian leaders were in dire straits, Stephen, either unable or unwilling, delayed sending them aid, although they were awaiting his help. When he heard that an army of Turks had set up camp before the city walls, he rode shrewdly to the mountains and observed the amount the enemy had brought. When he saw the fields covered with innumerable tents, in understandably human fashion he retreated, judging that no mortal power could help those shut up in the city. A man of the utmost probity, energetic, pre-eminent in his love of truth, thinking himself unable to bring help to them, certain that they would die, as all the evidence indicated, he decided to protect himself, thinking that he would incur no shame by saving himself for an opportune moment.

Guibert concludes his defense of Stephen's questionable behavior with a skillful use of counter-attack:

> And I certainly think that his flight (if, however, it should be called a flight, since the count was certainly ill), after which the dishonorable act was rectified by martyrdom, was superior to the return of those who, persevering in their pursuit of foul pleasure, descended into the depths of criminal behavior. Who could claim that Count Stephen and Hugh the Great, who had always been honorable, because they had seemed to retreat for this reason, were comparable to those who had steadfastly behaved badly?

One of the functions of the panegyric he composes for a martyred Crusader is to make Guibert's own rank clear, present, and significant:

We have heard of many who, captured by the pagans and ordered to deny the sacraments of faith, preferred to expose their heads to the sword than to betray the Christian faith in which they had been instructed. Among them I shall select one, a knight and an aristocrat, but more illustrious for his character than all others of his family or social class I have ever known. From the time he was a child I knew him, and I watched his fine disposition develop. Moreover, he and I came from the same region, and his parents held benefices from my parents, and owed them homage, and we grew up together, and his whole life and development were an open book to me.

He is a spokesman not only for aristocrats, but for the French, in spite of his emphasis on *per Deum* in his title, regularly emphasizing, throughout his text, the significance and superiority of the French contribution. At the end of Book One, Guibert insists that Bohemund, the major military figure in his history, was really French:

Since his family was from Normandy, a part of France, and since he had obtained the hand of the daughter of the king of the French, he might be very well be considered a Frank.

In Book Three, when the Franks win a significant victory, Guibert insists that the defeated Turks and the victorious Franks have not merely common but noble ancestors, thereby melding his two political commitments:

But perhaps someone may object, arguing that the enemy forces were merely peasants, scum herded together from everywhere. Certainly the Franks themselves, who had undergone such great danger, testified that they could have known of no race comparable to the Turks, either in liveliness of spirit, or energy in battle. When the Turks initiated a battle, our men were almost reduced to despair by the novelty of their tactics in battle; they were not accustomed to their speed on horseback, not to their ability to avoid our frontal assaults. We had particular difficulty with the fact that they fired their arrows only when fleeing from the battle. It was the Turk's opinion, however, that they shared an ancestry with the Franks, and that the highest military prowess belonged particularly to the Turks and Franks, above all other people.

Having praised the West at the expense of the East in the first book, in the second he praises the French at the expense of the Teutons, recounting a conversation he recently held with a German ecclesiastic, to show himself an ardent defender of ethnicity:

Last year while I was speaking with a certain archdeacon of Mainz about a rebellion of his people, I heard him vilify our king and our people, merely because the king had given a gracious welcome everywhere in his kingdom to his Highness Pope Paschalis and his princes; he called them not merely Franks, but, derisively, "Francones." I said to him, "If you think them so weak and languid that you can denigrate a name known and admired as far away as the Indian Ocean, then tell me upon whom did Pope Urban call for aid against the

Turks? Wasn't it the French? Had they not been present, attacking the barbarians everywhere, pouring their sturdy energy and fearless strength into the battle, there would have been no help for your Germans, whose reputation there amounted to nothing." That is what I said to him.

Guibert then turns to his reader, and provides a more extensive panegyric for his people, recalling pre-Merovingian accomplishments:

> I say truly, and everyone should believe it, that God reserved this nation for such a task. For we know certainly that, from the time that they received the sign of faith that blessed Remigius brought to them, they succumbed to none of the diseases of false faith from which other nations have remained uncontaminated either with great difficulty or not at all. They are the ones who, while still laboring under the pagan error, when they triumphed on the battlefield over the Gauls, who were Christians, did not punish or kill any of them, because they believed in Christ. Instead, those whom Roman severity had punished with sword and fire, French native generosity covered with gems and amber. They strove to welcome with honor not only those who lived within their own borders, but they also affectionately cared for people who came from Spain, Italy, or anywhere else, so that love for the martyrs and confessors, whom they constantly served and honored, made them famous, finally driving them to the glorious victory at Jerusalem. Because it has carried the yoke since the days of its youth, it will sit in isolation,[34] a nation noble, wise, war-like, generous, brilliant above all kinds of nations. Every nation borrows the name as an honorific title; do we not see the Bretons, the English, the Ligurians call men "Frank" if they behave well? But now let us return to the subject.

"Let us return to the subject," like the earlier injunction, "let us continue in the direction in which we set out," indicates Guibert's awareness of his tendency to perform "sorties."[35] At times he turns from the narrative to deliver a sermon, or to offer a biography of Mahomet, and, more than once, to lecture on ecclesiastical history. The apparent looseness of structure which results, a quality Misch attributed to the *Memoirs* as well, may be a symptom of Guibert's Shandy-like temperament, or may be evidence that the remarks he made about his style in an early aside to the reader apply equally well to his structure:

> Please, my reader, knowing without a doubt that I certainly had no more time for writing than those moments during which I dictated the words themselves, forgive the stylistic infelicities; I did first write on writing-tablets to be corrected diligently later, but I wrote them directly on the parchment, exactly as it is, harshly barked out.

Such a cavalier attitude towards the finished product was not characteristic of

---

34 Jeremiah 3.27,28.
35 A term Paul Zumthor introduced in "Roman et Gothique," in *Studi in honore di Italo Siciliano*, Florence, 1966, vol. II, p. 1227.

Guibert,[36] and seems to be in keeping neither with his declared penchant for difficulty, nor with his declared intention to raise the level of his style to match the significance of his subject:

> No one should be surprised that I make use of a style very much different from that of the *Commentaries on Genesis*, or the other little treatises; for it is proper and permissible to ornament a history with the crafted elegance of words; however, the mysteries of sacred eloquence should be treated not with poetic loquacity, but with ecclesiastical plainess. Therefore I ask you to accept this graciously, and to keep it as a perpetual monument to your name.

The seriousness of purpose and the apparent looseness of structure may perhaps be reconciled by considering that the literal level of events was a less urgent concern for Guibert than the significance of those events. In addition, he imagined himself not so much as a recorder of events, but as a competitor in a rhetorical agon, as the implied metaphor that he uses in describing his activity as a writer, *in hujus stadio operis excurrisse debueram*, "racing in a stadium," suggests.

In fact, in the course of composing his explicitly corrective version of the First Crusade, Guibert participates in several contests simultaneously; he "mollifies" the style and corrects the substance of previous writers on the Crusades; he argues for some miracles and against others; he utilizes and attempts to transcend both the Graeco-Roman and the Judaeo part of the Judaeo-Christian past. As a rhetorical performance, in both prose and verse, the results are impressive, since the *Gesta Dei per Francos* simultaneously reflects historical reality, and provides some insight into the workings of the mind of a gifted, early twelfth-century French cleric and aristocrat.

Summary of the
Gesta Dei per Francos

Characteristically, Guibert opens the *Gesta* defensively, justifying his choice of a modern topic by insisting upon the exceptional nature of the Crusade, as well as the exceptional nature of the French. The entire first book is devoted to a selective history of the Eastern Church and a denunciation of heresies, concluding with an extensive invective against Mahomet, compounding sex, excrement, and disease.[37] Guibert then moves forward in time, to the generation before the First

---

[36] For evidence that Guibert was remarkably fastidious in his attitude towards his literary production, or at least towards three of his theological compositions, see Monique-Cecile Garand, "Le Scriptorium de Guibert de Nogent," *Scriptorium* 31 (1977), pp. 3–29.

[37] See Robert Levine, "Satiric Vulgarity in Guibert de Nogent's *Gesta Dei per Francos*," *Rhetorica* 7 (1989), pp. 261–273.

Crusade, to describe a complaint about Muslim lust made by the Greek emperor to the elder Count Robert of Flanders. Guibert also complains about the Greek emperor's own excessive interest in erotic motivation for warriors.

Book Two begins with an account that amounts to little more than a panegyric of Pope Urban II, admired by Guibert at least partially because he is French. Guibert then compliments the French for their long-standing loyalty to the popes, and for their generally Christian behavior.[38] Guibert then proceeds to describe the rise of Peter the Hermit as leader of the poor people who misguidedly set out on the Crusade, a group whose lack of control outrages Guibert throughout the *Gesta*.[39] However, he quickly returns to giving an account of the aristocrats who took the cross, composing panegyrics for Godfrey, Baldwin, and Eustace of Bouillon, complimenting Godfrey in particular for his military victories in skirmishes with the Greek emperor. The second book ends with a description of some of the other leaders and their qualities.

In Book Three Guibert introduces Bohemund, describes the siege of Nicea, the battle of Dorylea, and adds the story about Baldwin's adoption by the ruler of Edessa (not to be found in the *Gesta Francorum*).

In Book Four the Crusaders arrive at Antioch and take up the lengthy siege. Guibert again adds material not to be found in the *Gesta Francorum*: one story involves the false stigmata of an abbot, another the martyrdom of a man know personally by Guibert.

In Book Five Guibert describes the taking of Antioch, the capture of Cassian and his decapitation by Armenians and Syrians, the prediction of eventual Christian victory by Kherboga's mother, the Crusaders themselves besieged in Antioch, the initial resistance to Peter's vision about the location of the Lance, and the desertion of the Crusade by Stephen of Blois, whom Guibert defends with his characteristic loyalty to aristocrats.[40]

Book Six offers the discovery of the Lance, a futile meeting between Peter the Hermit and Kherboga, the reported appearance of a celestial army, the Crusaders' defeat of Kherboga, and the lifting of the siege of Antioch. In addition, Ademar of Puy dies, the Crusaders attack Marrah, and Bohemund and Raymond of St. Gilles disagree about to whom Antioch belongs. The trial by fire of Peter

---

[38] Although he calls the pope a fine Latinist, instead of giving Urban's words at Clermont, Guibert rewrites them, "etsi non verbis, tamen intentionibus," "not word for word, but according to what he meant." For an attempt, on the basis of the various surviving representations of Urban's performance at Clermont, to determine what the pope actually said, see D.C. Munro, "The Speech of Pope Urban II at Clermont," *American Historical Review* XI (1906), pp. 231–242. For objections to Munro's technique, see Paul Rousset, *Les origines et les caractères de la première croisade*, Geneva, 1945, p. 58.

[39] See W. Porges, "The Clergy, the Poor, and the Non-Combatants on the First Crusade," *Speculum* 21 (1946), pp. 1–20; Jean Flori, "Faut-il réhabiliter Pierre l'Ermite?" *Cahiers de civilisation médiévale* XXXVIII (1995), pp. 35–54.

[40] See above, p. 10.

Bartholomew (not to be found in the *Gesta Francorum*) differs significantly and with clear polemical intentions from the scene in Fulcher; Guibert attributes the skepticism about the authenticity of the Lance to the death of Ademar. The book ends with the martyrdom of Anselm of Ribemont, and a mention of his letters, which Guibert will use later.

Book Seven is more than twice the length of any of the earlier books; in it the Crusaders reach Tripoli, negotiate successfully with its king, continue on through Palestine, reach Jerusalem, and begin the siege. As part of his extended panegyric of both brothers, Guibert now inserts the story of Godfrey cutting a man in half and wrestling with a bear (not in the *Gesta Francorum*), which permits him, by association, to modulate to the story of Baldwin refusing to be saved by having a soldier killed and examined for a similar wound, instead agreeing to substitute a bear. As he approaches the end of his task, Guibert loosens the structure of his narrative even more, providing a discussion of Near Eastern ecclesiastical politics, a description of some of the battles in which the Crusaders consolidated their control over Palestine, and a cadenza, dense with biblical quotations and some allegorical exegesis, on the significance of the Crusade itself. After providing an anecdote about the way in which children's combat inspired the soldiers, Guibert provides a brief discussion of the Tafurs, and describes the betrayal by the emperor that led to the death of Hugh Magnus. Next Guibert describes Stephen's disastrous expedition to Paphligonia, offers conflicting versions of Godfrey's death, mentions his replacement by Baldwin, and provides a flashback to Robert of Flanders' visit to Jerusalem twelve years before the Crusade (at which time, according to Guibert, an astrological prediction of a later Christian victory had been made). Guibert now tells a story about a man who defeated the Devil, then attacks Fulker of Chartres for his style, for his story about Pirrus betraying Antioch, and for his rejection of the authenticity of the Lance.

Guibert's Other Works

None of the salacious verse Guibert confesses to have written in his youth has survived.[41] Instead, in addition to the *Gesta Dei* and the *Monodiae*, the following writings, entirely on religious topics, have survived, and have been published in vol. 156 of Migne's *Patrologia Latina*:

Quo ordine sermo fieri debeat (Migne 21–32 and Huygens, 1993, 47–63).
Moralium Geneseos libri decem (Migne 32–338).
Tropologiae in prophetas Osee, Amos ac Lamentationes Jeremiae (Migne 337–488).
Tractatus de Incarnatione contra Judaeos (Migne 489–528).

---

[41] Labande, I.xvii, pp. 135ff.

Epistola de buccella Judae data et de veritate dominici Corporis (Migne 527–538 and Huygens, 1993, 65–77).

De laude sanctae Mariae liber (Migne 537–578).

De virginitate opusculum (Migne 579–608).

De pignoribus sanctorum libri quatuor (Migne 607–680 and Huygens, 1993, 79–175).

The Translation

In diction, syntax, word order, and complexity of expression, Guibert's Latin is more difficult than that of any other Latin historian of the First Crusade. I have tried to preserve as much of the complexity of the syntax as is tolerable in comprehensible English sentences. Guibert's penchant for alliteration, rhyming clausulae, and pithiness must usually be sacrificed. A characteristic example of the sonic loss occurs in my attempt to translate the sardonic description of Arnulf's elevation to patriarch:

> . . . dum vox magis quam vita curatur, ad hoc ut Iherosolimitanus fieret patriarcha vocatur. (RHC 4.233)

> and since a man's voice is of more concern than the life he has led, he was called to the patriarchy of Jerusalem.

I have followed the paragraphs of the latest edition, often longer than those to which twentieth-century readers are accustomed, to allow readers to check the original more easily. Passages which Guibert composed in verse are translated into prose and indented. Guizot's early nineteenth-century French translation, although at times erroneous or misleading, was very helpful.

Notes

Annotating Guibert's text in a truly satisfying manner would have produced a prologomenon to a synoptic history of the First Crusade.[42] Instead, I have tried to limit myself to providing: (1) information necessary to understand and to clarify the translation; (2) sources for Guibert's biblical and classical references; (3) modern names of cities and towns mentioned in the text;[43] (4) the names of

---

[42] A task for which Heinrich Hagenmeyer's *Chronologie de la première croisade*, Hildesheim, 1898–1901, provides a sound basis.

[43] Whenever possible, the modern spellings are taken from the Gazetteer provided in *A History of the Crusades*, ed. by Kenneth M. Setton and M.W. Baldwin, Madison, 1969, vol. I, pp. 626–666.

the meters in which Guibert composes the portions of his text in verse; (5) representative illustrations of the intertextual nature of the *Gesta Dei per Francos*.

Acknowledgements

I am grateful to Jessica Weiss for reading through the entire translation and making useful corrections and suggestions, to Mark Stansbury for reading through parts of the translation and making useful corrections and suggestions, and to the staff of The Boston University Office of Information Technology for help in solving problems involving word-processing.

BIBLIOGRAPHY

Albert of Aix, *Historia Hierosolymitana, Recueil des Historiens des Croisades, Historiens Occidentaux* IV, Paris, 1879, pp. 265–713.

Auerbach, Erich, *Literary language and its public in late antiquity and in the Middle Ages*, translated by Ralph Mannheim, New York, 1965.

Baldric of Dole, *Historia Hierosolymitana*, RHC.HO IV, pp. 1–111.

Benton, John, *Self and Society in Medieval France*, New York, 1970.

Boehm, Laetitia, 'Studien zur Geschichtschreibung des ersten Kreuzzuges Guibert von Nogent', Munich, 1954.

Bréhier, Louis (ed. and transl.), *Histoire anonyme de la première croisade*, Paris, 1924.

Bull, Marcus, *Knightly Piety and the Lay Response to the First Crusade*, Oxford, 1993.

Burstein, Eitan, "Quelques remarques à propos du vocabulaire de Guibert de Nogent," *Cahiers de civilisation médiévale* XXI (1978), pp. 247–263.

Cahen, C., *La Syrie du nord*, Paris, 1940, pp. 211–218.

Charaud, Jacques, "La conception de l'histoire de Guibert de Nogent," *Cahiers de civilisation médiévale* VIII (1965), pp. 381–395.

Damascus Chronicle, transl. A.R. Gibbs, London, 1932.

Daniel, Norman, *Heroes and Saracens*, Edinburgh, 1984.

Duby, Georges, *The Three Orders: Feudal Society Imagined*, Chicago, 1980 (original, Paris, 1978).

Edbury, Peter, and Rowe, John Gordon, *William of Tyre*, Cambridge, 1988.

Embricho of Mainz, *La vie de Mahomet*, ed. Guy Cambier, 1962.

Fulcheri Carnotensis Historia Hierosolymitana, ed. Heinrich Hagenmayer, Heidelberg, 1913.

Garand, Monique-Cecile, and Etcheverry, François, "Analyse d'écriture et macrophotographie; les manuscrits originaux de Guibert de Nogent," *Codices manuscripti* I (1975), pp. 112–122.

———, "Le Scriptorium de Guibert de Nogent," *Scriptorium* XXXI (1977), pp. 3–29.

Grundmann, Herbert, *Geschichtsschreibung im Mittelalters*, Göttingen, 1965.

Guenée, Bernard, *Histoire et culture historique dans l'occident medieval*, Paris, 1980.

Guibert de Nogent, *Autobiographie*, edited and translated by Edmond-Rene Labande, Paris, 1981.

Guibert de Nogent, *Gesta Dei per Francos*, RHC.HO IV, pp. 115–263.

Guizot, F., *Collection des mémoires relatifs à l'histoire de France*, Paris, 1823–35, v. 9.

Hagenmeyer, Heinrich, *Chronologie de la première croisade*, Hildesheim, 1898–1901.

——— (ed.), *Epistulae et chartae ad historiam primi belli sacri spectantes*, Innsbruck, 1901.

Huygens, R.B.C., *Guibert de Nogent: Quo Ordine Sermo Fieri Debeat; De Bucella Iudae Data et De Veritate Dominic Corporis; De Sanctis et Eorum Pigneribus*, Turnholt, 1993.

———, *La tradition manuscrite de Guibert de Nogent*, The Hague, 1991.

——— (ed.), *Guillaume de Tyre Chronique*, Turnholt, 1986, I and II.

Knoch, Peter, *Studien zur Albert von Aachen*, Stuttgart, 1966.

Labande, Edmond-Rene, "L'Art de Guibert de Nogent," in *Mélanges E. Perroy*, Paris, 1973, pp. 608–625.

Bibliography

Levine, Robert, "Satiric Vulgarity in Guibert de Nogent's *Gesta Dei per Francos*," *Rhetorica* 7 (1989), pp. 261–273.

Mayer, Hans Eberhard (transl. John Gillingham), *The Crusades*, Oxford, 1988.

Misch, Georg, *Geschichte der Autobiographie*, vol. 3, part two, first half, Frankfurt, 1959, pp. 108–162.

Monod, Bernard, "De la méthode historique chez Guibert de Nogent," *Revue historique* 84 (1904), pp. 51–70.

Morris, C., "Policy and Visions: The Case of the Holy Lance at Antioch," in J.B. Gillingham and J.C. Holt (eds.), *War and Government in the Middle Ages*, Cambridge, 1984.

Partner, Nancy, *Serious Entertainment*, Chicago, 1977.

Peeters, P., "Un témoignage autographe sur le siège d'Antioche etc.," in *Miscellanea historica Alberti de Meyer*, 2 vols., Louvain, 1946; I. 373–390.

Pickering, F.P., *Augustinus oder Boethius*, Berlin, 1967.

Porges, W., "The Clergy, the Poor, and the Non-Combatants on the First Crusade," *Speculum* 21 (1946), pp. 1–20.

Raoul of Caen, *Gesta Tancredi*, RHC.HO III, pp. 588–716.

Riley-Smith, Jonathan, *The First Crusade and the Idea of Crusading*, Philadelphia, 1986.

Robert the Monk, *Hierosolomytana expeditio*, RHC.HO III, pp. 717–802.

Rogers, R., *Latin Siege Warfare in the Twelfth Century*, Oxford, 1992.

Schreiner, Klaus, "Discrimen veri ac falsi," *Archive für Kulturgeschichte* XLVIII (1966), pp. 1–51.

Setton, Kenneth M., and Baldwin, M.W., *A History of the Crusades*, Madison, 1969, vol. I.

Smalley, Beryl, *Historians in the Middle Ages*, London, 1974.

Ward, John O., "Some Principles of Rhetorical Historiography in the Twelfth Century," in *Classical Rhetoric and Medieval Historiography*, edited by Ernest Breisach, Kalamazoo, 1985.

THE TRANSLATION

The Letter of Guibert to Lysiard

Some of my friends have often asked me why I do not sign this little work with my own name; until now I have refused, out of fear of sullying a pious history with the name of a hateful person. However, thinking that the story, splendid in itself, might become even more splendid if attached to the name of a famous man, I have finally decided to attach it to you. Thus I have placed a most pleasing lamp in front of the work of an obscure author. For, since your ancient lineage is accompanied by a knowledge of literature, as well an unusual serenity and moral probity, one may justly believe that God in his foresight wanted the dignity of the bishop's office to honor the gift of such reverence. By embracing your name, the little work that follows may flourish: crude in itself, it may be made agreeable by the love of the one to whom it is written, and made stronger by the authority of the office by which you stand above others. Certainly there were bishops, and others, who have heard something about this book and about some of my other writings; leaving them aside, my greatest wish was to reach you. In reading this you should consider that, if I occasionally have deviated from common grammatical practice, I have done it to correct the vices, the style that slithers along the ground, of the earlier history. I see villages, cities, towns, fervently studying grammar, for which reason I tried, to the best of my abilities, not to deviate from the ancient historians. Finally, consider that while taking care of my household duties, listening to the many cases brought to my attention, I burned with the desire to write, and, even more, to pass the story along; and while I was compelled outwardly to listen to various problems, presented with biting urgency, inwardly I was steadily compelled to persist in what I had begun. No one should be surprised that I make use of a style very much different from that of the *Commentaries on Genesis*, or the other little treatises; for it is proper and permissible to ornament a history with the crafted elegance of words; however, the mysteries of sacred eloquence should be treated not with poetic loquacity, but with ecclesiastical plainness. Therefore I ask you to accept this graciously, and to keep it as a perpetual monument to your name.

Preface to the book of the deeds of God
by means of the Franks

In trying to compose the present small work, I have placed my faith not in my literary knowledge, of which I have very little, but rather in the spiritual authority of the events themselves, for I have always been certain that it was brought to completion only by the power of God alone, and through those men whom he willed. Likewise, the story undoubtedly was written down by whatever men, even if uneducated, God willed. I am unable to doubt that He who guided their steps through so many difficulties, who removed the many military obstacles that lay before them, will implant within me, in whatever manner he pleases, the truth about what happened, nor will he deny to me the ability to choose the correct and fitting words. A version of this same history, but woven out of excessively simple words, often violating grammatical rules, exists, and it may often bore the reader with the stale, flat quality of its language. It works well enough for the less learned, who are not interested in the quality of the diction, but only in the novelty of the story, nor is it the case that the author should have spoken in a way that they do not understand. Those, moreover, who think that honesty nourishes eloquence, when they see that the words have been chosen less carefully than the narrative demands, and that the story is told briefly where the elaborate variety of mollifying[44] eloquence was appropriate, when they see the narration proceed bare-footed, then, as the poet says, they will either sleep or laugh.[45] They hate a badly performed speech, which they judge should have been recited in a much different way. The style of writers should fit the status of the events: martial deeds should be told with harsh words; what pertains to divine matters must be brought along at a more controlled pace. In the course of this work, if my ability is equal to the task, I should perform in both modes, so that haughty Gradivus[46] may find that his lofty crimes have been represented in matching words, and, when piety is the subject, gravity is never violated by excessive cleverness.[47] Even if I have been unable to follow these standards, nevertheless I have learned to admire or praise for the most part what is done well by someone else. Therefore I confess that I, with shameless temerity, but out of love of faith, have run the risk of being criticized by judges whom I do not know because, when they find that I have taken up this project with a vow to correct a previous work, they may value the second less than the first. Since we see a passion for grammar everywhere, and we know that the discipline, because of the number of scholars that now exist, is

---

[44] *paregorizantis*, "curative," a rare word, used by Augustine.
[45] Horace, AP 105.
[46] One of the names of Mars.
[47] Literally, never goes beyond Mercurial moderation.

now open to the worst students, it would be a horrid thing not to write, even if we write only as we are able, and not as we should, about this glory of our time, or even to leave the story hidden in the scabbiness of artless speech. I have seen what God has done in these times – miracles greater than any he has ever performed – and now I see a gem of this kind lying in the lowest dust. Impatient with such contemptuous treatment, I have taken care, with whatever eloquence I have, to clean what was given over to neglect more preciously than any gold. I have not boldly done this entirely on my own initiative, but I have faithfully promised others, who were eager for this to be done. Some asked that I write in prose; but most asked that it be done in meter, since they knew that I had, in my youth, performed more elementary exercises in verse than I should have. Older and more responsible, however, I thought that it should not be done with words designed to be applauded, or with the clatter of verse; but I thought, if I may dare to say this, that it deserved being told with greater dignity than all the histories of Jewish warfare, if God would grant someone the ability to do this. I do not deny that I set my mind to writing after the capture of Jerusalem, when those who had taken part in the expedition began to return; but because I did not want to be importunate, I put the task off. However, because, with the permission (I do not know if it is in accordance with the will) of God, the chance to carry out my wishes came about, I have gone forward with what I had desired piously, perhaps only to be laughed at by everyone, yet I shall transcend the laughter of some, as long as I may occupy myself with the daily growth of my creation, no matter what objections others may bark. If anyone does laugh, let him not blame a man who has done what he was able to do, whose intentions were sound; may he not instantly cauterize the fault in my writings, but if he utterly despises them, let him lay aside the war of words, rewrite what was badly done, and offer his own examples of correct writing. Furthermore, if anyone accuses me of writing obscurely, let him fear inflicting on himself the stigma of weak intellect, since I know for certain that no one trained in letters can raise a question about whatever I may have said in the following book.

In proceeding to offer a model to correct (or perhaps to corrupt) the history, I have first attempted to consider the motives and needs that brought about this expedition, as I have heard them, and then, having shown how it came about, to relate the events themselves. I learned the story, related with great veracity, from the previous author whom I follow, and from those who were present on the expedition. I have often compared the book's version of events with what was said by those who saw what happened with their own eyes, and beyond a doubt I have seen that neither testimony was discordant with the other. Whatever I have added, I have learned from eye-witnesses, or have found out for myself. If anything described is false, no clever critic may rightly accuse me of lying, I say, since he cannot argue, as God is my witness, that I have spoken out of a desire to deceive. How can it be surprising if we make errors, when we are describing things done in a foreign land, when we are clearly unable not only to express in words our own thoughts and actions, but even to collect them in the silence of our own minds? What can I say then about intentions, which are so hidden most of the time that they can scarcely be discerned by the acuity of the inner man? Therefore we should not be severely attacked if we stumble unknowingly in our words; but relentless blame should be brought to bear when falsity is willfully woven into the text, in an attempt to deceive, or out of a desire to disguise something. Furthermore, the names of men, provinces, and cities presented me with considerable difficulties; I knew some of the familiar ones were written down incorrectly by this author, and I do not doubt that in recording foreign, and therefore less known, names, errors were also made. For example, we inveigh every day against the Turks, and we call Khorasan[48] by its new name; when the old word has been forgotten and has almost disappeared, no use of ancient sources, even if they were available, has been made: I have chosen to use no word unless it were in common use. Had I used Parthians instead of Turks, as some have suggested, Caucasus and not Khorasan, in the pursuit of authenticity, I might have been misunderstood and laid myself open to the attacks of those who argue about the proper names of provinces. In particular, since I have observed that in our lands provinces have been given new names, we should assume that the same changes take place in foreign lands. For if what was once called Neustria is now called Normandy, and what was once called Austrasia is now, because of a turn of events, called Lotharingia, why should one not believe that the same thing happened in the East? As some say, Egyptian Memphis is now called Babylon. Instead of using different names, thereby becoming obscure or participating in polemics, I have preferred to make use of the common word. I was in doubt for a long time about the name of the Bishop of Puy, and learned it just before finishing this work, for it was not in the text from which I was working. Please, my reader, knowing without a doubt that I certainly had no more time for writing than those moments during which I dictated the words themselves, forgive the stylistic infelicities; I did not first write on wax tablets to be corrected diligently later, by I wrote them directly on the parchment, exactly as it is, harshly barked out. I inscribed a name that lacks arrogance, and brings honor to our people: *The Deeds of God through the Franks.* Here ends the preface to the history which is called the Deeds of God through the Franks, written by the reverend Dom Guibert, Abbot of the monastery of Saint Mary at Nogent, which is located near Coucy, in the district of Laon.

---

[48] An area in northeast Persia, but used as a general term for the Near East by the Western chroniclers of the First Crusade.

Book One

Sometimes, but not always incorrectly, certain mortals have developed the foul habit of praising previous times and attacking what modern men do. Indeed the ancients should be praised for the way in which they balanced good fortune with restraint, as well as for the way in which thoughtfulness controlled their use of energy. However, no discerning individual could prefer in any way the temporal prosperity of the ancients to any of the strengths of our own day. Although pure strength was pre-eminent among the ancients, yet among us, though the end of time has come upon us, the gifts of nature have not entirely rotted away. Things done in early times may rightly be praised because done for the first time, but far more justly are those things worth celebrating which are usefully done by uncultivated men in a world slipping into old age. We admire foreign nations famous for military strength; we admire Philip for his merciless slaughter and victories everywhere, never without relentless shedding of blood. We commend with resounding rhetoric the fury of Alexander, who emerged from the Macedonian forge to destroy the entire East. We measure the magnitude of the troops of Xerxes at Thermopylae, and of Darius against Alexander, with the terrible killing of infinite numbers of nations. We wonder at Chaldean pride, Greek bitterness, the sordidness of the Egyptians, the instability of the Asiatics, as described by Trogus Pompeius[49] and other fine writers. We judge that the early Roman institutions usefully served the common good and the spread of their power. And yet, if the essence of these things were laid bare, not only would their bravery be considered praiseworthy by wise men, but the relentless madness of fighting without good reason, only for the sake of ruling, would obviously deserve reproach. Let us look carefully, indeed let us come to our senses about the remains, I might have said dregs, of this time which we disdain, and we may find, as that foolish king said,[50] that our little finger is greater than the backs of our fathers, whom we praise excessively. If we look carefully at the wars of the pagans and the kingdoms they traveled through by great military effort, we shall conclude that none of their strength, none of their armies, by the grace of God, is comparable in any way to ours. Although we have heard that God was worshipped among the Jews, we know that Jesus Christ, as he once was among the ancients, today exists and prevails by clear proofs among the moderns. Kings, leaders, rulers and consuls, have collected vast armies from everywhere, and from among the so-called powerful of nations everywhere, have amassed hordes of people to fight. They, however, come together here out of fear of men. What shall

---

[49] Gnaeus Trogus Pompeius, a contemporary of Livy, wrote 44 books, of which only an epitome by Justin survives.

[50] I Kings 12.10; II Chronicles 10.10.

I say of those who, without a master, without a leader, compelled only by God, have traveled not only beyond the borders of their native province, beyond even their own kingdom, but through the vast number of intervening nations and languages, from the distant borders of the Britannic Ocean, to set up their tents in the center of the earth? We are speaking about the recent and incomparable victory of the expedition to Jerusalem, whose glory for those who are not totally foolish is such that our times may rejoice in a fame that no previous times have ever merited. Our men were not driven to this accomplishment by desire for empty fame, or for money, or to widen our borders – motives which drove almost all others who take up or have taken up arms. About these the poet correctly says:

> Quis furor, o cives, quae tanta licentia ferri,
> Gentibus invisis proprium praebere cruorem? (Lucan 1.8,9)

> What madness was this, my countrymen, what fierce orgy of slaughter
> . . . to give to hated nations the spectacle of Roman bloodshed?[51]

and:

> Bella geri placuit, nullos habitura triumphos.

> It was decided to wage wars that could win no triumphs.[52]

If they were taking up the cause of protecting liberty or defending the republic, they would be able to offer a morally acceptable excuse for fighting. Indeed, in the case of an invasion of barbarians or pagans, no knight could rightly be prevented from taking up arms. And if these conditions were not the case, then simply to protect Holy Church they waged the most legitimate war. But since this pious purpose is not in the minds of everyone, and instead the desire for material acquisitions pervades everyone's hearts, God ordained holy wars in our time, so that the knightly order and the erring mob, who, like their ancient pagan models, were engaged in mutual slaughter, might find a new way of earning salvation. Thus, without having chosen (as is customary) a monastic life, without any religious committment, they were compelled to give up this world; free to continue their customary pursuits, nevertheless they earned some measure of God's grace by their own efforts. Therefore, we have seen nations, inspired by God, shut the doors of their hearts towards all kinds of needs and feelings, taking up exile beyond the Latin world, beyond the known limits of the entire world, in order to destroy the enemies of the name of Christ, with an eagerness greater than we have seen anyone show in hurrying to the the banquet table, or in celebrating a holiday.[53] The most splendid honors, the castles and towns over which they held

---

[51] Translation by J.D. Duff, *Lucan*, Cambridge, 1969; "of one's own blood," is the more literal translation.

[52] Lucan, I. 8, 9, 12.

[53] Albert of Aix uses the same comparison several times within one paragraph to describe the

power, meant nothing to them; the most beautiful women were treated as though they were worthless dirt; pledges of domestic love,[54] once more precious than any gem, were scorned. What no mortal could have compelled them to do by force, or persuade them to do by rhetoric, they were carried forward to do by the sudden insistence of their transformed minds. No priest in church had to urge people to this task, but one man urged another, both by speech and by example, proclaiming his determination, both at home and in the streets, to go on the expedition. Every man showed the same fervor; the chance to go on the trip appealed both to those who had little property, and to those whose vast possessions or stored-up treasures permitted them to take the richest provisions for the journey. You would have seen Solomon's words clearly put into action, "the locusts have no king, yet they march together in bands."[55] This locust made no leap of good works, as long as he lay in the frozen torpor of deep sin, but when the heat of the sun of justice shone, he leaped forward in the flight of a double (or natural)[56] movement, abandoning his paternal home and family, changing his behavior to take on a sacred purpose. The locust had no king, because each faithful soul had no leader but God alone; certain that He is his companion in arms, he has no doubt that God goes before him. He rejoices to have undertaken the journey by the promptings of God's will, who will be his solace in tribulation. But what is it that drives a whole community unless it is that simplicity and unity which compels the hearts of so many people to desire one and the same thing? Although the call from the apostolic see was directed only to the French nation, as though it were special, what nation under Christian law did not send forth throngs to that place? In the belief that they owed the same allegiance to God as did the French, they strove strenuously, to the full extent of their powers, to share the danger with the Franks. There you would have seen the military formations of Scots, savage in their own country, but elsewhere unwarlike, their knees bare, with their shaggy cloaks, provisions hanging from their shoulders, having slipped out of their boggy borders, offering as aid and testimony to their faith and loyalty, their arms, numerically ridiculous in comparison with ours. As God is my witness I swear that I heard that some barbarian people from I don't know what land were driven to our harbor, and their language was so incomprehensible that, when it failed them, they made the sign of the cross with their fingers; by these gestures they showed what they could not indicate with words, that because of their faith they set out on the journey. But perhaps I shall treat these matters at greater length

---

joys of the Crusaders about to attack Ascalon: they are "tanquam ad convivium pergentes laetati," then the pagan prefect of Ramna, noticing that the Christians are singing and rejoicing, "tanquam ad epulas omnium deliciarum invitati essent," remarks: "Miror, et sufficienter mirari nequeo unde populus hic in tanta laetitia et voce exultationis glorietur, quasi ad convivium iturus." (RHC IV.492).

54 That is, children.
55 Proverbs 30.27.
56 The first printed edition offers "genuinae," where MS A offers "geminae."

when I have more room. Now we are concerned with the state of the church of Jerusalem, or the Eastern church, as it was then.

In the time of the faithful Helen, the mother of the ruler Constantine, throughout the regions known for the traces of the Lord's sufferings, churches and priests worthy of these churches were established by this same Augusta.[57] From church history we learn that, for a long time after the death of those just mentioned, these institutions endured while the Roman Empire continued. However, the faith of Easterners, which has never been stable, but has always been variable and unsteady, searching for novelty, always exceeding the bounds of true belief, finally deserted the authority of the early fathers. Apparently, these men, because of the purity of the air and the sky in which they are born, as a result of which their bodies are lighter and their intellect consequently more agile, customarily abuse the brilliance of their intelligence with many useless commentaries. Refusing to submit to the authority of their elders or peers, "they searched out evil, and searching they succumbed."[58] Out of this came heresies and ominous kinds of different plagues. Such a baneful and inextricable labyrinth of these illnesses existed that the most desolate land anywhere could not offer worse vipers and nettles. Read through the catalogues of all heresies; consider the books of the ancients against heretics; I would be surprised if, with the exception of the East and Africa, any books about heretics could be found in the Roman world. I read somewhere that Pelagius, unless I am mistaken, was a British heretic; but I believe that no one has ever been able to compose an account of the mistaken people, or their errors. The Eastern regions were lands cursed on earth in the work of its teachers,[59] bringing forth thorns and prickly weeds for those working it. Out of Alexandria came Arius,[60] out of Persia Manes.[61] The madness of one of them tore and bloodied the mantle of holy Church, which had until then no spot or wrinkle,[62] with such persistence that the persecution of Datian[63] seemed shorter in time, and more narrowly confined in space. Not only Greece, but, afterwards, Spain, Illyria, and Africa succumbed to it. The fictions of the other, although ridiculous, nevertheless deceived the sharpest minds far and wide with its trickery. What should I say about the Eunomians, the Eutychians, the Nestorians, how can I represent the thousands of hideous groups whose frenzy against us was so relentless, and against whom victory was so difficult, that the heresies seemed to be beheaded not with swords but with sticks? If we examine the early histories of the beginnings of their kingdoms, and if we chatter about the ridiculous nature of their kings, we must wonder at the sudden overthrowing and replacing of rulers brought about by Asiatic instability. Anyone who wants to learn about their inconstancy may look at the Antiochi and Demetrii, whirling and alternating in and out of power; the man flourishing in

---

57 That is, Helena.
58 Psalm 63.7
59 Genesis 3.17,18.
60 Died c. A.D. 336.

61 Died c. A.D. 274.
62 Ephesians 5.27.
63 A.D. 249–251.

power today may be driven tomorrow not merely from power, but from his native land, exiled by the fickleness of the peoples whom he had ruled. Their foolishness, both in secular behavior and in religious belief, has thrived until this day, so that neither in the preparation of the Eucharist, nor in the location of the Apostolic see do they have anything in common with us. But if making the sacrament out of leavened bread is defended with the apparently reasonable argument that using yeast is not harmful when it is done in good faith, and that the Lord had put an end to the old ways by eating lamb with unleavened bread, and celebrating the sacrament of his own body with the same bread, because there was no other bread, and he could not fulfill the law at that time in any other way, to them the use of unleavened bread, necessary at the time, did not seem a central part of the mystery, just as the dipping of the mouthful[64] was an indication not of the carrying out of the sacrament but of Judas' betrayal. If, I say, these things and others also can be proposed as either true or false, then what will they say about the Holy Spirit, those who impiously argue, in accordance with the vestiges of the Arian heresy, that He is less than the Father and the Son. Since they disagree, both in thought and in many of their actions, with the ancient laws of the fathers, and with the holy ritual of the Western Church, they have added this increment to their damnation: they claim that God limps, having inflicted upon him an inequality of his own nature. For if one is baptized according to the teaching of the Son of God, "in the name of the Son and the Holy Spirit," it is for this reason, that the three are one God; arguing that any of the three is less than the other is to argue that he is not God. Therefore the herd of such bulls among the cows of the people now shuts out those who have proved themselves worth their weight in silver, since some of our countrymen, stirred by the debate with the Greeks, have published splendid books on the office of the Holy Spirit. However, since God places a stumbling-block before those who sin voluntarily, their land has spewed forth its own inhabitants, since they were first deprived of the awareness of true belief, and rightly and justly they have been dispossessed of all earthly possessions. For since they fell away from faith in the Trinity, like those who fall in the mud and get muddier, little by little they have come to the final degradation of having taken paganism upon themselves; as the punishment for their sin proceeded, foreigners attacked them, and they lost the soil of their native land. Even those who managed to remain in their native land must pay tribute to foreigners. The most splendidly noble cities, Antioch, Jerusalem, and Nicea,[65] and the provinces, Syria, Palestine, and Greece, the seed-beds of the new grace, have lost their internal strength at the roots, while the Italians, French, and English, who migrated there, have flourished. I am silent about the fact that so many abuses have become customary in those worthless churches, that in many of these regions no one is made a priest unless he has chosen a wife, as though in observance of the apostle's statement that a man who is to be chosen should have only one wife. That this statement does not concern a man who has and uses a

---

[64] *buccella intinctio.*   [65] Iznik (Turkish).

wife, but does concern a man who had a wife and sent her away, is confirmed by the authority of the Western church. I am also silent about the fact that, against Latin custom, people of the Christian faith, regardless of whether they are men or women, are bought and sold like brute animals. To add to the cruelty, they are sent far from their native country to be sold as slaves to pagans. Finally, worse than all these, it appears that imperial law among them generally sanctions young girls (a freedom permitted everywhere as though it were just) being taken to become prostitutes. An example: if a man has three or four daughters, one of them is put in a house of prostitution; some part of the smelly lucre derived from the suffering of these unhappy women goes to the wretched emperor's treasury, while part goes to support the woman who earned it in such a base way. Hear how the clamor ascends mightily to the ears of the Lord of Hosts.[66] Moreover, the priests who are in charge of celebrating the divine sacraments prepare the Lord's body after they have eaten, as I have heard, and offer it to be eaten by anyone who is fasting. While they wander in these and similar paths of evil, and while they "follow their own devices,"[67] God has set up over them a new law-giver, "so that the people may know that they are mortal."[68] And since they, more wanton than the beasts of the field, have knowingly transgressed the limits set by their fathers, they have become objects of opprobrium. But just let me tell something about the authority upon which the nations of the East rely when they decide to abandon the Christian religion to return to paganism.

According to popular opinion, there was a man, whose name, if I have it right, was Mathomus, who led them away from belief in the Son and in the Holy Spirit. He taught them to acknowledge only the person of the Father as the single, creating God, and he said that Jesus was entirely human. To sum up his teachings, having decreed circumcision, he gave them free rein for every kind of shameful behavior. I do not think that this profane man lived a very long time ago, since I find that none of the church doctors has written against his licentiousness. Since I have learned nothing about his behavior and life from writings, no one should be surprised if I am willing to tell what I have heard told in public by some skillful speakers. To discuss whether these things are true or false is useless, since we are considering here only the nature of this new teacher, whose reputation for great crimes continues to spread. One may safely speak ill of a man whose malignity transcends and surpasses whatever evil can be said of him.

An Alexandrian patriarch died, I'm not sure when, and the leaderless church was divided, as usual, into various factions; the more eagerly each argued for the person whom he favored, the more strongly he argued against the person whom he opposed. The choice of the majority was a hermit who lived nearby. Some of the more discerning men often visited him, to find out what he was really like, and from these conversations they discovered that he disagreed with them about

---

[66] James 5.4.
[67] Psalm 80.13.
[68] Psalm 9.21.

the Catholic faith. When they found this out, they immediately abandoned the choice they had made, and, with the greatest regret, set about condemning it. Scorned, torn apart by bitter grief, since he had been unable to reach what he had striven for, like Arius, he began to think carefully how to take vengeance by spreading the poison of false belief, to undermine Catholic teaching everywhere. Such men, whose whole aim in life is to be praised, are mortally wounded, and bellow unbearably, whenever they feel that their standing in the community is diminished in any way. Seeing his opportunity with the hermit, the Ancient Enemy approached the wretch with these words: "If," he said, "you want certain solace for having been rejected, and you want power far greater than that of a patriarch, look very carefully at that young man who was with those who came to you lately – I shall recollect for you his clothing, his face, his physical appearance, his name – fill his vigorous, receptive mind with the teaching that lies near to your heart. Pursue this man, who will listen faithfully to your teachings and propagate them far and wide." Encouraged by the utterance, the hermit searched among the groups that visited him for the identifying signs of the young man. Recognizing him, he greeted him affectionately, then imbued him with the poison with which he himself was rotting. And because he was a poor man, and a poor man has less authority than a rich one, he proceeded to procure wealth for himself by this method: a certain very rich woman had recently become a widow; the filthy hermit sent a messenger to bring her to him, and he advised her to marry again. When she told him that there was no one appropriate for her to marry, he said that he had found for her a prophet who was appropriate, and that, if she consented to marry him, she would live in perfect happiness. He persisted steadily in his blandishments, promising that the prophet would provide for her both in this life and in the next, and he kindled her feminine emotions to love a man she did not know. Seduced, then, by the hope of knowing everything that was and everything that might be, she was married to her seer, and the formerly wretched Mahomet, surrounded by brilliant riches, was lifted, perhaps to his own great stupefaction, to unhoped-for power. And since the vessel of a single bed frequently received their sexual exchanges, the famous prophet contracted the disease of epilepsy, which we call, in ordinary language, falling sickness; he often suffered terribly while the terrified prophetess watched his eyes turning upward, his face twisting, his lips foaming, his teeth grinding. Frightened by this unexpected turn of events, she hurried to the hermit, accusing him of the misfortune which was happening to her. Disturbed and bitter in her heart, she said that she would prefer to die rather than to endure an execrable marriage to a madman. She attacked the hermit with countless kinds of complaints about the bad advice he had given her. But he, who was supplied with incomparable cleverness, said, "You are foolish for ascribing harm to what is a source of light and glory. Don't you know, blind woman, that whenever God glides into the minds of the prophets, the whole bodily frame is shaken, because the weakness of the flesh can scarcely bear the visitation of divine majesty? Pull yourself together, now, and do not be afraid of these unusual visions; look upon the blessed convulsions of the holy man with gratitude, especially since spiritual power teaches him at those moments about the things it will help you to know and to do in the future." Her womanly flightiness was taken in by these words, and what she had formerly thought foul and despicable now seemed to her not only tolerable, but sacred and remarkable. Meanwhile the man was being filled with profane teaching drawn by the devil's piping through the heretical hermit. When the hermit, like a herald, went everywhere before him, Mahomet was believed by everyone to be a prophet. When far and wide, in the opinion of everyone, his growing reputation shone, and he saw that people in the surrounding as well as in distant lands were inclining towards his teachings, after consulting with his teacher, he wrote a law, in which he loosened the reins of every vice for his followers, in order to attract more of them. By doing this he gathered a huge mob of people, and the better to deceive their uncertain minds with the pretext of religion, he ordered them to fast for three days, and to offer earnest prayers for God to grant a law. He also gives them a sign, because, should it please God to give them a law, he will grant it in an unusual manner, from an unexpected hand. Meanwhile, he had a cow, whom he himself had trained to follow him, so that whenever she heard his voice or saw him, almost no force could prevent her from rushing to him with unbearable eagerness. He tied the book he had written to the horns of the animal, and hid her in the tent in which he himself lived. On the third day he climbed a high platform above all the people he had called together, and began to declaim to the people in a booming voice. When, as I just said, the sound of his words reached the cow's ears, she immediately ran from the tent, which was nearby, and, with the book fastened on her horns, made her way eagerly through the middle of the assembled people to the feet of the speaker, as though to congratulate him. Everyone was amazed, and the book was quickly removed and read to the breathless people, who happily accepted the licence permitted by its foul law. What more? The miracle of the offered book was greeted with applause over and over again. As though sent from the sky, the new license for random copulation was propagated everywhere, and the more the supply of permitted filth increased, the more the grace of a God who permitted more lenient times, without any mention of turpitude, was preached. All of Christian morality was condemned by a thousand reproofs, and whatever examples of goodness and strength the Gospel offered were called cruel and harsh. But what the cow had delivered was considered universal liberty, the only one recommended by God. Neither the antiquity of Moses nor the more recent Catholic teachings had any authority. Everything which had existed before the law, under the law, under grace, was marked as implacably wrong. If I may make inappropriate use of what the Psalmist sings, "God did not treat other nations in this fashion, and he never showed his judgements to any other people."[69] The greater opportunity to fulfil lust, and, going beyond the appetites

---

[69] Psalm 146 (147).20.

of beasts, by resorting to multiple whores, was cloaked by the excuse of procreating children. However, while the flow of nature was unrestrained in these normal acts, at the same time they engaged in abnormal acts, which we should not even name, and which were unknown even to the animals. At the time, the obscurity of this nefarious sect first covered the name of Christ, but now it has wiped out his name from the furthest corners of the entire East, from Africa, Egypt, Ethiopia, Libya, and even the more remote coasts of Spain – a country near us. But now to describe how this marvelous law-giver made his exit from our midst. Since he often fell into a sudden epileptic fit, with which we have already said he struggled, it happened once, while he was walking alone, that a fit came upon him and he fell down on the spot; while he was writhing in this agony, he was found by some pigs, who proceeded to devour him, so that nothing could be found of him except his heels. While the true Stoics, that is, the worshipers of Christ, killed Epicurus, lo, the greatest law-giver tried to revive the pig, in fact he did revive it, and, himself a pig, lay exposed to be eaten by pigs, so that the master of filth appropriately died a filthy death. He left his heels fittingly, since he had wretchedly fixed the traces of false belief and foulness in wretchedly deceived souls. We shall make an epitaph for his heels in four lines of the poet:

> Aere perennius,
> Regalique situ pyramidum altius:

> (I have built a monument) more lasting than brass, taller than the royal site of the Pyramids . . .

So that the fine man, happier than any pig, might say with the poet:

> Non omnis moriar, multaque pars mei
> Vitabit Libitiam.

> I shall not die entirely, a great part of me shall avoid Hell.[70]

That is:

> Manditur ore suum, qui porcum vixerat, hujus
> Membra beata cluunt, podice fusa suum.
> Quum talos ori, tum quod sus fudit odori,
> Digno qui celebrat cultor honore ferat.

> He who has lived by the pig is chewed to death by the pig and the limbs which were called blessed have become pigs' excrement. May those who wish to honor him carry to their mouths his heels, which the pig has poured forth in stench.

What if there is some truth in what the Manicheans say about purification, that in every food something of God is present and that part of God is purified by

---

[70] Horace, *Odes* 3.30.1–2.

chewing and digesting, and the purified part is turned into angels, who are said to depart from us in belching and flatulence: how many angels may we believe were produced by the flesh eaten by these pigs and by the great farts they let go? But, laying aside the comic remarks intended to mock his followers, my point is that they did not think that he was God, but a just man and leader, through whom divine laws might be transmitted. They imagined that he had been taken up into heaven, with only his heels left as a monument for his faithful adherents, who visit them with great veneration, and condemn eating pork, because pigs consumed their lord with their bites.

After the pagan heresy had grown strong over a long time, and for many generations, the people whom we have mentioned above invaded Palestine, Jerusalem, and the Holy Sepulchre, and captured Armenia, Syria, and the part of Greece that extends almost to the sea which is called the Arm of Saint George. Among all the Eastern kingdoms, the Babylonian empire was from ancient times the most powerful, and ruled over many kingdoms. However, the kingdom of the Parthians, whom we, because of changes in the language, call the Turks, is preeminent in military matters, in horsemanship, and in courage, although it is a very small country. And so the Babylonian emperor occupied the areas we just mentioned with a large army, but in the course of time he lost them, as the Turks grew in number, and the Assyrians were defeated. More energetic, and in command of an astute boldness, they were attacking the empire of Constantinople and seemed about to besiege the city, when the Emperor of the Greeks, frightened by their frequent and relentless incursions, sent a letter to France, written to the elder Robert, Count of Flanders,[71] offering him reasons that might urge him to defend endangered Greece. He did not approach him because he thought that Robert, although extremely wealthy, and capable of raising a large force, could alone supply enough troops for the task, but because he realized that if a man of such power went on such a journey, he would attract many of our people, if only for the sake of a new experience, to support him. This count was truly as wise in military matters as he was perspicacious and discriminating in literary matters. He had once before gone to Jerusalem, for the sake of prayer, and, happening to pass through Constantinople on the way, had spoken with the emperor; as a result, on the basis of the great feeling of trust he had developed for him, the emperor was impelled to call upon him for aid. Since inserting the letter itself in this little work would produce a tedious effect, I have preferred to offer some of what was said, but clothed in my own words.

He complained that, "After Christianity was driven out, the churches which the pagans held had been turned into stables for horses, mules, and other animals. It was also true that they had set up in them temples, which they called Mahomeries, and they carried out all kinds of filthy activity in them, so that they

---

[71] Robert I, Count of Flanders, 1071–1093. The letter is printed in *Epistulae et chartae ad historiam primi belli sacri sectantes*, edited by Heinrich Hagenmayer, Innsbruck, 1901, pp. 129–136.

had become not cathedrals, but brothels and theaters. Moreover, there would be no purpose to my mentioning the slaughter of Catholics, since the faithful who died received in exchange eternal life, while those who survived led lives wretchedly bound by the yoke of slavery, harsher, I believe, than what those who died endured. They took virgins and made them public prostitutes, since they were never deterred by shame or feeling for marital fidelity. Mothers were violated in the presence of their daughters, raped over and over again by different men, while their daughters were compelled, not only to watch, but to sing obscene songs and to dance. Then they changed places, and the suffering, which is painful and shameful to speak of, was inflicted upon the daughters, while the filthy activity was adorned by the obscene songs of the unfortunate mothers. Finally reverence for all that was called Christian was handed over to the brothel. When the female sex was not spared (an action which might be excused since it is at least in accord with nature), they became worse than animals, breaking all human laws by turning on men. Their lust overflowed to the point that the execrable and profoundly intolerable crime of sodomy, which they committed against men of middle or low station, they also committed against a certain bishop, killing him. How can this urgent lust, worse than any insanity anywhere, which perpetually flees wisdom and modesty, and is enkindled more powerfully the more it is quenched, control itself among human beings, whom it befouls with couplings unheard of among beasts, actions to which Christians may not give a name. And although, according to their own judgement, these wretches may have many women, that is not enough, but they must stain their dignity at the hog-trough of such filth by using men also. It is not surprising that God could not tolerate their ripe wantoness, and turned it into grief, and the earth, in its ancient way, cast out the excrement of such destructive inhabitants." Therefore, after he had expressed his great fears about the siege of Constantinople, which would follow the crossing of the Arm of Saint George by his enemies, he added, among other remarks, the following: "This great city is most deserving of every kind of help if for no other reason than to prevent the six apostles whose bodies are buried here from being burned by unbelievers, or buried in the swirling sea." And certainly nothing is more true. For that city, not only superior for its monuments of the saints, but also famed for the merit and renown of its founder, and particularly for the divine revelation which transformed it from a very old little town into a miraculous city and a second Rome, is worthy of having the whole world come together to help it, if that were possible. Then, after speaking of the apostles, the emperor said that they had the head of John the Baptist, which (although it was not true) seemed to be covered with hair and skin, as though alive today. Now if this were true, one would have to investigate the head of John the Baptist that is glorified by the monks at Angers. Now we are certain that two John the Baptists did not exist, nor did the one man have two heads, which would be impious to say. In this matter, one should consider the frequent but not deadly error, which particularly assails the churches of France, regarding the bodies of saints: two different places claim to have the same martyr or confessor, but a single entity cannot occupy two spaces simultaneously. This mistaken contention arises from the fact that saints are not permitted to enjoy the peace of the permanent burial they deserve. And I do not doubt that their bodies are covered with silver and gold out of motives lower than piety; open and extremely foul avarice drives them to collect money by displaying bones and dragging them around in wagons. These things would stop if, as in the case of the Lord Jesus, their limbs were shut up in locked tombs.

However, setting these things aside, let us go on. The emperor added that if neither the prevention of such evil, nor the love of the aforementioned saints inspired them to perform this task, then at least greed for gold and silver, of which there was a plentiful supply in his region, might entice them. Finally he offered an argument that has no power over men with self-control, saying that they would be drawn by the pleasure of seeing the most beautiful women, as though the beauty of Greek women were so great that they would be preferred to the women of Gaul, and for this reason alone, the Frankish army would march to Thrace. While this foul tyrant was offering this argument, he should have kept in mind that for this very reason the most powerful adversity had descended upon him and his people; in a well-known proclamation, he had issued an order throughout the land that families with several daughters give one of them up to prostitution, and place in his own treasury money gained from the disgusting experience. In addition, he had issued another edict, ordering families with several sons to have one castrated, thus rendering their bodies, deprived of virility, weak and effeminate, no longer fit for military service. Even worse, they were cut off from producing progeny for the future, who might have been looked for as aid against their enemies. Therefore he who had brought destruction upon himself was now compelled to seek help from foreigners. In addition, one should note that this emperor had received the purple not by legitimate succession, but because he had been one of the officers of the palace, under the ruler whose name, unless I am mistaken, was Michael, who had put him in charge of[72] the larger group of Western soldiers, whose natural probity made them the best of the emperor's men, and the emperor's bodyguard. Gathering boldness from the men he commanded, he undertook a coup against his own prince. Invading the city of Constantinople, he captured his ruler, cruelly deprived him of his eyes, and placed him under close guard in a certain town. Then he usurped imperial power entirely without legal right. Compelled by necessity, as we said above, he sought the Franks. But after he saw such remarkable leaders assembled, distinguished both for their impeccable conduct and military ability, he envied the size of the forces, but envied their wisdom even more. When they successfully completed what they had set out to do, his envy of the ability of our men grew even greater; after the victory at Jerusalem, the emperor feared that they might turn their victorious arms against him, especially since they had learned that, among

---

[72] Michael VII Ducas, Parapinaces, 1071–1078.

the nations in that area, he was their most powerful rival. We also heard, however, before the beginning of the journey had been announced, that the emperor's mother, a sorceress, had predicted that a man of Frankish origin would take his empire and his life from him. Judging by events, Bohemund tried to fulfill this oracle, attacking the emperor with such force, and compelling him so often to flee from battle, that a large part of the provinces fell into his hands. Since his family was from Normandy, a part of France, and since he had obtained the hand of the daughter of the King of the Franks, he might be very well be considered a Frank.

HERE ENDS THE FIRST BOOK OF THE DEEDS OF GOD AS PERFORMED BY THE FRENCH.

Book Two

Pope Urban, whose name was Odo before becoming pope, was descended from a noble French family[73] from the area and parish of Rheims, and they say, unless the report is in error, that he was the first French pope. A cleric, he was made a monk of Cluny, after the abbot of glorious memory who aided Hugo;[74] not long afterwards he was made prior, and then, because of his abilities, he was appointed bishop of the city of Ostia, by order of Pope Gregory VII; finally, he was elected supreme pontiff of the Apostolic See. His greatness of spirit was made manifest when he urged that the journey be undertaken, because when he first showed how it was to be done the whole world was astonished. His death, resplendent in miracles, attests to the state of his mind. According to what the bishop who succeeded him at Ostia wrote,[75] many signs were seen after he was dead and buried; a certain young man stood at his tomb, and swore by his own limbs that no sign had ever been given or might be given by the merit of Urban, who was called Odo. Before he could move a step, he was struck dumb, and paralyzed on one side; he died the next day, offering testimony to the power of Urban. This great man, although honored with great gifts, and even with prayers, by Alexius, prince of the Greeks, but driven much more by the danger to all of Christendom, which was diminished daily by pagan incursions (for he heard that Spain was steadily being torn apart by Saracen invasions), decided to make a journey to France, to recruit the people of his country. It was, to be sure, the ancient custom for pontiffs of the apostolic see, if they had been harmed by a neighboring people, always to seek help from the French: the Pontiffs Stephen and Zacharias, in the time of Pepin and Charles,[76] took refuge with them; Pepin made an expedition to Ticinum to restore to the church its patrimony, and to place Stephen back on his throne.[77] Charles compelled King Desiderius,[78] by the mere threat of combat, to return what he had seized by force. More respectful and humble than other nations toward blessed Peter and pontifical decrees, the French, unlike other peoples, have been unwilling to behave insolently against God. For many years we have seen the Germans, particularly the entire kingdom of Lotharingia, struggling with barbaric obstinacy against the commands of Saint Peter and of his pontiffs.[79] In their striving, they prefer to remain under a daily,

---

[73] He was the son of Eucherius, master of Lageri.
[74] Elected Abbot of Cluny in 1049.
[75] Odo, nephew of Urban II.
[76] Stephen II, 752–757; Zacharias, 741–752.
[77] Pepin compelled Astolphus to restore Ravenna and other cities to Stephen in 755.
[78] Last Lombard king, 756–774.
[79] A reference to the struggle between Emperor Henry IV and Gregory VII; see Uta-Renate Blumenthal, *The Investiture Controversy*, Philadelphia, 1988.

or even eternal excommunication rather than submit. Last year while I was arguing with a certain archdeacon of Mainz about a rebellion of his people, I heard him vilify our king and our people, merely because the king had given a gracious welcome everywhere in his kingdom to his Highness Pope Paschal and his princes; he called them not merely Franks, but, derisively, "Francones."[80] I said to him, "If you think them so weak and languid that you can denigrate a name known and admired as far away as the Indian Ocean, then tell me upon whom did Pope Urban call for aid against the Turks? Wasn't it the French? Had they not been present, attacking the barbarians everywhere, pouring their sturdy energy and fearless strength into the battle, there would have been no help for your Germans, whose reputation there amounted to nothing." That is what I said to him. I say truly, and everyone should believe it, that God reserved this nation for such a great task. For we know certainly that, from the time that they received the sign of faith that blessed Remigius brought to them until the present time, they succumbed to none of the diseases of false faith from which other nations have remained uncontaminated either with great difficulty or not at all. They are the ones who, while still laboring under the pagan error, when they triumphed on the battlefield over the Gauls, who were Christians, did not punish or kill any of them, because they believed in Christ. Instead, those whom Roman severity had punished with sword and fire, native French generosity encased in gold and silver, covered with gems and amber. They strove to welcome with honor not only those who lived within their own borders, but they also affectionately cared for people who came from Spain, Italy, or anywhere else, so that love for the martyrs and confessors, whom they constantly served and honored, made them famous, finally driving them to the glorious victory at Jerusalem. Because it has carried the yoke since the days of its youth, it will sit in isolation,[81] a nation noble, wise, war-like, generous, brilliant above all kinds of nations. Every nation borrows the name as an honorific title; do we not see the Bretons, the English, the Ligurians call men "Frank" if they behave well? But now let us return to the subject.

When the pope crossed our borders, he was greeted with such great joy by crowds in the cities, towns, and villages, because no one alive could remember when the bishop of the apostolic see had come to these lands. The year of the incarnate Word 1097 was hastening to its end,[82] when the bishop hastily convoked a council, choosing a city in Auvergne, famous for the most learned of all bishops, Sidonius, although its name has now been changed to Clermont. The council was even more crowded because of the great desire to see the face and to hear the words of such an excellent, rarely seen person. In addition to the

---

80 Paschal came to France in 1107, with Philip I on the throne. Isidore of Seville (IX.ii.101) offers two derivations for "Franks." "Franci a quodam proprio duce vocari putantur. Alii eos a feritate morum nuncupatos existimant." The Archdeacon of Mainz clearly was referring to their animal-like behavior.

81 Jeremiah 3.27, 28.

82 An error by Guibert or by the scribe; the council of Clermont began on 18 November 1095.

multitudes of bishops and abbots, whom some, by counting their staves, estimated at approximately 400, learned men from all of France and the dependent territories flowed to that place. One could see there how he presided over them with serene gravity, with a dignified presence, and, if I may use the words of Sidonius, with what peppery eloquence[83] the most learned pope answered whatever objections were raised. It was noted with what gentleness the most brilliant man listened gently to the most vehemently argued speeches, and how little he valued the social position of people, judging them only by God's laws.

Then Philip, King of the French, who was in the thirty-seventh year of his reign, having put aside his own wife, whose name was Berta, and having carried off Bertrada, the wife of the Count of Anjou, was excommunicated by the pope, who spurned both the attempts by important people to intercede for the king, and the offers of innumerable gifts. Nor was he afraid because he was now within the borders of the kingdom of France. In this council, just as he had planned before leaving Rome and seeking out the French for this reason, he gave a fine speech to those who were in attendance. Among other things which were said to exceed the memories of the listeners, he spoke about this project. His eloquence was reinforced by his literary knowledge; the richness of his speech in Latin seemed no less than that of any lawyer nimble in his native language. Nor did the crowd of disputants blunt the skill of the speaker. Surrounded by praiseworthy teachers, apparently buried by clouds of cases being pressed upon him, he was judged to have overcome, by his own literary brilliance, the flood of oratory and to have overwhelmed the cleverness of every speech. Therefore his meaning, and not his exact words, follow: "If, among the churches scattered through the whole world, some deserve more reverence than others because they are associated with certain people and places, then, because of certain persons, I say, greater privileges are granted to apostolic sees; in the case of places, some privilege is granted to royal cities, as is the case with the city of Constantinople. We are grateful for having received from this most powerful church the grace of redemption and the origin of all Christianity. If what was said by the Lord remains true, namely that "salvation is from the Jews," and it remains true that the Lord of the Sabbath has left his seed for us, lest we become like those of Sodom and Gomorrah, and that Christ is our seed, in whom lies salvation and blessing for all people, then the earth and the city in which he lived and suffered is called holy by the testimony of Scripture. If this land is the inheritance of God, and his holy temple, even before the Lord walked and suffered there, as the sacred and prophetic pages tell us, then what additional sanctity and reverence did it gain then, when the God of majesty took flesh upon Himself there, was fed, grew up, and moving in his bodily strength walked here and there in the land? To abbreviate a matter that could be spun out at much greater length, this is the place where the blood of the Son of God, holier than heaven and earth, was spilled, where the body, at whose death

---

[83] Sidonius Apollinarus uses "piperata facundia" in Book VIII, epistle xi, of the *Poems and Letters*, ed. W.B. Anderson, Cambridge, 1984, vol I.

the elements trembled, rested in its tomb. What sort of veneration might we think it deserves? If, soon after our Lord's death, while the city was still in the possession of the Jews, the Evangelist called it sacred, when he said, "Many bodies of the saints that have been asleep here have awoken, and come to the holy city, and they have been seen by many, "[84] and it was said by the prophet Isaiah, "His tomb will be glorious,"[85] since this very sanctity, once granted by God the sancti-fier himself, cannot be overcome by any evil whatsoever, and the glory of his tomb in the same way remains undiminished, then, O my dearly beloved brothers, you must exert yourselves, with all your strength, and with God leading you and fighting for you, to cleanse the holiness of the city and the glory of the tomb, which has been polluted by the thick crowd of pagans, if you truly aspire to the author of that holiness and glory, and if you love the traces that he has left on earth. If the Maccabees once deserved the highest praise for piety because they fought for their rituals and their temple, then you too, O soldiers of Christ, deserve such praise, for taking up arms to defend the freedom of your country. If you think you must seek with such effort the thresholds of the apostles and of others, then why do you hesitate to go to see and to snatch up the cross, the blood, and to devote your precious souls to rescuing them? Until now you have waged wrongful wars, often hurling insane spears at each other, driven only by greed and pride, for which you have deserved only eternal death and damnation. Now we propose for you battles which offer the gift of glorious martyrdom, for which you will earn present and future praise. If Christ had not died and been buried in Jerusalem, had not lived there at all, if all these things had not taken place, surely this fact alone should be enough to drive you to come to the aid of the land and the city: that the law came from Zion and the word of God from Jerusalem. If all Christian preaching flows from the fountain of Jerusalem, then let the rivulets, wherever they flow over the face of the earth, flow into the hearts of the Catholic multitude, so that they may take heed of what they owe to this overflowing fountain. If "rivers return to the place whence they flow, so that they may continue to flow,"[86] according to the saying of Solomon, it should seem glorious to you if you are able to purify the place whence you received the cleansing of baptism and the proof of faith. And you should also consider with the utmost care whether God is working through your efforts to restore the church that is the mother of churches; he might wish to restore the faith in some of the eastern lands, in spite of the nearness of the time of the Antichrist. For it is clear that the Antichrist makes war neither against Jews, nor against pagans, but, according to the etymology of his name, he will move against Christians. And if the Antichrist comes upon no Christian there, as today there is scarcely any, there will be no one to resist him, or any whom he might justly move among. Accord-ing to Daniel and Jerome his interpreter, his tent will be fixed on the Mount of Olives, and he will certainly take his seat, as the Apostle teaches, in Jerusalem, "in

---

[84] Matthew 27.53.
[85] Isaiah 11.10.

[86] Eccl. 1.7.

the temple of God, as though he were God,"[87] and, according to the prophet, he will undoubtedly kill three kings pre-eminent for their faith in Christ, that is, the kings of Egypt, of Africa, and of Ethiopia. This cannot happen at all, unless Christianity is established where paganism now rules. Therefore if you are eager to carry out pious battles, and since you have accepted the seedbed of the knowledge of God from Jerusalem, then you may restore the grace that was borrowed there. Thus through you the name of Catholicism will be propagated, and it will defeat the perfidy of the Antichrist and of the Antichristians. Who can doubt that God, who surpasses every hope by means of his overflowing strength, may so destroy the reeds of paganism with your spark that he may gather Egypt, Africa and Ethiopia, which no longer share our belief, into the rules of his law, and "sinful man, the son of perdition,"[88] will find others resisting him? See how the Gospel cries out that "Jerusalem will be trodden down by the Gentiles, until the time of the nations will be fulfilled."[89] "The time of nations" may be understood in two ways: either that they ruled at will over the Christians, and for their own pleasures have wallowed in the troughs of every kind of filth, and in all of these things have found no obstruction (for "to have one's time" means that everything goes according to one's wishes, as in "My time has not yet come, but your time is always ready,"[90] and one customarily says to voluptuaries, "You have your time;") or else the "time of nations" means the multitudes of nations who, before Israel is saved, will join the faith. These times, dearest brothers, perhaps will now be fulfilled, when, with the aid of God, the power of the pagans will be pushed back by you, and, with the end of the world already near, even if the nations do not turn to the Lord, because, as the Apostle says, "there must be a falling away from faith."[91] Nevertheless, first, according to the prophecies, it is necessary, before the coming of the Antichrist in those parts, either through you or through whomever God wills, that the empire of Christianity be renewed, so that the leader of all evil, who will have his throne there, may find some nourishment of faith against which he may fight. Consider, then, that Almighty providence may have destined you for the task of rescuing Jerusalem from such abasement. I ask you to think how your hearts can conceive of the joy of seeing the holy city revived by your efforts, and the oracles, the divine prophecies fulfilled in our own times. Remember that the voice of the Lord himself said to the church, "I shall lead your seed from the East, and I shall gather you from the West."[92] The Lord has led our seed from the East, in that he brought forth for us in a double manner[93] out of the Eastern land the early progeny of the Church. But out of the West he assembled us, for through those who last began the proof of faith, that is the Westerners (we think that, God willing, this will come about through your deeds), Jerusalem's losses will be restored. If the words of Scripture and our own

---

87 II Thess. 2.4.
88 II Thess. 2.3.
89 Luke 21.24.
90 John 7.6.

91 II Thess. 2.3.
92 Isaiah 43.5.
93 Presumably Peter and Paul.

admonitions do not move your souls, then at least let the great suffering of those who wish to visit the holy places touch you. Think of the pilgrims who travel the Mediterranean; if they are wealthy, to what tributes, to what violence are they subjected; at almost every mile they are compelled to pay taxes and tributes; at the gates of the city, at the entrances of churches and temples, they must pay ransoms. Each time they move from one place to another they are faced with another charge, compelled to pay ransom, and the governors of the Gentiles commonly coerce with blows those who are slow to give gifts. What shall we say about those who have taken up the journey, trusting in their naked poverty, who seem to have nothing more than their bodies to lose? The money that they did not have was forced from them by intolerable tortures; the skin of their bones was probed, cut, and stripped, in search of anything that they might have sewed within. The brutality of these evil-doers was so great that, suspecting that the wretches had swallowed gold and silver, they gave them purgatives to drink, so that they would either vomit or burst their insides. Even more unspeakable, they cut their bellies open with swords, opening their inner organs, revealing with a hideous slashing whatever nature holds secret. Remember, I beg you, the thousands who died deplorably, and, for the sake of the holy places, whence the beginnings of piety came to you, take action. Have unshakable faith that Christ will be the standard-bearer and inseparable advance guard before you who are sent to His wars."

The superb man delivered this speech, and by the power of the blessed Peter absolved everyone who vowed to go, confirming this with an apostolic benediction, and establishing a sign of this honorable promise. He ordered that something like a soldier's belt, or rather that for those about to fight for the Lord, something bearing the sign of the Lord's passion, the figure of a Cross, be sewn onto the tunics and cloaks of those who were going. If anyone, after accepting this symbol, and after having made the public promise, then went back on his good intentions, either out of weak regretfulness, or out of domestic affection, such a person, according to the pope's decree, would be considered everywhere an outlaw, unless he came to his senses and fulfilled the obligation which he had foully laid aside. He also cursed with a horrible anathema all those who might dare to harm the wives, sons, and possessions of those who took up God's journey for all of the next three years.

Finally, he entrusted the leadership of the expedition to the most praiseworthy of men, the bishop of the city of Puy (whose name, I regret, I have never discovered or heard). He granted him the power to teach the Christian people as his representative, wherever they went, and therefore, in the manner of the apostles, he laid hands upon him and gave him his blessing as well. How wisely he carried out his commission the results of this wonderful effort demonstrate.

And so, when the council held at Clermont at the octave of blessed Martin in the month of November was over, the great news spread through all parts of France, and whoever heard the news of the Pontiff's decree urged his neighbors and family to undertake the proposed "path of God" (for this was its epithet).

The courtly nobility were already burning with desire, and the middle-level knights were bursting to set out, when lo the poor also were aflame with desire, without any consideration for the scarcity of their resources, and without worrying about suitably disposing of their homes, vineyards, and fields. Instead, each sold his assets at a price much lower than he would have received if he had been shut up in a painful prison and needed to pay an immediate ransom. At this time there was a general famine, with great poverty even among the very wealthy, since even though there were enough things, here and there, for sale for some people, they had nothing or scarcely anything with which those things could be bought. Masses of poor people learned to feed often on the roots of wild plants, since they were compelled by the scarcity of bread to search everywhere for some possible substitute. The misery that everyone was crying out about was clearly threatening to the powerful people as they watched, and, while each man, considering the anguish of the starving mob to be of little importance, became fastidiously parsimonious, fearing that he might squander the wealth for which he had worked hard by spending money too easily, the thirsty hearts of the avaricious, who rejoiced that the times smiled upon their brutal rates of interest, thought of the bushels of grain they had stored through the fertile years, and calculated how much their sale would add to their accumulating mountains of money. Thus, while some suffer terribly, and others swiftly go about their business, Christ, "breaking the ships of Tarshish with a powerful wind,"[94] resounded in everyone's ears, and he "who freed those who were in adamantine chains" broke[95] the shackles of those desperate men whose hearts were ensnared by greed. Although, as I just said, hard times reduced everyone's wealth, nevertheless, when the hard times provoked everyone to spontaneous exile, the wealth of many men came out into the open, and what had seemed expensive when no one was moved, was sold at a cheap price, now that everyone one was eager for the journey. As many men were rushing to depart (I shall illustrate the sudden and unexpected drop in prices with one example of those things that were sold), seven sheep brought an unheard-of price of five cents. The lack of grain became a surfeit, and each tried to get whatever money he could scrape together by any means; each seemed to be offering whatever he had, not at the seller's, but at the buyer's price, lest he be late in setting out on the path of God. It was a miraculous sight: everyone bought high and sold low; whatever could be used on the journey was expensive, since they were in a hurry; they sold cheaply whatever items of value they had piled up; what neither prison nor torture could have wrung from them just a short time before they now sold for a few paltry coins. Nor is it less absurd that many of those who had no desire to go, who laughed one day at the frantic selling done by the others, declaring that they were going on a miserable journey, and would return even more miserable, were suddenly caught up the next day, and

---

[94] Psalm 47.8.   [95] Psalm 77.7.

abandoned all their good for a few small coins, and set out with those at whom they had laughed.

> Who can tell of the boys, the old men, who were stirred to go to war? Who can count the virgins and the weak, trembling old men? Everyone sang of battle, but did not say that they would fight. Offering their necks to the sword, they promised martyrdom. "You young men," they said, "will draw swords with your hands, but may we be permitted to earn this by supporting Christ."[96]

Indeed they seemed to have a desire to emulate God, "but not according to knowledge,"[97] but God, who customarily turns many vain undertakings to a pious end, prepared salvation for their simple souls, because of their good intentions. There you would have seen remarkable, even comical things; poor people, for example, tied their cattle to two-wheel carts, armed as though they were horses, carrying their few possessions, together with their small children, in the wagon. The little children, whenever they came upon a castle or a city, asked whether this was the Jerusalem to which they were going.

At that time, before people set out on the journey, there was a great disturbance, with fierce fighting, throughout the entire kingdom of the Franks. Everywhere people spoke of rampant thievery, highway robbery; endless fires burned everywhere. Battles broke out for no discernible reason, except uncontrollable greed. To sum up briefly, whatever met the eye of greedy men, no matter to whom it belonged, instantly became their prey. Therefore the change of heart they soon underwent was remarkable and scarcely believable because of the heedless state of their souls, as they all begged the bishops and priests to give the sign prescribed by the above-mentioned pope, that is, the crosses. As the force of powerful winds can be restrained by the gentle rain, so all of the feuds of each against the other were put to rest by the aspiration imbedded undoubtedly by Christ Himself.

While the leaders, who needed to spend large sums of money for their great retinues, were preparing like careful administrators, the common people, poor in resources but copious in number, attached themselves to a certain Peter the Hermit, and they obeyed him as though he were the leader, as long as the matter remained within our own borders. If I am not mistaken, he was born in Amiens, and, it is said, led a solitary life in the habit of a monk in I do not know what part of upper Gaul, then moved on, I don't know why, and we saw him wander through cities and towns, spreading his teaching, surrounded by so many people, given so many gifts, and acclaimed for such great piety, that I don't ever remember anyone equally honored. He was very generous to the poor with the gifts he was given, making prostitutes morally acceptable for husbands, together with generous gifts, and, with remarkable authority, restoring peace and treaties where there had been discord before. Whatever he did or said seemed like something

---

[96] These seven elegiacs are the first verses Guibert inserts in the *Gesta Dei*.
[97] Rom. 10.2.

almost divine. Even the hairs of his mule were torn out as though they were relics, which we report not as truth, but as a novelty loved by the common people. Outdoors he wore a woolen tunic, which reached to his ankles, and above it a hood; he wore a cloak to cover his upper body, and a bit of his arms, but his feet were bare. He drank wine and ate fish, but scarcely ever ate bread. This man, partly because of his reputation, partly because of his preaching, had assembled a very large army, and decided to set out through the land of the Hungarians. The restless common people discovered that this area produced unusually abundant food, and they went wild with excess in response to the gentleness of the inhabitants. When they saw the grain that had been piled up for several years, as is the custom in that land, like towers in the fields, which we are accustomed to call "metas" [98] in every-day language, and although supplies of various meats and other foods were abundant in this land, not content with the natives' decency, in a kind of remarkable madness, these intruders began to crush them. While the Hungarians, as Christians to Christians, had generously offered everything for sale, our men willfully and wantonly ignored their hospitality and generosity, arbitrarily waging war against them, assuming that they would not resist, but would remain entirely peaceful. In an accursed rage they burned the public granaries we spoke of, raped virgins, dishonored many marriage beds by carrying off many women, and tore out or burned the beards of their hosts. None of them now thought of buying what he needed, but instead each man strove for what he could get by theft and murder, boasting with amazing impudence that he would easily do the same against the Turks. On their way they came to a castle that they could not avoid passing through. It was sited so that the path allowed no divergence to the right or left. With their usual insolence they moved to besiege it, but when they had almost captured it, suddenly, for a reason that is no concern of mine, they were overwhelmed; some died by sword, others were drowned in the river, others, without any money, in abject poverty, deeply ashamed, returned to France. And because this place was called Moisson, and when they returned they said that they had been as far as Moisson, they were greeted with great laughter everywhere. [99]

When he was unable to restrain this undisciplined crowd of common people, who were like prisoners and slaves, Peter, together with a group of Germans and the dregs of our own people, whose foresight had enable them to escape, reached the city of Constantinople on the calends of August (July 30). But a large army of Italians, Ligurians, Langobards, together with men from parts of countries beyond the Alps, had preceded him, and had decided to wait for his army and the armies of the other Frankish leaders, because they did not think that they had a large enough army to go beyond the province of the Greeks and attack the Turks. By order of the emperor they had been granted permission to buy everything they wanted, and to conduct business in the city, but, on the advice of this prince,

[98] Classical Latin for a conical column.
[99] In French, *moisson* means "harvest."

they were forbidden to cross the Arm of Saint George, which was the sea that provided a border with the Turks, because he said that it was sure destruction for so few men to go up against so many. But they were not held back by the decency of the people of the province, nor were they mollified by the emperor's affability, but they behaved very insolently, wrecking palaces, burning public buildings, tearing the roofs of churches that were covered with lead, and then offering to sell the lead back to the Greeks. Disturbed by such foul arrogance, the emperor instructed them to delay their crossing of the waters of the Arm no longer. Once they had made the crossing, they continued to behave as they had on the other side; those who had taken a vow to fight against the pagans fought against men of our own faith, destroying churches everywhere, and stealing the possessions of Christians. Since they were not subject to the severity of a king, who might correct their errors with judicial strength, nor did they reflect soberly upon divine law, which might have restrained the instability of their minds, they fell to sudden death, because death comes to meet the undisciplined, and the man who cannot control himself does not last long.

When they finally reached Nicomedia,[100] the Italians, Lombards, and Germans, unable to bear the pride of the Franks, separated from them. For the Franks, as their name indicates,[101] were famous for their great energy, but, in large groups, unless they are restrained by a firm hand, they are fiercer than they should be. And so the people from beyond the Alps, having separated, as we just said, from the Franks, chose as their leader a certain Rainald, and entered the province which is called Romania.[102] Four days march from Nicomedia, they came upon a castle which its builder had been pleased to call Exorogorgum,[103] and which, since it had been abandoned by its inhabitants, lay open to the troops, who immediately rushed in. The inhabitants had fled out of fear of the invaders; desperate to save themselves, they gave no thought to carrying with them their goods, of which they had a considerable amount. Thus the troops found an abundance of food there, and they ate their fill. When the Turks discovered that the Christians had occupied the castle, they laid siege to it with great force. In front of the entrance to the city was a well, and below it, not far from the city walls, another well, where their leader Rainald cleverly set an ambush, to keep an eye on the Turks. Soon the Turks who were being watched advanced towards the city, and on the day on which the memory of the blessed Michael was

---

100 Izmit, on the Sea of Marmara. The *Gesta Francorum* begins here. A more specific account of the difficulties that produced the separation from the Franks can be found in Albert of Aix, RHC IV.284.

101 "Franci a quodam proprio duce vocari putantur. Alii eos a feritate morum nuncupatos existimant. Sunt enim in illis mores inconditi, naturalis ferocitas animorum." "The French are thought to derive their name from one of their leaders. Others think that they derive their name from the ferocity of their behavior. For they are naturally fierce." (Isidore of Seville, *Etymologies*, ed. W.M. Lindsay, Oxford, 1962, vol. 2).

102 Asia Minor, or the entire Byzantine empire.

103 Xerigordo, according to Anna Comnena; today, Eski-Kaled.

celebrated,[104] the duke and his retainers were attacked, and many of those who lay in ambush were killed, while others were forced to return in disgrace within the battlements. The surrounding Turks attacked so relentlessly that the Crusaders were prevented from drawing water. They became so thirsty that they drew blood from their horses and asses, and were compelled to drink the blood. Some, by dipping their belts and rags into a cistern, and squeezing the liquid into their mouths, seemed to find some relief. Others, horrible though it is to say, drank their own urine,[105] while others dug a hole and placed themselves in the hole they had dug, covering their parched breasts with the recently dug up earth, in the belief that they might relieve their burning insides with a bit of moisture. The bishops and priests who were present, and were themselves suffering in the same way, seeing that the dangers were hideous and human help unavailable, offered consolation, continuing to promise heavenly rewards. For eight days their suffering continued. While they all seemed to be subject to the same misery, they did not all hope for God's mercy in the same way; those who had been the leaders plotted treacherously to save themselves. Rainald, who lead them in prosperity, secretly and foully concluded a pact with the Turks, promising to betray to them all the soldiers he commanded. And so he marched out as though about to go to battle with them, but while pretending to lead them in this way, he and many of his own men fled to the Turks, and he remained with them from then on; the others were captured. Some of the prisoners were challenged about their faith, and ordered to renounce Christ, but they proclaimed Christ with steady heart and voice, and were decapitated.

> And now Christ will have new honors, like those he had long ago, ornamenting our age with new martyrs. How fragrant are the laurels on the brows of those who prepare to offer their throats to the swift blade! I shall call them happy who endure those few moments: their firm faith has brought them eternal life. Now the least of us need despair no longer, having dared what can scarcely be imitated.[106]

The Turks divided up among themselves some of the captives, whose lives they had spared, or rather reserved for a more painful death, and submitted them to dismal servitude at the hands of cruel masters. Some were exposed in public, like targets, and were pierced by arrows; others were given away as gifts, while others were sold outright. Those to whom they were given took them back to their own homes, bringing some of them to the region called Khorasan, and others to the city of Antioch, where they would endure wretched slavery under the worst masters imaginable.

---

104 September 29, 1096.

105 Guibert here rejects the perhaps more pathetic scene in the *Gesta Francorum* (Bréhier, 8): "alii mingebant in pugillo alterius et bibebant."

106 Eight elegiacs.

They underwent a torture much longer than that endured by those whose heads were severed swiftly by the sword. A cruel master drives them, subjecting them to painful labor; everywhere the pious man serves the ungrateful man. The conscientious worker is flogged; the faithful man, who performs eagerly and competently, is punished. What he sees, what he hears, what he does during the day, because he resists doing evil, becomes foul torture. I have no doubt that their suffering was more excruciating than three days of torture on the rack.[107]

These were the first martyrs God made in the nearly desperate state of our modern times.

Meanwhile Peter, about whom we spoke earlier, often troubled by the folly of his retinue, disturbed by frequent losses, finally gave the reins of leadership over to a well-born man, a powerful warrior from beyond the Seine, whose name was Walter,[108] in the hope that those whom he had been unable to control by warnings might at least be restrained by military authority. Walter hurried, together with his insane army, to reach Civitot,[109] a city that is said to be located above Nicaea.[110] When the Turks, who were keeping track of our movements, found out, they hurried to Civitot, eager to act out their great ill will. Half-way there, they met up with the above-mentioned Walter and his group, and they killed him and a great many of his men. Peter, called the Hermit, unable to restrain the insanity of the men he had gathered together, was afraid of being caught up in their undisciplined, improvident folly, and wisely retreated to Constantinople. The Turks attacked them without warning, and, finding some of them asleep, and others not only without weapons, but unclothed as well, immediately killed them all. Among them they found a certain priest performing mass, and they killed him in the very act of completing the sacrament; while he was sacrificing to God, they sacrificed him at the same altar.

What better host can be offered to God than the flesh of him who becomes a victim for his God. What prayer did he utter from the depths of his heart when the trumpets of battle sounded? The victors tore them to pieces, the clangor of arms resounded, and the wretched band of fugitives howled. The fine priest embraced the altar, holding the sacred host closely. "Good Jesus," he said, "you are here as my protection. Since I am holding you, let the hope of flight disappear. I shall enter into an eternal pact with you. I am killed, and you, God, shall carry out the sacred things we have begun."[111]

---

107 Ten elegiacs.
108 Sometimes given the epithet, "sine habere," "the Penniless."
109 Gemlik, now abandoned.
110 Iznick, on the lake of the same name.
111 Twelve Asclepiadeans. At this point, the *Gesta Francorum* gives only "quemdam sacerdotem missam celebrantem, quem statim super altare martirizaverunt," "a priest celebrating mass, whom they immediately martyred on the altar."

Those who were able to escape fled to the city of Civetot. The depths of the sea received some, who, unable to escape, preferred to choose their death rather than have it thrust upon them. Others sought out the mountains and hid among the rocks, while others hid in the woods. After they had captured or taken vengeance on those they found outside, the Turks quickly attacked those who were hiding inside the castle and they set up a siege, bringing wood to start a fire. They lit fires for those who were being besieged, thinking that the fire would burn those inside the castle. However, in accordance with God's judgement, the whole force of the fire fell upon the Turks, and burned some of them, while none of it reached our men. They continued to attack, however, and the town was captured. Those whom they found alive they tied up and then, as had been done to the others before them, they were sent to the various provinces from which the enemy had come, to endure perpetual exile. These things happened in the month of October. When the treacherous emperor was informed of the disaster that had befallen the faithful, the wretch was elated with joy, and ordered that the remaining troops be given permission to cross the Arm of Saint George, and to retreat to the nearer parts of Greece. When he saw them return to the territory over which he had power, he forced them to sell their arms to him. Such was the end of the group under the command of Peter the Hermit. We have followed this story without interrupting it so that we might show that Peter's group in no way helped the others, but in fact added to the audacity of the Turks. And now we shall return to the men we have passed over, who followed the same path that Peter did, but in a far more restrained and fortunate way.

Duke Godfrey, the son of Count Eustace of Boulogne, had two brothers: Baldwin, who ruled Edessa, and succeeded his brother as King of Jerusalem, and who still rules there; and Eustace, who rules in the county he inherited from his father. They had a powerful father, who was competent in worldly affairs, and their mother was, if I am not mistaken, a learned Lotharingian aristocrat, but most remarkable for her innate serenity and great devotion to God. The joys she received from such exemplary sons were due, we believe, to her profound religious belief. Godfrey, about whom we are now speaking, had received a duchy in Lotharingia as his maternal heritage. All three, in no way inferior to their mother in honesty, flourished in great military deeds, as well as in the restraint of their behavior. The glorious woman used to say, when she marveled at the result of the journey and the success of her sons, that she had heard from the mouth of her son the duke a prediction of the outcome long before the beginning of the expedition. For he said that he wanted to go to Jerusalem not as a simple pilgrim, as others had done, but forcefully, with a large army, if he could raise one. In accordance with this divinely inspired intuition, fortune later smiled on his project. The three brothers, heedless of the great honors they already had, set out on the journey. But even as Godfrey was wiser than his other brothers, so he was equipped with a larger army. He was joined by Baldwin, Count of Mons, son of Robert, the paternal uncle of the young Count of Flanders. With the splendid knightly ceremony and spectacle, the band of powerful young men entered the

52

land of the Hungarians, in possession of what Peter was unable to obtain: control over his army. Two days before Christmas, the first of the French leaders to arrive, they reached the city of Constantinople, but their lodgings were outside the city. The treacherous emperor, frightened when he heard that the brilliant duke had arrived, offered formal, but grudging signs of respect, and offered him permission to dwell in front of the walls, in a suburb of the city. And so, after accepting the emperor's offer, the duke and each of his men sent their own squires to get straw and whatever was necessary for their horses from wherever they could. While they were thinking that they could go safely and securely wherever they wished, the foul prince secretly ordered the men around him to kill, without making any distinctions, all of the men who were carrying out the duke's instructions, wherever they found them. When Baldwin, the duke's brother, found out about this, he set an ambush; when he discovered the Turcopolitans violently attacking his own men, he forcefully attacked them, as was right. And with God's favor he won such a victory that he captured sixty of them; he killed some of them and handed others over to his brother the duke. When news of this event reached the impious emperor, he was filled with self-reproach. Made more cautious by this event, the duke left the suburb of the city where he had been staying, and set up camp outside of its borders. However, as evening approached, the emperor, unable to put aside his anger, hastily collected an army and began hostilities against the duke and his men. Forcefully accepting the challenge, the duke defeated them and drove them in flight back into the city, killing seven men. After this fortunate turn of events, the duke returned to his encampment, and remained there for five days, while he and the emperor negotiated a treaty. The frightened emperor asked that the duke cross the Arm of Saint George, promising in return that he would order to be brought to them supplies of whatever kinds of food were to be found in Constantinople and that he would give alms to their poor. And this was done.

Since we have spoken about the duke and his journey up to this point, I must return to the leaders of central France; I shall give a brief sketch of who they were, by what roads they traveled, and what the outcome of their efforts was. The Bishop of Puy, a man to be admired for his life, knowledge, teaching, and wisdom in military affairs, together with a large group of his countrymen, chose to set out through the land of the Slavs. Earlier I expressed my regret at not knowing his name, and for being unable to learn it from the history of which I seem to be the interpreter; finally, however, through those who knew him on that expedition, and who were familiar with him, I learned that this precious man's name was Adhemar.

Among the rest of the leaders, it seems to me that Hugh the Great, the brother of Philip the King of the Franks, must be dealt with first. Although others were wealthier or more powerful, he was second to none in birth or in the probity of his behavior. He was most justly celebrated for being forceful in arms, serenely secure in his noble birth, and, even more important, humble towards every sacred order, forthright and restrained. Certain leaders attached themselves to him, thinking that they would make him king if it happened that, after the Gentiles were driven out, the occupation of the land came about as a result of battle.

After him came Count Stephen, a man endowed with such power that, according to report, he controlled as many castles as the year has days. His generosity was unexcelled, his presence very pleasing, his performance in council sober, steady, and thoughtfully mature; he so excelled in his activities as a knight, that the entire holy army chose him as their chief magistrate and general for the duration of the battle against the Turks. His wife was the wisest of women, the daughter of King William the elder, who had conquered the kingdoms of the English and the Scots. If we wish to praise her wisdom, generosity, bountifulness, and opulence, I fear lest, by praising his wife, we cast a shadow on the magnificent man, which he has earned now that he has been deprived of her. Robert the younger, son of Robert the elder, to whom the emperor had sent a letter, with great eagerness took charge of building up their forces; he gave up the county of Flanders, which he had ruled with great military skill, to become a fellow soldier on the journey with those who had chosen to become exiles for Christ. The rest of the present history will indicate how steadily he carried out what he had begun. Leaving behind their superb wives and their fine sons, they put aside whatever they felt great affection for, choosing instead exile. I say nothing about their honors and possessions, which are outside our concerns. But what surprises us most is the way in which loving husbands and wives, attached even more closely to each other by the bond of children, could be separated, when there was no present danger to either.

It would hardly be right to remain silent about Robert, Count of Normandy, whose bodily indulgences, weakness of will, prodigality with money, gourmandising, indolence, and lechery were expiated by the perseverance and heroism that he vigorously displayed in the army of the Lord. His inborn compassion was naturally so great that he did not permit vengeance to be taken against those who had plotted to betray him and had been sentenced to death, and if something did happen to them, he wept for their misfortune. He was bold in battle, although adeptness at foul trickery, with which we know many men befouled themselves, should not be praised, unless provoked by unspeakable acts. For these and for similar things he should now be forgiven, since God has punished him in this world, where he now languishes in jail, deprived of all his honors.

Each of the illustrious leaders was followed on the journey by many lesser princes, whom we shall not list at this point, because it might seem to be distracting, and we shall perhaps have better reason for naming them in the course of the narration. Who can count the masters of one, two, three, or four castles? There were so many that the siege of Troy could scarcely have brought so many together. At the time that this expedition was being undertaken by the magnates of the kingdom, and a meeting was being held by them with Hugh the Great, with Philip the king present, at Paris, in the month of February, on the eleventh day of the month, a lunar eclipse took place just before midnight. Little by little the moon turned to the color of blood, until it had turned completely and hideously blood red, but at dawn an unusually bright splendor shone around the circle of the moon.

Soon afterward stars seemed to fall from the skies, like a heavy rain. This was so like a portent that many churches considered it to be one, and they instituted public prayers to avert the punishment that it might signify, and they wrote down the time of the event. Soon after, in the month of August, on the eighth day, just before sunset, the part around the center of the moon turned black, and many people saw this happen. It should be said that, although the moon normally undergoes eclipses when full, nevertheless some of these changes of colors are manifestations of portents, and are customarily recorded in the pontifical books and in the deeds of kings. Other things were also seen, most of which we shall pass over.

Raymond, Count of Saint Gilles is placed last, not because he is of no worth, but to complete the list. Because he lived at the furthest edge of France, he has offered us less information about his activities; but he ennobles the telling of this history, from the beginning to the end, with the model of his great virtue and constancy. Having left behind his own son to rule his land, he brought with him his present wife and the only son he had had with her. Raymond was older than the other leaders, but his army was in no way inferior, except perhaps for the Provencal habit of talking too much. When this large force of powerful knights, having traveled over the road which we customarily take to Rome, arrived in Apulia, they had contracted a great many illnesses, and many died, because of the great heat of the summer, the foul air, and the strange food. To cross the sea they gathered at different ports:

> many went to Brundisi, pathless Hydrus (Otrante) received others, while the fishy waters of Bari welcomed others.[112]

Hugh the Great did not wait for his men and the knights of the princes who were his allies, but hastily and unwisely went to the port of Bari, and after a fortunate sea-journey, arrived at Dyrrachium.[113] He should have considered that at the prospect of so many men, such great numbers of knights and foot soldiers, all of Greece, as one might say, trembled to its very foundations. And although other leaders had greater repute among us than he, nevertheless, among foreigners, and particularly among the Greeks, who are the laziest of men, his unbounded fame as the brother of the King of France preceded him. Therefore, when the leader appointed by the emperor to govern that place saw such a well-known man without a large retinue about him, he seized the opportunity to make something out of his isolation. He took the man and ordered him to be conducted carefully and respectfully to Constantinople, with one purpose in

[112] Two dactyls, the second line borrowed from Horace, Sat. I.97.
[113] Durazzo.

mind: that he might promise the frightened prince that he would not harm his life or honor. Thus what happened to this famous man weakened the courage of the great leaders who came after him, for the cleverness of the treacherous prince compelled the others, either by force, or in secret, or by imprecations, to do what he had done. But now the end of this book has come.

Book Three

When the vast army drawn from nearly all the Western lands approached Apulia, word of the arrival of that multitude reached Bohemund, son of Robert who was called Guiscard, a man of remarkable greatness. At that time he was engaged in besieging Amalfi. After the messenger had made his way through the crowd of people, he told Bohemund the reasons for the journey: they were hastening to free Jerusalem, the Lord's tomb, and the sacred places which were being abused there, from the power of the Gentiles. He also told him of the kind of people, of how many fine men, as I might say, left their honorable positions and were striving with unheard-of eagerness to join this expedition. He asked if they were carrying arms, packs, what insignia of this new pilgrimage they were wearing, and finally, what war-cries they called out in battle. He replied that the Franks were carrying their usual arms, and that they had sewn the sign of the cross on their shoulders or elsewhere, out of any material or rag they had at hand; they had renounced individual battle-cries as arrogant, and instead they all humbly and faithfully shouted in battle, "God wishes it." His heart was deeply stirred by these words, and, inspired by God, he was stung by conscience; he ordered that his most precious mantle be brought to him, and he had it cut up into little crosses; he put one on himself, and gave out the other crosses to be worn by those of his men who subscribed to the cause to which he had dedicated himself. The knights who had followed him to this siege also experienced a sudden change of heart, and set out on the same journey that their leader had chosen. Such a crowd of knights made this choice at that moment that Bohemund's brother, Count Roger of Sicily, grieved deeply that he was robbed of nearly all of his retainers at this siege.

But I should say a few words about Bohemund's parentage, and about the steps by which he proceeded to this position of honor. Robert, whose surname we have given as Guiscard, was from Normandy, and was born to a family of no great distinction. He went from there to Apulia, but whether he left his native land voluntarily or was driven from it I don't know. There, by some means or other, he earned horses and arms to become a knight. He assembled, from various places, a group of thieves to help him in his endeavours, took over certain castles, with the aid of disgraceful treachery, occupied some other castles after wearing them down with frequent attacks, laid sieges to wealthy cities, and compelled them to surrender. To finish in a few words, this "new man" extended his power, conquering at will to such an extent that the verses on his epitaph read, "he drove him out whom the Ligurians, Rome, and Lake Leman recognized as king",[114] that is,

---

[114] This single elegiac may contain a scribal error, confusing Alemannus with Lemanus (Lake

Henry Augustus, a man favored by fortune with innumerable, almost continual victories.

Parthia, Arabia, the phalanx of Macedonians did not protect Alexis,[115]

the prince of the Greeks, who has often been our concern. Having defeated him often, Robert, they say, would have worn the crown in the city of Constantinople in a few days, had a draught of poison not suddenly snatched his life from him. Anyone who wishes today may see the power of his son Bohemund who, obliterating the low origin of his family, married the daughter of Philip, King of France, and tried to take by violence the empire of the above mentioned King Alexis. While his brother Roger returned to Sicily, unhappy that he had lost so many men of all ranks, that it seemed that the whole people was about to go off to Jerusalem, Bohemund collected the troops and supplies that were necessary for such an expedition, embarked with his army, and with a favoring wind easily reached the Bulgarian shore. His retinue was filled with many wise knights and great princes, among whom was Tancred, who was, if I am not mistaken, the son of a certain marquis and Bohemund's sister. Tancred's brother, whose name was William, had set out before him with Hugh the Great. In addition there was Richard of the First City,[116] a remarkably good-looking man, whom we saw perform the office of delegate to the King of the Franks, to ask for the hand of Constantia as wife for Bohemund. Then, when he and his men entered the land of Bulgaria, they found a great supply of every kind of food. When they arrived in the valley of Andropolitanus,[117] they remained there waiting for the rest of the fleet to finish the journey. When everyone had arrived, the leaders met, and Bohemund told his plan to his men, ordering everyone alike who was about to pass through territory inhabited by Christians to behave peacefully, to do no harm, and not to depopulate the land of those whose rights they had come to protect; they should take, as peacefully as possible, and after having paid for it, only the food that they needed. They went forward, and as they passed from city to city, from field to field, from camp to camp, they found abundant trade everywhere, until they arrived in the province called Castoria, and there they solemnly celebrated Christmas, remaining for several days. They asked the people of the province for permission to trade, but they refused to grant permission, fearing that our men, whom they considered warriors, not pilgims, wanted to destroy their land and crush them. Angered, their restraint now turned to fury,

---

Geneva). The epitaph reads:

> Hic terror mundi Guiscardus, hic expulit urbe
> Quem Ligures regem, Roma, Alemannus habet.
> Parthus, Arabs, Macedumque phalanx non texit Alexim,
> At fuga; sed Venetum, nec fuga, nec pelagus.

[115] A single dactylic hexameter.

[116] In the Latin, "de prima civitate Richardum," glossed (p. 152) as "Richardum de Principatu, vel Principem."

[117] Edirne (Turkish) in Bulgaria.

and they seized horses, cows, asses, and whatever else was useful. Then they left Castoria and entered Pelagonia, where they came upon a fortified town of heretics, which they attacked on every side, compelling them to surrender. They then burned it to the ground, together with its inhabitants. From there they went to the river called the Baudarus.[118] Bohemund moved forward with part of his knights and left the rest in the hands of a certain one of his counts. When the emperor's army, which was not far off, learned of this, it attacked the count, who was now without the aid of Bohemund, who had gone on ahead of him, and the count's men were thrown into confusion by the attack of the enemy. When brave Tancred heard of this, he swiftly turned back, leaped into the river mentioned above, and swam back to those who were being attacked. He then assembled the nearly two thousand men who swam behind him, found the enemy, who were fighting fiercely against his own men, and attacked them with equal fierceness, quickly overcoming them. Many of them were captured and brought before Bohemund in chains. To them the prince said, "Why do you pursue my people, the people of Christ? I am not trying to overthrow your emperor." They replied, "We do nothing by our own deliberation. We are soldiers who earn money by carrying out the orders of the emperor; whatever he tells us to do we do." When the splendid man heard this, he let them go, without punishment and without ransom. This battle took place on the fourth day of the week, which among Christians is called the beginning of the fast.[119]

The emperor Alexis, when he heard of Bohemund's exemplary action, then sent for the councilor upon whom he most relied, and told him to lead the magnanimous duke, together with his army, through his own land, and into his own presence at Constantinople. While the army was passing through all the towns and cities of the empire, an imperial edict commanded all the inhabitants of these regions to see to it that Bohemund and his men had a supply of everything that could be bought. However, although the army was allowed to proceed through the provinces, none of Bohemund's men was permitted to enter the walls of any city. The knights were about to invade a certain fort that seemed abundant with supplies, but the illustrious man forbade it, partly out of respect for the laws of the land, partly to avoid offending the emperor, or rather, he did not want to break the pact he had just made with him through intermediaries. Angry at their foolish attempt, and particularly at Tancred, he forbade them to go on. This happened in the evening. The next morning the inhabitants of the fort came out, bearing the banners of the Cross before them, demonstrating their humility and religious belief to Bohemund. He greeted them affably and courteously, thanked them, and sent the contented people back to the town. Then they reached a city called Serra, where they pitched their tents, and successfully traded in the marketplace. Here Bohemund was reconciled with his two courtly prefects. In keeping with the recent treaty and with the law of the land, he ordered that

---

118 Today, the Vardar.
119 Ash Wednesday.

everything which had been taken from the inhabitants be restored to them. Then they proceeded to the outskirts of a city called Rusa,[120] where a crowd of Greeks, both aristocrats and commoners, rushed to greet the noble man, offering all kinds of merchandise. They made camp there three days before the feast of the Lord. Bohemund then left his retinue behind and set out for Constantinople, together with a few of his knights, to confer with the emperor. In the meanwhile Tancred was in charge of the army, and when he saw that food was difficult to purchase with empty purses, he decided to leave the major routes and move along the less frequented ones, where a greater supply of necessary items for everyone might be found. Therefore he lead them from the public way, out of consideration for the poor, and entered a valley abundantly supplied with different kinds of food. There the people piously celebrated Easter (April 5, 1097). When Alexis heard that Bohemund was coming to meet with him, he ordered that he be given the most respectful welcome, and that he be given quarters just outside the city wall.[121] When he arrived, he was invited to speak with the emperor; he went and was received in secret.

Meanwhile Duke Godfrey, together with his brother Baldwin and the Count of Saint-Gilles, each leading a strong group of men, reached the outskirts of Constantinople. The perfidious Alexis, who once was thought to be eager for support against the Turks, gnashed his teeth in the bitterness of his anger, and pondered on a means to bring about the total destruction of the large army that was, as he thought, about to attack him. But God, whose force drove this pious army, watched over them so well that no occasion presented itself for the scoundrel to harm them; furthermore, cut off from all possibility of doing harm, the wretch was stricken with great fear. The people of Constantinople were disturbed at the sight of so many battalions assembling, and they held a meeting to determine what to do. Fearful that the city would be crushed by the great number of men who were arriving, and that the provinces would be taken over and devastated, they decided, after considering several alternatives, that their tyrant should demand an oath from the Franks that they would never harm him or his people. When our leaders learned of this, they showed great contempt and scorn. They understood clearly that if the initial army happened to deviate from this pact, it would be necessary for such a large army, stripped of all resources by poverty, to wage war against the perfidious prince, contrary to the oaths they had taken. "And certainly," they said, "even if no fear of what might happen in the future weighed upon us, the fact that we had been compelled by the puny Greeks, laziest of all people, to swear an oath would be to our eternal shame. We cannot doubt that they would say that we, willy-nilly, had submitted to their rule." The emperor came to mighty Bohemund about this matter, and was ready to entice him whom he greatly feared with gifts, for Bohemund had often defeated him in

---

[120] Today, Ruskujan.

[121] "outside of the city wall" is my version of "brugo," uninhabited land, a field not under cultivation.

battle; Alexis concentrated particularly on Bohemund, because he regarded him as his greatest rival. Therefore he offered him land the other side of Antioch, whose length would take fifteen days to cross, and whose width would take no less than eight days to cross. The great man's firmness was broken by this offer, and what Hugh the Great had promised, compelled by necessity and the enticement of money, Bohemund agreed to swear to on condition that if Alexis reneged on what he had agreed to, he himself would not have to carry out what he had sworn to. If anyone asks why he and the others relaxed their firmness by swearing oaths to the tyrant, he should understand that the leaders were helping their fellow soldiers in God out of necessity, for they would have been in dire poverty if they had been denied their pay. Alexis swore oaths also, stating, "that he would come with them, at the head of his own army, aid them on land and on the sea, and he would order that food be brought from everywhere for them to purchase; if they suffered any losses, he would indemnify them fully; finally, he would not wish or allow anyone on this expedition, to the extent that he had the ability, to be harassed, harmed, or killed."

The Count of Saint-Gilles had established camp in the outskirts of Byzantium before the entire army had arrived, and the tyrant sent a messenger to ask the count to do what the others had done, that is, offer him homage. The cleverness of the insolent tyrant demanded this, but the wisdom of the glorious count set about devising a way to take vengeance against the envy of the scoundrel. But the leaders, that is, Godfrey, Hugh the Great, and Robert of Flanders, and the others, said that they would never take up arms against someone who was considered to be a Christian. Bohemund added that if Raymond waged war against the emperor, and thereby broke the oath he had given the emperor, he himself would take the emperor's part. And so the count, after consulting with his closest advisors, swore to protect the life and honor of the impious Alexis, and that he would not for his own sake or to aid others work to destroy him. When they considered the clause about hommage, he said that he would rather undergo mortal danger than submit to such a proposition. Meanwhile Bohemund's army drew near to the towers of Constantinople. Having learned what oaths the emperor had exacted, Tancred, together with the men he was leading (almost the entire forces of Bohemund), quickly crossed the Arm of Saint George. The army of the Count of Saint-Gilles had scattered, setting up its tents at the edge of the city. Bohemund remained with the emperor, so that he might more easily supervise the carrying out of the imperial edict which ordered the people beyond Nicaea to bring food from everywhere to his army. Duke Godfrey had gone ahead, together with Tancred, to Nicomedia, a city founded by Nicomedes, who, according to a poem, won a battle against Caesar, but did not triumph.[122] Each of them remained there with his troops for three days. The duke, considering that the roads were filled with obstacles, and that an army as large as theirs could not

---

[122] Suetoniuis, Caesar 80: *Gallias Caesar subegit, Nicomedes Caesarem.*

make its way along them, since the road that Peter the Hermit's men had used could not accommodate so many men, sent three thousand men ahead of him, with axes and hoes to widen the roads and make them passable as far as Nicea. The road was incredibly difficult, filled with sharp stones, and moving over steep mountains. Those who were in the lead widened the road by cutting up the rocks, and they placed crosses of iron and wood on tall stakes, so that our men, when they saw these signs aloft, would not wander from the road. Finally they came to Nicea, the central city of Armenia, and the chief city of Bythinia, famous for the synod of 318 fathers, but even more famous for the declaration of *Omousion*, and the condemnation of Arius. The next day was the sixth of May, and they pitched their camps in the area around the city, on the third day after they had left Nicomedia. Before the army of Bohemund arrived, they say that there was such a shortage of bread that one loaf of bread cost twenty or thirty pennies. But when Bohemund appeared, he brought a great quantity of food by land and by sea, and suddenly a plentiful supply of everything necessary flowed.

On the day of the Ascension of Our Lord, they began to attack the city from all sides, to draw up machines, to erect ladders, prepare fire-bombs, and to fire at the ramparts of the walls and towers with their crossbows.[123] The siege of the city was undertaken with such sharp fervor that within two days they had undermined the walls. The Turks, who held the city, sent messengers to other cities, asking for them to bring help, and to enter without fear by the southern gate, since that part was not under siege, and presented no obstacle to those wishing to bring help. On that very day, however, the sabbath after the Ascension of Our Lord, the entrance of that gate was being guarded by the Count of Saint-Gilles and the Bishop of Puy. An event occurred there that was truly noteworthy. This same noble count, faithful to God, strong and competent in arms, surrounded by a no less competent army, found in front of him enemy reinforcements hurrying towards the town. Relying in his spirit upon divine assistance, he attacked and conquered the Turks, compelling them to flee, and slicing most of them to pieces. Hideously defeated, the Turks went about finding new forces with which they enthusiastically decided to go to battle again, carrying ropes with which they proposed to tie up our men and bring them back to Khorasan. Encouraged by this empty hope, they began, in single file and step by step, to descend from the top of the mountain that towered over the city. They were welcomed with pleasure by our men, as was fitting, and they left their severed heads as proof of our victory. After the Turks fled, our catapults and slings fired the severed heads into the city to terrify the Gentiles. However, the Bishop of Puy of blessed memory and Count Raymond of Saint-Gilles, pressing forward to weaken the city, attacked a tower near their own camp by digging tunnels to undermine its foundations. After the miners were in place to carry this out, they were given protection by men with bows and crossbows, by men swinging balearic ropes, and by others defending

---

[123] For whatever facts can be assembled about the siege, see R. Rogers, *Latin Siege Warfare in the Twelfth Century*, Oxford, 1992, pp. 16–25.

the sappers. Thus the tower was undermined to the depths of its foundation, while the collapsing wall was held only with beams and poles; when the base of the foundation had been entirely demolished, they set fire to the beams:

> When cloudy night brought quiet to both sides, the weakened tower fell in ruins, but because night is less appropriate for fighting, the Franks stopped, refusing to harm the Turks at night.[124]

The Turks, however, worried about their safety, very wisely got up, and, in the same place, rebuilt the wall so quickly and of such strength that the next day our men could find no way of doing them any harm. Meanwhile, two men arrived, the most celebrated for deeds of arms and the wealthiest counts, whom we have already mentioned, accompanied by many knights, whose arrival filled the whole army of the Lord with joy: Robert, Count of Normandy, and Count Stephen of Chartres.

Thus Bohemund besieged the city from the front, Tancred from the side, Duke Godfrey from a third position, the Count of Flanders from a fourth, the Count of Normandy from a fifth, and the Count of Saint-Gilles and the Bishop of Puy from a sixth. They set about besieging it, so that none of the besieged could get in or out. There one could see gathered the flower of the armed force, or the wisdom, the nobility, of the fame of all of France, dressed in the breastplates and helmets of knights; those who were skilled at counting the number of people in an army thought that there were about 100,000 men. I do not think that anyone could count the whole crowd of foot-soldiers, or of those who attended knights. The latter group not only performed the tasks that servants and slaves normally perform for soldiers, but they took part in the siege, and in the battles themselves, like lions, with bravery like that of their betters, as though they were accustomed to wielding now arms, now tools of any sort, whether for war, or for any other task necessary.

> No speech will be able to tell how much the integrity of those powerful warriors shone forth at that time. No land on earth will ever see soldiers of such nobility fighting together. If you wish, I shall relate the story of every kingdom, speak of battles done everywhere; none of these will be able to equal either the nobility or the force of these men. They left their paternal lands, abandoned conjugal bonds, their children were unattractive to them, remaining at home was a punishment for them; in every knight the desire for martyrdom burns. When the mob is carried away by the promise of bloodshed, who can find anyone who is unmoved? Everyone is lion-hearted, pleased to see the walls of Nicea surrounded. The field shone with the reins of horses, and the shape and sound of their trappings gives pleasure to everyone. Their armor burns more brightly once it has drunk the sun's rays. Their helmets, shields with yellow bronze, and belts blaze. You would have seen them, like a storm, beating the walls down with their battering rams. The Frankish spears penetrated their

---

[124] Four dactylic hexameters.

hard limbs, and their sharp swords broke many of their bones. The wooden tower strove to drive the Turks from the lofty walls. The battle rages hand-to-hand, and spears were hurled on both sides; hardly any of them missed. Unexpected death laid some men low. Heavenly glory then made our men strong; they exposed their bodies to what was fated. They rejoiced in seeking rewards through death. Every weary man became bold and aggressive, driven by hope for a better life. The crimes of souls greedy of praise are far distant. Every man believed that, if war granted him a breath of fame, Christ was the one who gave it. No one who performed a noble act took credit for it.

We will not be able to compare the Scythian triumphs over Darius with these, nor could the great, manly efforts of Cyrus be known, which Tomyris had finished off with a bag of gore.[125] You would have mourned the outcome, good Pyrrus, looking upon Tarentum; you babble uselessly of taking on new wars with elephants. Once, twice, three times Hanibal's men cut down the Quirites like wheat, but they were at last defeated and left the city. Although under Caesar there was a ten-year fight without loss, let it be clear that the sojourn in the fields of Gaul was harmful. The task took very little time, and was entirely successful. Since God was involved, everything turned out well in the end. Those who died as martyrs had a glorious fate, and those who did not judged that the suffering mitigated their sins.[126]

Part of the city was bordered by a long, broad, stagnant lake, upon which the enemy was seen launching boats, freely going in and out, carrying wood and fodder and other necessary items. Our leaders held a meeting about this activity, and they agreed to send a delegation to the prince of Constantinople, to urge him to send as many ships as possible to the city of Civitot, where there was a port, and to collect a great number of bulls to carry the ships over the mountains and through the forests until they reached the above-mentioned lake. The plan was discussed and carried out quickly, urged on by the prince; those who are called the Turkopoles, that is, the knights of his court, were sent on the expedition. When the boats were brought, in accordance with the emperor's orders, they remained still on the day that they were brought. That night, however, they put the boats on the lake, and the Turkopoles, very well equpped with weapons, got into them. In the morning the fleet assembled, and proceeded slowly towards the city, as though they were bringing tribute. The Turks, who were amazed at the sight of the ships, could not decide whether they were their own, or the emperor's. After they understood that what they were seeing was an enemy force, they grew weak with a fear of death, but the more they groaned and wept the more our own men were pleased and gave thanks to the Lord. This misfortune severely enfeebled the enemy, who now lost faith in themselves and their allies, and sent a legation to the emperor, offering to surrender the city, if he could get permission from the Franks for them to leave with their wives, sons, and

---

[125] Tomyris dips Cyrus' head in a bag of blood in Herodotus I CCV. Tibullus (IV.i.143ff.) alludes to the story, and Valerius Maximus (IX.x) uses the story to illustrate vengeance.
[126] Ninety-nine Adonic verses kata stichon, followed by 13 dactylic hexameters.

adequate provisions. The tyrant graciously favored their request, and not only granted it without punishing them, but, to bind them even closer to himself, brought them to Constantinople. He had one principal object in doing this: in case of a disagreement with the Franks, he would advantageously have men with whom to oppose them. The siege had lasted seven weeks and three days, and many of our men received the gift of martyrdom in that place. It is undoubtedly true that those who went to their death in defense of the true faith certainly may be numbered among those who are with God; having paid with their blood, they have earned celestial rewards. Those who died of starvation are certainly their equals, and a great number died there in that way. For if, according to the Prophet, speaking historically, "It was better for those killed by the sword than for those killed by hunger,"[127] since the latter undoubtedly were tortured to death by daily pain, they will not, it is right to believe, be deprived of the more noble crown of martyrdom.

After the city had surrendered, and the Turks had been brought to Constantinople, the tyrannical prince was extremely pleased to have regained the city, and he gave our leaders countless gifts; he also made substantial charitable contributions to all the poorest people. As a result, those who were neither powerful nor poor, whom his generosity had overlooked, grew envious and hostile towards the leaders. And, in a way, it was not unjust. They had fought the battles; they were the ones who had carried out the entire siege, hauled the engines of war, fired the catapults; to conclude briefly, I say that they carried, "the burden and heat of the day."[128] On the day that they left the captured city they reached a bridge in whose vicinity they remained for two days. On the third day, at the first feeble glimmerings of dawn, they arose, moved about blindly in what little light there was, and went down two separate roads, forming two groups. For two days they marched in two separate divisions. One contained Bohemund, Robert of Normandy, and Tancred, together with a large contingent of knights; the Count of Saint-Gilles, Duke Godfrey, the Bishop of Puy, Hugh the Great, and the Count of Flanders were leading the other group through pathless territory. On the third day, an innumerable, terrible, and nearly overwhelming mass of Turks suddenly rushed upon Bohemund and his men. You would have seen them speaking melodramatically about the fear that they expected our men, frightened at their unexpected attack, to feel as they shouted their war-like battle-cry in the horrible tones of their language. Under attack by an immense force, the extraordinary man was not frightened into acting unwisely, but immediately ordered everyone to halt, unroll the tents, and establish camp quickly. Before his orders had been carried out, he addressed his own knights: "If you keep in mind the expedition that you joined, having considered why it was necessary, then go forward; attack them like men, defend your honor and your life, and you, foot soldiers, pitch the tents carefully." When he had finished, the Turks attacked suddenly and swiftly,

[127] Lamentations 2.9
[128] Matthew 20.12.

hurling javelins, and fighting in their usual fashion by fleeing as they fired arrows into the breasts of their pursuers. Aware of what they had promised, mindful of their vaunted strength, the Franks clearly understood that they were numerically overmatched, but they fought with energetic bravery against their furious enemies. The Count of Normandy, properly mindful of his father's military valor and noble ancestry, performed mighty deeds of arms, fighting off the enemy, and offering a fine example of resistance to our momentarily frightened army. God was also present, so that the women who had accompanied them stood by their men, constantly bringing water to refresh the knights. Indeed, their encouragement and advice did more to make the men more tireless and inventive than the water did to refresh them. But when Bohemund became troubled by the extreme inequality of the contest, he sent a messenger to those who had gone off separately, Raymond the Count of Saint-Gilles, Duke Godfrey, Hugh the Great, the Bishop of Puy, and others of their retinues, telling them to come very quickly, because battle was imminent. Thus they say:

> If they would like to see the beginnings of a battle with the Turks, what they want is now here: come quickly.[129]

And so Godfrey, worthy of the title of duke, a model warrior, accompanied by Hugh the Great, who took after his father in military ardor, courageous as befitted one descended from kings, like a leopard, I might say, together with his retinue, raced to the battle as eagerly as to a feast. Then the Bishop of Puy,

> strengthened the army not only with his shining arms, but with his counsel and sacred prayers; if they had been hesitant, he ignited the army.[130]

Then the Count of Saint-Gilles, older and wiser with experience and very reliable in council, surrounded by his Provençal soldiers, burst forth. When our men saw the enemy army face-to-face, they wondered where in the world such an infinite number of people had come from. Turks, Arabs, and Saracens stood out among the others, both in number and in nobility; there was a smaller number of auxiliaries and people from less illustrious nations. There you would have seen the heights of the mountains and the slopes of the hills grow dense with this profane mass, and all the plains were covered with countless throngs. And so our leaders exhorted their men, "If you have devoted to God the army in which you now serve, if you have given up your countries, homes, wives, children, and your bodies, and if these bodies have only survived to be offered for the glories of martyrdom, how, I ask, can you be terrified at this sight? The wisdom of one of you, derived from faith in God, is more powerful than the superstitions of this entire heap of rabble. If death is to be your lot, the heavenly kingdom and a joyful death await you; if you remain alive, and persevere in your faith, certain victory

---

[129] Two dactylic hexameters.
[130] Three dactylic hexameters.

awaits you, and after victory, glory, and after glory, greater courage, and then great opulence from the enemy's treasures. Whatever happens, you will be secure, you have nothing to fear; no delay or doubt should stand in your way. Therefore surrender your minds and bodies to the faith of the Lord of the Cross, and take up arms against this pile of husks, these little creatures who are hardly men at all." Then they drew up their battle lines in an orderly fashion, with great-hearted Bohemund on the left flank, together with the Count of Normandy, valiant knight, Tancred, and Richard who was called "of the first city." The Bishop of Puy, however, moving through the mountains from enemy territory, was surrounding the Turks; Count Raymond rode on the left flank. On the right flank, Duke Godfrey, Robert of Flanders, Hugh the Great, and the other warriors, powerful because they took up their positions on behalf of Christ. Oh good God, who knows men's thoughts, how many tears were shed for you during these preparations! How much pious remorse and how many pious confessions rose up out of the minds of all of these men! Who could judge adequately how much sensitivity was in the hearts of all these men whose hopes were placed only in You? O Christ, with what grief did holiness and sinfulness cry out to you. They wept, and called upon pious Christ with their pious sighs, when, lo, all the soldiers crossed themselves; I do not say that they were as brave as lions, but, what is more fitting, brave as martyrs, bearing the banners against the enemy throng.

> The Arabs, Persians, and ferocious Turks soon fled; the savage people showed their backs to the Christians. It was a rout, and the wretched army ran in all directions; the Arabs ran like rabbits. Prodigious was the slaughter of the fleeing army; we hardly had enough swords to do all the killing. Swords became dull with cutting so many limbs; they cut men down the way reapers cut wheat with a scythe. Here they cut a head, here a nose, here a throat, here a pair of ears; a belly is sliced open; everyone in their path dies. Hands become stupified, arms grow stiff with gore. No one resists them and remains alive; lassitude overcomes the infidels. Their breasts blindly receive the baneful assault.[131]

The number of enemy defeated is said to have been 460,000, not counting the Arabs, whose number was too great to be counted.[132] At first, indeed, crying out in despair of their lives,

> they ran in fear to their tents,[133]

where they seized what they could with their hands and fled. For a whole day our men pursued them very closely, piling up the spoils they took from the fleeing enemy; and so, after drawing considerable amounts of blood, they took comfort

---

[131] Fourteen elegiacs.

[132] The *Gesta Francorum* had given the number as 360,000, Anselm of Ribemont as 260,000 (Bréhier 49).

[133] An elegiac couplet.

in the copious sums of money, in the precious garments, and in the herds of cattle which they took from the fleeing men. From the third until the ninth hour the destruction, or rather Arabian slaughter, of this battle raged. Two leaders of distinguished name, Geoffrey of Mont Scabieuse, and William, brother of Tancred, and many others whose names are entrusted to the notice of God alone, died there. Here we can clearly see the signs of Christian power; and if we marvel at the inequality of a battle between so few men and so many, we must attribute the results entirely to the aid of Christ. For if in the ancient text it is said of the Jews who had not yet separated from God, "one will pursue a thousand, and two will put to flight ten thousand,"[134] then it seems to me no less true of this victory, since human understanding cannot hope to fathom how so many men could be defeated by so few. But perhaps someone may object, arguing that the enemy forces were merely peasants, scum herded together from everywhere. Certainly the Franks themselves, who had undergone such great danger, testified that they could have known of no race comparable to the Turks, either in the liveliness of spirit, or energy in battle. When the Turks initiated a battle, our men were almost reduced to despair by the novelty of their tactics in battle; they were not accustomed to their speed on horseback, nor to their ability to avoid our frontal assaults. We had particular difficulty with the fact that they fired their arrows only when fleeing from the battle. It was the Turk's opinion, however, that they shared an ancestry with the Franks, and that the highest military prowess belonged particularly to the Turks and Franks, above all other people.

While they were being defeated in this manner, and were fleeing day and night from the face of the Franks, the prince who ruled Nicaea,[135] frightened out of his mind, after the siege had ended, happened to meet a group of ten thousand Arabs, who said to him, "O least of men, why are you fleeing in miserable fright?" He replied, "I thought that I had destroyed and killed every last Frank, and I thought that I would deliver them to eternal captivity; I assumed that I would conquer them as they moved forward in small groups, and I would bind them and lead them away to distant lands. But a large army appeared, and the fields and mountains were covered with great numbers of them, and they seemed to occupy every inch of our entire land." The capture which he mentioned referred to the army of Peter the Hermit, and the multitude that followed to those who lately had subjugated Nicaea. "There, when we had seen an army of so many people, with divisions growing like wheat, against whom we judged correctly that we stood no chance of defending ourselves (for there was no safe place), we thought it best to escape imminent death by fleeing swiftly. Although we are now at some distance, nevertheless we are shaken by the terrible memory of those men whom we saw, and the momentary encounter has left us frightened of their ferocity. If you have any faith in my report of what happened, you will retreat

---

[134] Deut. 32.30.
[135] Kilidj-Arslan.

from this place because, if their forces find you here, you will undoubtedly pay
for your folly many times over." They decided that what they heard was credible,

quickly reversed direction,[136]

and scattered all over Romania.

Meanwhile our men were intent on pursuing the fleeing Turks, who, when
they passed through cities and forts, boastfully proclaimed that they had conquered the Franks, thus deluding the inhabitants of the lands through which they
traveled with lying words. "We have defeated the Christian armies," they said,
"and deprived them of all desire for combat. Therefore let us into your cities, and
welcome gratefully those who go to such lengths to protect you." Then they
entered the cities, stripped the churches of their ornaments, carried off the wealth
of public buildings, and set about carrying off gold and silver, various kinds of
animals, and whatever else might be of use to them. For this purpose, they
abducted the sons of Christians as slaves, and consigned to the flames other
things that were less useful, constantly in fear of our coming up behind them.
Afterward, in searching for the infidels through pathless solitudes, our men
entered a deserted, pathless, waterless land, from which the pitiful men emerged
scarcely alive. They suffered from hunger and thirst; nothing edible could be
found, but the cruel deprivation seemed sometimes to be relieved by rubbing
their hands with the spikes.[137] Certainly many noble knights died there, and the
desert, to which they were unaccustomed, took the lives of many horses. The
feeble succumbed to the relentless hardship. The great lack of horses and carts
compelled them to use cattle, goats, rams, and what is more amazing, dogs, to
carry whatever supplies were appropriate to their size. From there they moved on
to a province rich in what they needed, and they reached the city of Iconia,[138]
famous for its tolerance of Paul and his writings. Meanwhile, the inhabitants of
this province urged our men to provide themselves with supplies, and to bring
water in bags with them, because they would not be able to find any water on the
entire next day's journey. They did so, and moved on until they reached the bank
of a river, where they rested for two days. And so those who made up the
vanguard reached Trachias,[139] where a large Turkish phalanx had assembled for
the sole purpose of finding a way to trouble the army of Christ. When our men
came upon them, they attacked them with their usual boldness. The enemy
swiftly took flight,

like an arrow launched from a cross-bow.[140]

Thus our men, now that the gate was open, entered the city and they remained

---

[136] One hexameter.
[137] Spikes of cactus, perhaps, for making flour?
[138] Konya (Turkish).
[139] Ereghli (Turkish).
[140] One dactylic hexameter.

there for four days. There Tancred, Bohemund's nephew, and Baldwin, Duke Godfrey's brother, left the encampment of the army, not out of a desire to avoid fighting, but because of the ardor of their spirits, and they entered a certain valley, which they call in that language Bothrentot. And so Tancred, uncomfortable with a partner, separated from the duke's brother, and, together with his men, attacked Tarsus, renowned for the precious birth of the special apostle.[141] Turks from the city rushed out to join battle with our men as they approached, but, as they were about to join battle, they sought refuge in the city from which they had come. Tancred gave rein to his horse in pursuit of the enemy, and set up his camp in a position that blockaded the gate of the city. Baldwin soon arrived to besiege the city, set up camp on the other side, and asked Tancred if he and his army might share in the taking of the city. Tancred angrily refused, since he wanted control of the city and the trophies of victory for himself alone. And so night fell, and the crowd of Turks, uncomfortable with the siege, and well aware of the strength and persistent nature of the besieger, fled in haste. When they had been forced out, those who remained in the city, the Gentiles of that land, which is to say those who were Christians, came out to our men during the night, and cried out, "Franks, hurry, enter the city, since the alien race has fled, so great was their fear of your strength." At dawn, the leaders surrendered the city, and when they learned that there was a fight about who should control the city, they said, "We choose to rule over us the man whom we saw yesterday battling so fiercely with the Turks." Baldwin instantly urged Tancred that they enter the city together, so that each might set about taking the spoils with all his might. Tancred wisely replied, "Our plan was to fight the Turks, not to rob Christians, particularly since they have voluntarily chosen me, and do not want anyone else." Although he had said this, Tancred took into account the fact that Baldwin's army was larger and better supplied, and yielded to him, willingly or unwillingly, for the moment. During his retreat two very fine cities, Athena[142] and Manustra,[143] yielded themselves to him, together with many castles.

Since no chance to talk about Baldwin may offer itself later on, I wish to insert a few details about how well things turned out for him. Near Edessa, a city in Mesopotamia, as we understand from reports of people who have been there, a certain man became leader[144] and ruled over the Christian province as a duke, protecting it from the incursions of Gentiles not by arms, but by paying protection-money. Worn out with age and illness, with a wife as old as he, and without children, when he heard that the Franks were at the borders of Mesopotamia, he very much wanted to find someone from among the Frankish nobility to adopt, who, in exchange, would defend with arms and strength the land that

---

[141] Paul.
[142] Adana.
[143] Mamistra (medieval), Mopsuestia (classical), Msis (Armenian), Misis (Turkish).
[144] Thoros.

he had defended only with money. One of the knights of his household, aware of his desire, happened to be speaking with Baldwin. When he aroused the hope of obtaining the dukedom if he permitted himself to be adopted by the above mentioned old man, the count believed him and, accompanied by the knight, he went to Edessa. Welcomed even more warmly than he had hoped, he was adopted as a son by both. The method of adoption, in accordance with the customs of this nation, is said to have been like this: the old man directs him to strip himself naked and put on a linen inner garment, which we call a chemise, and he embraces him, and confirms the entire transaction with a kiss; both the old man and the old woman do this. When this was finished, the citizens perceived that the old man had been stripped of the high honor, and they made a secret pact immediately to besiege the court in which he and Baldwin were staying. They remembered whatever harmful things the old man had done to them. And so during the siege, when his newly adopted son wanted to fight back with Frankish boldness, the old man, admirably faithful, prevented him, saying that he knew for certain that he could by no means be delivered from the hands of the mob, while Baldwin would be in great danger if he took up his defense. Thus after many imprecations he persuaded him not to fight back, and when tearful Baldwin said that he would prefer to die with him, the old man pushed him away, and pleaded with the besiegers to kill him if they wished, but to spare the new prince. And they did in fact kill him, but in the meantime Baldwin, with great effort, managed to hold on to the power he had gained by adoption and, mindful of the recent treachery, brought in Frankish knights and servants for his own protection. A little later, at Christmas, another conspiracy was formed, to kill the new duke on that holy day. The attempt did not remain hidden from Baldwin, who told the members of his retinue who were Franks to appear in church wearing their cuirasses and helmets, as though prepared for battle; foot-soldiers were to bring their lances, swords, and battle-axes, and to move about everywhere in their gear. When this had been done, the inhabitants of the city understood that the ruler had been alerted, and he himself proceeded to the church with a large contingent of armed men, participated in the divine service, yet said nothing that day. But the next day he called the citizens of Edessa together and charged them with treason, compelled them by law to confess, and did not permit them to deny what they had proposed to do. And so, after the leaders of the entire city had been convicted, some had their feet cut off, some their hands, others their ears and noses, others their tongues and lips, and all of them were castrated and sent into exile in various distant places. Finally, when no one remained who might incite the crowd against him, Baldwin experienced the rewards and happiness of such a dukedom. Thereafter he led a prosperous and rich life, ruled several cities, among which Seleucia[145] stood out as the best known since antiquity. After the death of

---

[145] Selevgia (West Armenian), Silifke (Turkish).

his brother Godfrey, who had ruled at Jerusalem, Baldwin moved from this dukedom to that of Jerusalem, but from this he derived no increase in earthly felicity, but only more blessed labor in the service of God – that is, continual battle against the Gentiles.

The Third Book of the Deeds of God by the Franks Ends.

Book Four

I think that no one can justifiably ridicule me for undertaking this task. For although I did not go to Jerusalem, and to this day am unacquainted with many of the people and places, I think that these conditions in no way hinder the general usefulness of what I do, if the things which I have written or shall have written have been taken from men whose testimony is endowed with truth. If anyone objects that I did not see, he cannot object on the grounds that I did not hear, because I believe that, in a way, hearing is almost as good as seeing. For although, "What has been thrust into the ears stirs the mind more slowly than those things which have appeared before reliable eyes,"[146] nevertheless, who doubts those historians who wrote the lives of the saints, who wrote down not only what they saw with their own eyes, but what they drunk up from what others have understood and told them? For if the narrator is reliable and, as one reads, "testifies to what he saw and heard,"[147] then stories told by those who speak the truth about events no one has seen are clearly acceptable as true. If there is anyone who objects, and who despises this undertaking, he has the option, if he wishes, of offering corrections. Whoever is displeased with what we have done may write his own version.

Thus the Lord's army, led by Raymond, Count of Saint-Gilles, Bohemund, Godfrey, and many others, entered Armenia, rejoicing at the possibility of Turkish attacks. On their way they took a fort which was difficult to approach, so that any attempt to attack it seemed futile. A pagan of that district, a certain Symeon, well known for having a Christian surname, asked our leaders for control of that area, so that he could guard it against Turkish attacks. They did not refuse the favor he requested, and he remained there, intending to guard the land. Then our men moved on and reached Cappadocian Caesarea.[148] After they left the province of Caesarea, they reached a very lovely, wealthy city,[149] which the Turkish army had been besieging for three weeks before the arrival of our army. But their siege produced no results. When our men approached, the citizens voluntarily surrendered the city. A certain knight called Peter of the Alps asked that the leaders grant him the right to protect the region in the name of the Emperor of the Greeks and of our own leaders. His request was willingly granted, since the meritorious fidelity of the petitioner was well known. As the day then drew to a close, Bohemund heard that a large but insignificant group of the enemies who had earlier besieged this city was moving ahead of our men. And so, taking with him only his immediate retinue, he set out in pursuit, but did not find those whom he sought. Now the army reached a town called Coxon,[150] where they

---

146 Horace, *Ars Poetica*, 180–181.
147 John 3.32.
148 Kayseri.

149 Placentia, or Comana.
150 Goksun.

found great abundance of useful supplies. The inhabitants of this place happily opened their gates to our men, and for three days fed them properly and well.

After the Count of Saint-Gilles heard that the Turks, who usually supplied the garrison for the city of Antioch, had left the stronghold, he sent part of his army ahead to take possession of the city and to maintain control of it. He chose four men from among the leaders of his army, of whom three had the same name, that is, Peter, and the fourth was called William of Montpellier, a man well know among us for his feats of arms, and he gave them 500 knights to lead. And so, not far from the above-mentioned city, they entered a valley and in that valley found a fort, and there they heard that the Turks, with a large army, were in control of the city of Antioch, and in addition they learned that the Turks were making great preparations of men and arms, to defend themselves against the French, in case they attacked. Therefore one of those Peters we named above, whose surname had been derived from a place called Roaix, separating himself from his companions, entered a valley of a town named Rugia,[151] where he found Turks and Saracens, with whom he fought. After killing many of them, he pursued the others. The Armenians took notice of this and, pleased with the man's bravery, and impressed by his unusual boldness against the Turks, surrendered voluntarily to his command. Quickly thereafter he was given control of a city named Rusa[152] when its inhabitants capitulated, and several other forts surrendered to him. The rest of the army departed from Coxon, the city we mentioned, and marched through high mountains along incredibly rocky paths so narrow that no one could pass the man in front of him, but each man had to proceed one step at a time, stepping carefully, in single file. A deep gulley lay beneath the narrow, rough path, so that if a horse happened to push up against another horse, he would fall to instant death. There you would have seen armed men, who, having just been converted by the hardship and starvation of the journey from knights into foot-soldiers, were suffering wretchedly, smashing their fists, tearing their hair, begging for the relief of death, selling their shields, helmets, and all of their arms, regardless of their true worth, for three or four, perhaps five cents. When they could find no buyer, they threw their shields and other fine equipment into the gulley, to disencumber their weakened, endangered bodies. When they finally emerged from these rocks and precipices, after unbearable suffering, they entered a town called Marasim,[153] whose inhabitants came forth joyfully to meet them, bring abundant supplies to sell to the soldiers. The rich earth replenished the exhausted men, until the presence of their leader Bohemund, who was following those who were waiting for him there, was restored to them.

Finally they arrived in the plains where the renowned city of Antioch was situated, whose particular glories, beyond those by means of which she flourished in this world, are those which grew out of her Christian fame. Pharphar was the name of the river on which she was located. When our men had reached a

---

[151] Riha, perhaps.
[152] Rouveha, perhaps.

[153] Marash.

place near the bridge over that river, some of them, who had been assigned the task of forming the vanguard of the army, met up with a large force of Turks, who were well supplied with provisions, and were hurrying to bring aid to the besieged. When our men saw them, they charged with Frankish ferocity, and almost instantly defeated them and scattered them in all directions. Like charging rams, they tore them to pieces, and the Turks threw away the arms that only moments before had been able to inspire terror. The mass of foot-soldiers fled through their own lines, in their haste and confusion wounding and crushing their own allies. The madness of pride now felt humiliation, and the man who anticipated taking pleasure in heaping up destruction upon us was now happy if he could get himself out alive, even though dishonored. Those who had come to bring aid to the besieged were turned into instant, filthy piles of cadavers. The Almighty mercifully converted what they had brought to aid the besieged into gifts for the besiegers. Thus after they had been destroyed, like grain crushed by hail, great quantities of grain and wine fell into our hands, and the foot-soldiers acquired the valuable horses, camels, mules, and asses that remained. And so our men built camps on the shore of the above-mentioned river. Bohemund, together with 4000 of his best men, undertook a blockade of the city's gate, and remained on guard all that night to prevent anyone from getting in or out. The next day, the twelfth calends of November,[154] the fourth day of the week, in the middle of the day, the army arrived, set up camp, and began a blockade of three of the city's gates; the fourth gate was left free, since it was inaccessible to the besiegers because of the great height of the surrounding mountains, and the narrowness of its paths. However, not only the inhabitants, but the Turks themselves who were inside the city were so frightened by us that none of them came out to fight us. No one put up any resistance, but instead they behaved as though we had come to the market, and this pretence of peace continued, as though a truce had been declared, for fifteen days. The city was surrounded by signs that augured well for beginning this siege; fresh abundance of everything necessary to sustain life was vividly present; I am surprised that at that time the crusaders found abundant grapes hanging on the vines everywhere, wheat shut up not in granaries, but in ditches and underground pits. The trees had plenty of apples, and whatever made their lives more comfortable was supplied by an extremely fertile soil. The Armenians and the Syrians, who formed the entire population of the city (except for the Turks, who, as I mentioned earlier, were not permanent residents), since they inhabited the city itself, and were titular Christians, visited us in great numbers, and told them whatever they had learned among us. They enticed the Franks with their deceptive, repeated lies, and, whispering in their ears, using the most flattering terms, they claimed that they shunned the Turks, although they did not allow their own wives to go beyond the city limits; when they left the Franks, and were back in the city, they reported to the Turks whatever news they had been

---

[154] October 21, 1097.

able to gather about the weaknesses of the Christian side. Thus, informed by the Syrians about our plans, the Turks from time to time rushed out from the city to sneak up upon our men and attack them as they were searching for food, and they covered over the most used paths and made unexpected attacks upon them as they sought the mountains and the sea, never permitting them to rest from ambush or open attack. Not far off was a fort named Harenc[155] in which they had placed a garrison of the fiercest Turkish warriors, who made frequent raids upon the Franks when they were unprepared. Our leaders, unwilling to suffer such affronts, sent a large force of cavalry and infantry to find out where those who were doing so much harm to their men were concealing themselves. When they found their hiding place, they at first attacked them, but then, cleverly simulating flight, they permitted themselves to be brought to a position where they knew that Bohemund was waiting in ambush. At that point, two of our men died in pursuit of the Turks. Coming out of his hiding-place, Bohemund fell upon the enemy, leading the group who appeared to have turned their backs, delivering the punishment they deserved by attacking the Turks with all his forces. He killed many of them, made others prisoners, and brought those he had captured back to the gate of the city, where, to terrify the citizens who were watching, he ordered that they be decapitated. Some of the citizens, however, climbed to the top of this gate and wore out our men by discharging so many arrows that a cloud of missiles flowed in the midst of Bohemund's camp, and one woman died when struck by one of the arrows. Finally the leaders consulted with each other, and decided to set up a fort at the top of a mountain which they called Malregard, and which, as a formidable stronghold, might serve to drive away the Turks. Thus the fort was being constructed, and there you would have seen the greatest princes laboring at carrying rocks. There no poor man might complain that he had to endure hardships inflicted upon him by the power of great men, since those who were in charge would permit themselves no rest in bringing the work to completion. For they knew by the instinct of pious nature, even if they had not read it, what Marius, according to Sallust, said, "If you behave gently, but rule the army firmly, you will be a master, not a general."[156] And when the fort was built, the leaders took turns guarding it. Christmas was near, and the grain and other food for the body began to diminish severely, and throughout the army everything that was for sale was expensive. There was no energy to go even a moderate distance to seek food; within the territory held by those who called themselves Christians almost nothing to eat could be found; no one could go into the Saracen region without a large military force. Therefore, compelled by hunger, the leaders held a meeting to discuss how to deal with the danger of such a large group of men starving unless something were done for them. Finally they decided to send part of the army to search everywhere for supplies, while the others maintained the siege they had undertaken. Bohemund then said, "If, O powerful

---

[155] Aregh.   [156] Sallust, Jugurtha 85.

soldiers, it seems prudent to you, I, with the support of the army of the Count of Flanders, shall devote myself to the effort of procuring food." The offer was accepted gratefully by the younger men, since they were worn out by greater thirst and more urgent need for food. The day after the Lord's Nativity, which was the second day of the week, had been celebrated, with what emotion and energy they could muster, the two princes just mentioned, together with 20,000 foot-soldiers and cavalry, set out as swiftly and as energetically as they could to attack the Saracen provinces.

Meanwhile the Turks, Arabs, Saracens, and other Gentiles, who had assembled from Jerusalem, Damascus, Aleph,[157] and other places, with one purpose in mind, to bring aid, hastened to Antioch in large numbers. They had heard that the Christians were coming into their own lands, to gather food and other supplies; as dusk fell, they moved in formation towards the place where they had learned our men were, with an eagerness that would soon be turned to grief. They divided themselves into two lines of battle, setting the first in front of us, and moving to position the other behind us. But the Count of Flanders, trusting in divine power, with the sign of the Cross fixed to his heart and body, relying confidently on the excellent Count Bohemund, attacked the enemy with the courage to be expected of such men. The battle began, but from the first moment of contact the enemy turned in flight. The battle turned into a victory, and many a sharp spear shattered in the bodies of those who had turned their backs to flee. The enemy's shields were battered by long ashwood lances that were struck with such force that they dwindled into slivers. No helmet prevented a head struck by the edges of the Crusaders' swords from being wounded; and they found the stitching of their so-called impenetrable cuirasses too fragile. Armor protected no part of the body; whatever the barbarians thought firm was weak; whatever the Franks touched shattered. The field was covered with innumerable corpses, and the thick pile of dead men disturbed the evenness of the grassy field. Everywhere the earth, sprinkled with the hateful blood of Gentiles, grew dark. Those who survived the carnage we inflicted saved their lives by their speed afoot, and were pleased to unburden themselves of their spoils, not out of generosity towards us, but to increase their speed. Our state of mind changed utterly: fear changed into courage, battle into victory, mourning into joy, hunger into plenty. He who was naked now had clothing, those who were on foot now had chariots, the poor man had money, the man who had been cast out now danced with gratitude and joy.

While these things were going on, the fact that Bohemund and the Count of Flanders were not present at the siege was not hidden from the Turks who were in control of Antioch. Made more confident by their absence, they came out, though cautiously, to challenge us in battle more often, trying to find out where the besiegers were weakest. Finally, seeing a day, the third day of the week, that seemed apt for trying their courage, they made a sudden assault, and killed many

---

[157] Aleppo.

of our foot-soldiers and knights, who were caught unaware. The magnificent Bishop of Puy lost a mainstay of his court, the man who was his standard-bearer, who was among those who perished. Had not the the river upon whose banks their camp was pitched separated them, the carnage among the Christians would have been very great. Meanwhile, Bohemund was on his way back, having pillaged the Saracen provinces; he was traveling through the mountainous area in which Tancred was staying, thinking that there he might be able to find something to help the men besieging Antioch. Although some of our men had carried off whatever they could see, many found nothing at all, and returned empty-handed, that is, without anything that could be eaten. Bohemund, however, never without a plan, when he saw them wandering about unsuccessfully, spoke these words, "If you are looking for material with which to sustain life, if you want to provide adequately for the bodily needs dictated by hunger, then while you search for food do not risk your lives. Stop scurrying through the pathless mountains, since you know that your enemies are preparing hidden traps for you in these horrible, desolate places. Let the army move forward united, for each is made stronger by the presence of the other, so that if one part is attacked violently, the other may offer assistance. For even as a sheep, if it escapes from the shepherd's grasp, is exposed to the wolf's jaws, so the knight, if he wanders forth alone from the tents of his companions, invariably becomes a plaything for plunderers. Therefore remain together with each other and with your men, and rather eat very little food than feed upon rare delicacies in permanent captivity. To go out and come back together, to take pleasure in being together, to do nothing rash, these are the things that sensible men do; anyone who wanders away wishes to die." He spoke, and returned to his companions, without enriching the besiegers in any way by his return. But the clever Armenians and Syrians, when they saw that the army's food was running out, and there was nothing left to buy, traveled about among all the places that they knew, bought grain, and brought it back to the army that was suffering from a lack of supplies. They sold the grain at inordinate prices, so that the amount of grain a single ass could carry brought eight of their besants, which they called "purpled," approximately 120 sous. Clearly those who could not possibly pay such a price were in great danger of succumbing to a terrible crisis of hunger. And if the leaders were already becoming hard pressed to pay such a price, what could he do who, for all his previous wealth, was now all but a pauper?

> Great torture had come upon them; lack of food was crushing them; the madness of hunger laid low the highest by exhausting their strength. Bread was far off, and they had neither the meat of cattle nor of pig: the hands of the indigent had torn up the grass far and wide. Whatever food they had finally had disappeared. Their limbs were weak, and they had lost heart. The skin of those who had nothing to eat was stretched with dreadful swelling. Without nourishment their strength ebbed, and they died. A brief torment delivered those who were killed in battle, but those who were hungry were tortured at length; therefore protracted death brought them a greater reward. Clearly

angelic bread fed those who rejoiced in the finest reward for their sufferings, the more they bore the burden of agonies. Others fought, struggling to endure various misfortunes, and scarcely anything went in their favor; they preferred unhappiness to joy. Now they struggled to follow Christ, bearing a double cross, rejoicing that they had surpassed His commands, who had imposed upon them only one cross. Hideous hunger gnawed at their weak hearts, and their dried-up stomachs cracked open; suffering racked their bowels, and destroyed their thinking. Disease ate away at their minds, already attacked by the ferocity of battle, and both day and troubling night threatened slaughter. Their minds were sharp although their strength was slight; their illness refreshed the energy of the soul, and they did not fear to go forth to shed blood.[158]

Meanwhile, William, who was called the Carpenter, not because he was a craftsman in wood, but because he prevailed in battle like a carpenter, by cutting men down, and who was from beyond the Seine, powerful in words, but less so in action, *magni nominis umbra*, "the shade of a great name,"[159] a man who set out to do things too great for him, but finished nothing, who when he set out for Jerusalem took from his poor neighbors the little that they had to provide himself shamefully with provisions for the journey, this man, I say, unwilling to suffer hunger, while he could see others much needier than he remaining faithful, silently fled. His reputation in war was for boasting only, and not for deeds done. In Spain, when a Frankish expedition took place against pagans who had come from Africa, he, whose boldness was entirely confined to words, retreated like a wretch, leaving countless men stranded by his flight. This probably took place by the will of God, so that divine judgement may show that those men whom public repute has made famous are worse than everyone else, and less capable of bearing difficulties. Nor is this evident in his case alone, but it is very clearly the case among others, whose names I shall pass over, that those whose reputation for martial ferocity among us had been pre-eminent became weaker than rabbits when they took their place in the Lord's army. The more their conduct deviated from the true path, the more contemptible it should be held. While they were here in France, fighting unjustly, making beggars with their criminal looting, they clearly should have been afraid that their souls would undergo certain damnation; but there, where they had every chance of eternal life, their sinful cowardice was evident.

Then, like the stars that, according to the Apocalypse (6.13; 8.10; 9.1) were seen to fall from the sky, Peter, the celebrated Hermit about whom we spoke previously, also foolishly fled.

Why do you follow this plan, Peter? Why do you forget the meaning of your name? If Peter is originally "stone," which designates something solid, what do you mean by thinking of flight? Stone cannot easily be moved. Stay your steps and recollect your old hermitage, your earlier fasting. You should have joined

---

[158] Eleven stanzas of sapphics.   [159] Lucan I.135.

your bones to your skin,[160] you should have stretched your stomach with the least roots, fed it with the grass eaten by cattle. Why do you remember immoderate eating? That is not the monastic rule, nor what you learned from the woman who gave you birth; or let your own teachings drive you. Even as you compelled people to go on this journey, and have made them into paupers, so you should go before them, carrying out the commandments that you have taught them. Once he abstained from grain, eating only fish and wine. For a monk, more pious food would be leeks, cress, turnips, cardamum, nuts, filberts, barley, lentils, and herbs, without fish or wine, but with crumbs of bread.[161]

And so the refugees from the pious siege and from the holy suffering were pursued by Tancred, a man steady in the pursuit of Christ's business, who followed and caught them; and, as was right, heaping abuse on them, he brought them back. He placed no faith in their promises to return until each had sworn on his faith to return to the sacred army and to submit to whatever judgement the leaders might make about their desertion. Therefore William, willing or unwilling, was compelled to return, and he was brought to the court of the magnificent Bohemund, outside of which he remained awake all night. The next day, at dawn's early light, he was led into the presence of this fine prince. To Peter, covered with the shame he had earned for himself, the leader said, "Although the name of the Frankish race, stands forth with regal majesty everywhere, and although France, the mother of virtue and resolve in accordance with God's will has sent forth men who until now have been the most morally unblemished, she bore you, you, useless babbler and most impure of all men, to her own disgrace and infamy, as though you were some kind of monster. O good Father of all things, what kind of Carpenter did we have, who, like a construction-worker with a pick-axe, hacked away, with lances and swords, at the backs of the Gentiles? See how the craftsman has worn out a thousand swords with the strength of his blows, and single-handedly slain the pagan people while we merely rested. Where is that haughty firmness, that quickness with words that was nourished at the Loire and at the Seine, which has resulted in so little action, but in so much steady, thundering speech? Alone,

he had been able to aid the laboring moon,[162]

yet, foully sluggish, he has done nothing useful whatever. Certainly it is in accord with your great strength that the man who had betrayed the people of the Lord in Spain exert himself in Syria to achieve the full measure of honor. Let it be so. Certainly it suits you to do nothing else; in this way you will receive the most generous reward for behavior that has been so wretched." Now his derisory speech began to make the Franks who were standing there feel shame, and with

---

160 i.e., become emaciated.
161 Fourteen heptameters.

162 Juvenal 6.443.

difficulty they restrained the angry man from speaking. Tempering his severity, the illustrious man spared the wretch, and was content to exact from him the oath to continue the journey to Jerusalem, whether prosperity or penury attended them. And William promised that Tancred, who had prevented him from escaping, would henceforth be his friend, if he decided to behave in a manly fashion. After these words were spoken, they came to a mutual agreement. A short time later, that remarkable Carpenter, who, when he was out of harm's way, once threatened to be executioner to the Turks, forgot his oath, and that profligate of fidelity did not hesitate to flee furtively again. However, let no one be surprised that the army, although pious, had suffered such want, since it is clear that, with the great crimes they had committed, they struggled against receiving the divine gifts which would have been theirs had they behaved properly. Such need afflicted them, and they were so horribly overcome by lack of food, that if any of our men happened to move any distance from the army, anyone else from the army who found him alone would kill him, even for the slightest gain. Such utter devastation raged among our men that scarcely a thousand horses could be found in so great an army; everyone was in beastly agony from a lack of food, which did not prevent, but rather inspired some men to criminal actions. Tortured by divine punishment, many of them were brought to remember their true selves by repenting; despairing of their own strength, they were driven by hope for something better to rely on God alone, the only true support in such tribulation. Under these circumstances they learned increasingly that the more they watched their supplies diminish and their strength ebb away, the more they were taught to submit with appropriate humility to God, for whom they believed all things possible.

Moreover, one of the delegates of the tyrannical emperor, whose name, unless I am mistaken, was Tetigus, and who was present at this siege, was a man heavy with age; his nose had been cut on some occasion or other, and for this reason he had a golden nose. A skilled liar, compelled by fear of the Turks as well as driven by the danger of starvation, he addressed the leaders: "Necessity compels your excellency, O finest of leaders, to recognize how hard pressed we are by internal suffering, and how much we are goaded on by external fears. Since battle threatens us outwardly, while hunger insistently gnaws at us inwardly, there seems to be no refuge for us anywhere, no solace that would permit us to catch our breath. If in your wisdom it seems appropriate, grant me permission to go back to Byzantium, and I shall see to it that grain, wine, wheat, meat, cereal, cheese, and various other necessary items be brought here by a large fleet. I shall also see to it that constant commercial traffic in these items will be established by imperial decree. By land, all of Greece will send to you horses and whatever other animals and supplies may be useful. The emperor himself, who has not known of your great need until now, as soon as he hears of your distress, will provide aid to you in your great need. And I myself swear to carry out faithfully what I have promised; and when I have finished these tasks I shall certainly not be afraid to present myself here again to undertake the labors of this siege. If you fear that I am leaving your camp because of hunger, lo, my tents and my men shall remain here with you. Although I am leaving them for a while, I shall not be able finally to value them lightly." He spoke, and charmed the ears of the leaders with his smooth, elaborate speech. Then he left, not at all fearing what punishment his perjury might incur. Having fabricated a complete lie, he never afterwards gave a thought to what he had promised.

The presence and strength of the enemy began to constrain us so greatly that none of our men presumed to leave his tents or the encampment for any business whatever. In addition, within the camp, famine, like a madness, plagued them. For if, as they say, "nothing does more harm than hunger wrung from the unwilling," what suffering do you think they endured, to what crosses were they constantly condemned, without a single, even false, consoling hope, as they laid siege each day to the impenetrable walls? The ordinary people, eaten away by poverty, wandered through various provinces; driven by the lack of food, some began to wander towards Cyprus, others to Romania, while others made their way to the mountains. But the frequent forays of the Turks had closed off the road to the sea. In short, there was no exit for our men.

When Bohemund heard that a very large army of Turks was approaching the Crusaders' camp, he called the other leaders together and said, "Since the very small part of our army that remains seems insufficient and too weak to fight a single battle, nor can it be split into two parts to carry on two battles, we should consider, if we are going to fight the attacking Turks with whatever kind of army we can muster, which soldiers to leave to continue the siege of the city, and which to defend our tents. Therefore, if it seems reasonable to you, let us assign the best part of the finest infantrymen to guard the besieged city; in our judgement, the strongest knights should be put up against the madness of the Turks." He spoke, and none of the leaders spoke against his plan.

The enemy army now set up camp near the fort called Areg, which was close to the city, across the river Pharphar. The day was ending, and Bohemund, having summoned the entire army, came out of the camp and quickly set up camp between the river and the lake next to it. In the morning he swiftly instructed sentinels to determine the size of the Turkish forces, as well as what they were doing and where they were located, and then to report to him as quickly as possible. They had advanced a short distance and begun to search out the enemy, whose advance could be clearly heard, when they saw an infinite number of soldiers, divided into legions of two battalions, appear before them. They were followed by a very large group of foot-soldiers. As soon as they saw them the sentinels returned: "The enemy," they said, "is at hand; see to it that they find you strong and prepared." Then, to stir up his brothers in Christ and fellow-sol-diers, Bohemund said, "O finest knights, your frequent victories provide an explanation for your great boldness. Thus far you have fought for the faith against the infidel, and have emerged triumphant from every danger. Having already felt the abundant evidence of Christ's strength should give you pleasure, and should convince you beyond all doubt that in the most severe battles it is not you, but Christ, who has fought. In the face of any attack, what desperate folly can enter the mind of you who have thus far, with God's assistance, escaped harm greater than any men have ever encountered, and who have achieved triumphs impossible for mere human beings? I ask only that you place your trust in your own experience, so that at last no human force may now resist us. Fortify your minds, proceed carefully, and strive mightily to emulate Christ, who carries your banners, as he usually does, and call upon him." They responded by shouting that they would behave faithfully, energetically, and prudently, and they entrusted to him, because he was the most experienced in battle, the task of dividing up the army; Bohemund ordered each leader to collect his liege men and to draw them up into individual battle lines. Six lines were drawn up, as he had directed, each to attack the enemy in separate formations, and five of them cautiously marched forward. Bohemund followed behind with his own group, to offer help if needed. Drawn up in this manner, closely packed and filled with courage, our troops went forth to fight, each man encouraging the other by his close presence, so that no one, to the extent that it depended upon each individual, would allow the conflict to falter.

Swiftly the enemy came forth with curved spears; as their courage grew warm, they pricked their horses with their spurs, and the air was shaken with wild clamor on both sides. The battle-lines clashed, the Turks threw their javelins, the Franks thrust their weapons through the breasts of their enemies. Swords grew dull from striking blows, the collision of steel made a splitting noise. The swift right hand, thirsting for the filthy blood, inflicted sword-wounds. Like a line of flying crows, like a countless flock of thrushes, thus the arrows blocked the celestial light, crowding and darkening the air with the hail of spears. Arms resounded, horses were caught up in the charge, bronze echoed. They grieved for the losses and rejoiced in the successes, making for wild discord.[163]

When the entire force of the army behind the vanguard poured into the hideous strife, the sharpness of our men began to grow dull under the fierce assault of the enemy; as their numbers grew, our men began to lose some of their previous ardor. When Bohemund, who was waiting in the rear with reinforcements, saw this, he gnashed his teeth in rage. He sent for his constable, Robert, the son of Girardus, and gave him the following directions, "Go, and make use of the courage which you should now show, and which is right for such a great task; keep in mind the purpose of this effort, and understand that our motive is to aid all of Christianity by redeeming Jerusalem for God and liberating his tomb. It is clear to you that to carry out this task divine rather than human aid is necessary. Go then, and offer your bravery for the suffering Christ, and do not let such an opportunity find you slow to act, for God may be preparing to give you great glory." Inflamed by these words, relying on God with his whole soul,

---

163 Fourteen dactylic hexameters.

He sprung forward, and tore at the thick crowd of enemies with his sword, holding aloft the standards of the duke, which inspired such awe that wherever they appeared the spirits of our men were uplifted, and he raged like a lioness who, bereft of her cubs, kills anyone in her way. The sword carved a path, cut through the dense battalions, smashing everyone who got in the way, pointing the way for the soldiers who followed.[164]

When our men saw that the familiar standard of Bohemund was not faltering in the least, and the constable was raging with such eagerness against the Turks, they all took heart and attacked with such force that flight was the only protection the enemy could hope for. Our men fell upon the fleeing Turks, who were running at great speed, helter-skelter, and we did not cease cutting them down and decapitating their bodies all the way to the narrow bridges of the Pharphar. After such slaughter, the Turks entered the fort of Areg, which I mentioned above, looted it entirely, set it afire, and then fled, never to return to it. However, the perfidious Armenians and Syrians, who had awaited the outcome of the battle without taking sides, so that they could join the side to whom victory was granted, when they saw the Turks vanquished, moved forward and blocked the roads, killing the Turks as they tried to go by. The painful indigence of our men was somewhat alleviated with what was taken from the conquered enemy; horses and money provided relief, and even more so, our growing triumphs vitiated the Turkish reputation for fierceness. After the victory, they cut off the heads of one hundred of those who had fallen in battle, and hung them before the walls of Antioch for the besieged Turks to look at. It is, of course, the custom of the Gentiles to keep the decapitated heads and to display them as a sign of victory. While these things were going on, the Babylonian emperor sent ambassadors to the leaders of our army, congratulating them for what they had done to the Turks; in addition, he promised, although falsely, that he would become Christian, if our people would grant and restore to him what the Turks had taken from his kingdom. We had said earlier that the Babylonian empire was far more powerful than the other eastern kingdoms, but that the Turks, more ferocious in arms and in spirits, had usurped much of their territory. Those who had remained to maintain the siege of the city had fought bitterly with the inhabitants, not merely at one point, but at every gate of the city. This triumph occurred on the fifth day before the Ides of February,[165] the day before the beginning of the fast. It was right that on the day before Christians were to fast they grew fat on what they most desired, the blood of their evil enemies. The Franks, in their fervent victory celebrations, thanked God for granting them so many of their prayers, and went back to their camps, loaded with booty. The Turks, on the other hand, ashamed to be seen, would have made their way, if they could, through secret passages, back to their native lands.

Then the leaders of the army, considering the many humiliations they were

---

[164] Seven dactylic hexameters.   [165] February 9.

suffering from the attacks of the besieged people, held a meeting and decided, to prevent the chance of any diminution of their forces, to build, at the gate of the city, where the pagan temple was located, a fort by means of which they could restrain, to some extent, the enemy's forays. All the junior officers assented to this plan. Then the Count of Saint-Gilles was the first to speak: "I shall provide for and protect the fort; you must help build it only." Bohemund said, "If it please you, I promise to go with this count who has offered his services, to the Gate of Saint Simeon, where we shall both supervise those who do the work. Let the others continue the siege, and prevent the enemy from getting out of the city." And so the count and Bohemund then proceeded to the Gate, as they had proposed. Those who had remained to build the castle began to work, but the Turks made a sudden, violent attack on the beginnings of the structure. With their sudden attack they compelled our men to flee, killing many of them, bringing a day of grief to the Franks. The next day the Turks learned that some of our leaders had left the siege and gone to the Gate of Saint Simeon. They prepared a large force and quickly moved to encounter those who were returning from the Gate. When they saw the count and Bohemund, together with a large military force, coming towards them, they began to shout and utter hideous noises. They surrounded our men on all sides, inflicting terrible wounds on them, hurling spears, firing arrows, and savagely killing them. Their attack was so severe that our men scarcely were able to escape into the nearby mountains, or wherever else ·escape seemed possible. Those who were, in a manner of speaking, swifter than winged horses, escaped; anyone whom the swift pagans found slower, however, died. In this disaster, as it was considered, a thousand of our men perished; those who were found, because of their proven faith, to be acceptable, received glorious rewards after death for their sufferings. For those who needed to expiate their sins, the outpouring of blood alone was the most potent way to purge their guilt. In great anguish because of such a misfortune, and separated from his companions because he had taken a shorter road, Bohemund, with a few of his knights, whom he found banded together, returned to the siege. Driven to distraction by the death of so many of their own men, sobbing bitterly, crying out to Christ, they moved out against those who had inflicted such pain upon them, and reached the field of battle. Confident because of their recent victory, the cohorts of the enemy stood firm, expecting to perform exactly as they boasted they had performed against Bohemund and the count. Against these proponents of evil the loving God in his mercy arranged a proper remedy for his suffering people. Therefore these famous men, moved by grief and compassion for their dead brothers, with the sign of the Lord's cross fixed on their foreheads and in their hearts, hurled themselves with all their strength against the enemy. As soon as they saw this, the enemy fled towards the Pharphar river, intending to cross the strait. In their hasty flight the mass of men was jammed together in the attempt to cross, and as the wedge of knights and infantry piled up in a very small space, struggling to pass each other, men knocked each other down. Our men watched all this very carefully, and when the crowd of fugitives seemed to thicken, a fall was more effective than a wound. If any man fell into the water and tried to get out either by hanging on to the columns of the bridge, or by swimming to dry land, our men located on the shore forced him back into the water to drown. The signs of carnage were so great that the Pharphar seemed to flow with blood, not with water. The sounds made there by the vanquished and the victors, by the dying and by those who were forcing them to die, were so terrible that the highest vault of the heavens seemed to resound with their shrieks. The air became clouded with arrows and other kinds of missiles, and the brightness of the solar globe was covered by a shower of flying spears. The women of the city who were Christian stood on the ramparts of the wall, feeding upon the sight; as they watched the Turks perish and submit to calamity they groaned openly, but then turned their faces away and secretly applauded the fortunate course events had taken for the Franks. The Armenians and Syrians, although they were Christian, were compelled to fire arrows at us; some even did so willingly. Twelve of the principal enemy leaders, called "satraps" in the Chaldean language, and "emirs" in the barbaric tongue, fell in battle on this occasion, as well as many others, amounting to perhaps 1500 of the wealthiest and most important people, upon whom the entire defense of the city rested. Those who survived the carnage no longer hurled their customary insults at our men; their boisterous, scurrilous chattering ceased. On that day their daily joy was turned into grief.

> Then oncoming night separated the enemies; strength and arms dropped from their agitated minds.[166]

This victory for us resulted in an apparent dimunition of their strength and force, and their derisory remarks entirely ceased. Moreover, the short supply of many things whose lack pressed our men was amply replenished, thanks to God's benevolence. At daylight the next day, some of the Turks came forth from the city to collect the bodies of their dead; they found some, but others had disappeared, carried off in the bed of the river. They buried those they found in the temple called the Mahometry, on the other side of the Pharphar, near the gate of Antioch. In these tombs they buried cloaks, gold besants, bows and arrows, and many other utensils that I shall refrain from describing. When they heard about these funeral ceremonies, our men armed themselves and entered the cemetery, broke open the tombs, took out the bodies, heaped them up and dropped them into a deep pit. Then they decapitated them and had the heads brought to their own tents, in order to calculate accurately the number they had killed, with the exception of the bodies that the ambassadors of the Babylonian emperor transported on the backs of four horses, as evidence of the victory won over the Turks. When the Turks saw this, they suffered more bitterly from the uncovering of the bodies than from the killings themselves. Now they did not restrain their grief with a few modest tears, but, putting aside all shame, they screamed in public agony. Three

---

[166] Two dactylic hexameters.

days later they began building the fort mentioned above, with the very stones they had taken from the tombs of the Gentiles that they had broken open. When the fort was finished, the besieged town began to suffer exceedingly, and their discomfort became even greater. Our own men were now free to go where they wished, and even the mountain paths, which previously had been treacherous, were now favorable for searching for food. With all the roads shut off to the Turks, one section near where the fort and the temple next to the fort were located, seemed to offer the possibility of entering and leaving the river. If we properly equipped this fort, which belonged to us, none of the enemy could have hoped to have found a way out. A meeting was held, and the leaders decided that they would choose one of our men to guard the fort, to fortify it carefully, and to defend it faithfully, so that the pagans might be kept from wandering through the mountains and fields, and might be cut off from entering or leaving the city. When they were looking for someone fit for such a task, Tancred, who earned and still deserves the title of a wise young man in the Lord's wars, unable to restrain himself, broke in at this point, saying, "If I were to know what future advantages for me might result from the present hard task, then I might under-take, carefully and with the aid of my retinue, to strengthen this fort, and I shall try to block our enemies from moving along the roads they are accustomed to use." Pleased with his generous offer, the leaders immediately promised to give him 400 silver marks. Displeased with the offer, which seemed not to match the magnitude of the task, Tancred nevertheless agreed; and so, lest he be considered cowardly if he refused, he gathered his knights and clients quickly and resolutely, took charge of the fort, and cut the enemy off from the possibility of getting out through the city's gates. By this means he inflicted upon them the greatest scar-city of food for their horses, as well as a great dearth of wood and other necessary items. This outstanding man chose to remain there resolutely, cutting off all traffic, and he set about surrounding the city and setting up a vigilant blockade. On the very day on which he entered the fort, a large group of Armenians and Syrians came through the mountains, bringing supplies of all sorts to the be-sieged city. This superb knight, to ensure that the task he had begun would have a positive outcome, intercepted them, compelled by God more than by his own boldness, and seized a great amount of grain, wine, oil, and other no less neces-sary supplies. The good man could no longer complain that while he was carry-ing out such a holy task God was forgetful of him, but he had learned, for the first time, from this remarkable good fortune that he would never again lack bodily necessities, and that he would not lack eternal reward from God, after His earthly assistance. The Turks were entirely prevented from leaving the city or moving around outside the walls, but were compelled to make do with what they could find within the city walls, until Antioch was under siege.

In the course of this siege the strength of Christian law flourished greatly, and, if anyone was convicted of a crime, he submitted to the severe judgement of the leaders of the army. Moreover, sexual crimes were punished with particular severity, and this was just. Those who were surrounded by atrocious deprivations, who seemed to be exposed to the swords of the enemy every day, if God were not protecting them, should not have been at the mercy of lustful thoughts. And how could pleasure enter where the fear of death was ceaselessly present? So it happened that merely speaking of a prostitute or of a brothel was considered intolerable, and they feared dying beneath the swords of the pagans if they committed such a crime. If any of the unmarried women was found to be pregnant, she and her pimp were submitted to hideous punishments. A certain monk of the most prestigious monastery, who had fled from the cloister to go on the expedition to Jerusalem, moved not by piety but by whim, was caught with a certain woman, and convicted, if I am not mistaken, by a trial by fire. Then they were stripped naked and led, by order of the Bishop of Puy and others, through all the nearby camps, and beaten in the cruellest fashion with whips, to the terror of the onlookers.

The above-mentioned Bishop of Puy assiduously exhorted men to be more patient in their sufferings and more careful about their vices; he let no Sunday or holiday go by without preaching the authority of holy writ through every corner of the camp. He enjoined every priest, bishop, abbot, and cleric whom he met and who seemed educated, to do the same.

It seems to me worthwhile, since the word "abbot" has made its way into my work, to tell about a certain abbot who, when this journey was first proposed among our people, finding himself without sufficient funds for the pilgrimage, cut into his forehead by I know not what means the sign of the cross, which ordinarily was made out of some kind of material and affixed to clothing. It did not look as though it had been painted on, but as though it had been inflicted, like stigmata received in battle. After he had done this, to make the trick look authentic, he claimed that an angel had appeared to him in a vision and placed it there. His hopes were not disappointed; when the restless crowd, always avid for novelty, heard this story, the man was innundated with gifts, both from people in and from people outside of his own region. Such a trick, however, could not be hidden from the eyes of those who looked at him carefully, because a slimy liquid seemed very clearly to ooze from the forcefully inscribed lines that formed the cross itself. Finally he set out on the crusade, was present at the siege of Antioch, displayed what he had fabricated, although others had seen through it for some time, and did not hide his intention to gain money. He behaved well there, and was very useful in instructing the Lord's army. He wished to emulate God, but he did not do this the way a wise man would. He was so outstanding that after the capture of Jerusalem he was made abbot of the church of the blessed Mary in the vale of Josaphat,[167] and later was made Archbishop of Caesarea, metropolis of Palestine. It is an indubitable fact that had the solace of the divine Word not been administered with great frequency to them, their patient perseverance would never have survived the hunger and hardships of war. Therefore we may say that

---

[167] Rom. 10.2.

those among them who were circumspect in their lives and endowed with wisdom were not less but more valuable than those who fought the enemy in hand-to-hand combat. He who provides encouragement that strengthens a wavering mind certainly is greater than the person to whom his exhortation provides strength, especially when the advisers and the advisees share the same suffering.

What shall I say finally about those who, on this same expedition, were sanctified in various places by becoming martyrs? They were not only priests, learned men, but warriors, and ordinary people, who had had no hope of confession, but were called to this glorious fate. We have heard of many who, captured by the pagans and ordered to deny the sacraments of faith, preferred to expose their heads to the sword than to betray the Christian faith in which they had once been instructed. Among them I shall select one, a knight and an aristocrat, but more illustrious for his character than all others of his family or social class I have ever known. From the time he was a child I knew him, and I watched his fine disposition develop. Moreover, he and I came from the same region, and his parents held benefices from my parents, and owed them homage, and we grew up together, and his whole life and development were an open book to me. Although he was already an outstanding knight, he was a singularly expert warrior, but entirely free from sexual vice. He was well-known at the court of Alexis, the Emperor of Constantinople, for he often traveled in his service. To consider his manner of living: although he had been blessed with wealth by fortune, he was considered to be unusually generous in giving alms; he attended divine services so regularly that he seemed to lead a life more like that of a bishop than a knight. When I recall his steadfast prayer, his pious words, and his generosity in giving gifts, I am extremely pleased with his holy purpose, but also with my own good fortune in having known him. I witnessed him perform acts that entitled him to nothing less than a martyr's death. I certainly take pride, as all those who were able to know him may take pride, in having known him, since I do not presume to say that I was his friend. Whoever saw him knew without a doubt that he had seen a martyr. Captured by the pagans, who demanded that he renounce the Christian faith, he asked these unbelievers to delay until the sixth day of the week. They readily agreed, thinking that his stubbornness would be altered, and when the day arrived, and the Gentiles in their madness pressed him to agree to their demand, he is reported to have said, "If you think that I have put off the sword hanging above my head because I wanted to enjoy a few more days alive, and not because I wanted to die on the day on which my Lord Jesus Christ was crucified, then it is fitting that I give evidence of how a Christian mind thinks. Get up, then, and kill me for the example that you want, so that I may restore my soul to him for whom I die, who on this day gave his own life for mankind." Having said this, he stretched his neck out to the sword that hung over him, and when his head was cut off, he was carried to God, whose death he had longed to imitate. His name was Matthew, as his name indicates, "given to God."

Book Five

In addition to the spiritual reward this little work of mine may bring, my purpose in writing is to speak as I would wish someone else, writing the same story, would speak to me. For my mind loves what is somewhat obscure, and detests a raw, unpolished style. I savor those things which are able to exercise my mind more than those things which, too easily understood, are incapable of inscribing themselves upon a mind always avid for novelty. In everything that I have written and am writing, I have driven everyone from my mind, instead thinking only of what is good for myself, with no concern for pleasing anyone else. Beyond worrying about the opinions of others, calm or unconcerned about my own, I await the blows of whatever words may fall upon me. And so let us take up what we have begun, and calmly bear the judgements that men bark at us.

We do not think it possible for anyone to tell what happened at the siege of Antioch, because, among those who were there, no one can be found who could have seen everything that happened everywhere in the city, or who could have understood it entirely in the order in which it happened. Since we have already briefly touched upon the privations and misfortunes of war that they suffered, it now seems proper to pass on to how they managed to end the siege, and what the fruits of such labor were.

One of the Turkish leaders in the city was called Pyrrus; having become familiar with Bohemund by some means or other, he began communicating with him by frequent messengers, and they often informed each other about what was happening on both sides. As their friendship grew, kindled by their steady conversations, little by little Bohemund began to propose that the city, over which the Turk had significant power, be surrendered to the Christians, and that he accept Christianity. He promised him, if he did these two things, that he would receive greater wealth, along with greater honor than he had ever had. After these offers had been made not once, but many times, attracted by the reward, he consented, and wrote a letter like this, "I am in charge of three towers: I shall hand them over to you; at whatever hour you please, or whatever time is convenient, I shall gladly permit either you or whomever you wish to enter them." Hope now began to lift Bohemund's spirit greatly, and while he waited to enter the city, his handsome face shone with inward pleasure. Fearing that, at the moment the city was being betrayed, one of our leaders might seize control of the whole city for himself, he cleverly called the leaders of the army together.

"It is no secret," he said, "O excellent peers, what starvation, what cold, what harsh vigils you have had to endure while besieging this city; clearly a deadly weariness, for which there is no known remedy, has descended equally on all of our people, the highest, the lowest, and those in between. I ask you to hold a meeting among yourselves, to consider whether you will give power over this city to one of us, if he is able to obtain its surrender. It seems to me right, if someone, whether by force, or in secret, or by bribery, manages to gain entrance, that everyone categorically agree to grant him rule over the city." The attitude of the leaders was very much at odds with Bohemund's; with angry frowns they said, "It is not right that, after the work and the fear have been shared by all, and undertaken without seeking the honor of a reward, and when danger has hung in an equal balance over all, that rule over the city, struggled for so long and through so much pain, by so many great men, should be granted to any one man. For who does not think it just, that, since the struggle raged for everyone, the rest and his own share after the victory rightly belongs to everyone." Unhappy with these developments, weighing in his troubled mind what he had heard, Bohemund left. Suddenly, news came to the leaders that an innumerable army, formed from among the barbarous nations that were their enemies, was forming to come to the aid of Antioch. After a swift change of mind, they called a meeting, and said to each other, "Should Bohemund take the city by some trick, we might permit him to possess it, with this one condition: if the emperor supplies the help he has promised us, and carries out with matching generosity what he has offered and sworn to give us, we must ourselves hand over the city to the emperor's jurisdiction. Should he fail us, the entire city will be given over to Bohemund, as he requested." When he found out what they had said, the splendid man was reassured, and repeated his imprecations to Pyrrus every day, seducing him with promises and praise. "Lo," he said, "fine Pyrrus, you see that opportunity smiles in the working out of these matters. Therefore, I say, do not delay, lest you lose what we have labored together for, because it is discovered, God forbid, by someone." Pleased with Bohemund's message, Pyrrus promised that his efforts would in no way be delayed. And, lest the effect of the daily delay create anxiety in the noble man, Pyrrus secretly sent his own son to Bohemund, informing him that he faithfully looked forward to the surrender of the city. "Tomorrow," he said, "at the first light, collect the entire force of the Franks' army, with horns blowing, and order them to proceed some distance from the encampment, as though they were going to make one of their usual raids on Saracen territory; but then bring them back immediately through the mountains on the right. I shall wait inside the city for your return, ready to admit immediately into the towers which seem to be under my control those whom you choose to send." Bohemund eagerly hastened to carry out the plan he had heard; summoning one of his retainers, he ordered him to carry out the office of herald, circulating throughout the Franks' camp, telling them to prepare themselves with the greatest care, as though they were proceeding into the land of the Saracens. Without delay, the wisdom of the servant carried out the command of the leader directly, nor did the men of France refuse to comply. At last Bohemund told the joy in his heart to Duke Godfrey, to the Count of Flanders, to the Count of Saint-Gilles, and to the Bishop of Puy; trusting the promises of Pyrrus, he said that Antioch would be surrendered to him that night. Therefore, when the army was drawn up in the order we have described, the knights were ordered to march through the plain;

the band of foot-soldiers marched through the mountains. Throughout the night they marched, and before dawn offered its first rays, they stood before the towers over which the blessed traitor vigilantly stood watch.

When Bohemund got down from his horse, he spoke to the Franks with a tone of unusual authority, "Go forward, and breathe free of the anxiety which you have long endured; climb the ladder built for you; let me detain you no longer – seize the city you have been hoping for so long. Long under subjection to the Turks, it will now surrender, God willing, to your custody." The Franks reached the ladder, which was attached and very firmly tied to the walls of the city, offering a way to ascend to the sixty men who, when they reached the towers, were given authority over them. However, because so few Franks had climbed up, Pyrrus, waiting, and anxious, not for our men but for himself, as became very clear later, feared that the outcome of the betrayal he had undertaken would lead to his own destruction, and he cried out brusquely in Greek to those near him, "We have too few Franks." With these words he eagerly called upon Bohemund to proceed quickly, before the inhabitants knew that the Franks were assembling. But a certain Lombard servant, understanding that Pyrrus was complaining about the absence of Bohemund, hastened as quickly as he could to the man who was being sought. "Why," he said, "are you behaving so foolishly? Why do you carry out such an arduous task so slowly? See how we now have obtained control of three towers; why do you watch the doubtful outcome of this affair from a distance? Wake up, move your forces, place yourself in the midst of the action." Very swiftly now he hastened with his men to the ladder, and he revived the hopes both of the good traitor and of those who had already climbed the wall. Immediately those who already occupied Pyrrus' towers, waiting for the Franks to assemble from all sides, began to shout with great joy, "God wishes it!" Those who were standing before the walls, about to climb up, shouted the same thing with all their might. With great competitiveness each tried to climb the wall first; once up the ladder, they took over the towers, and other towers, as quickly as possible. Whoever stood in their way was put to death; among those who died was Pyrrus' brother. Meanwhile a ladder broke, and the great crowd of our men below, and those who had preceded them, were sorely troubled; those on the top of the wall feared that they were cut off from aid, and those at the bottom feared that those who had climbed up could not receive support. But great effort quickly made a way. There was a hidden gate to their left; it was not remarkable that it could not be seen at night; even during the day it was hardly ever seen, since it was located in a place where there was little traffic. By tapping the wall, however, impelled by urgent need, they found it; immediately they ran up to it, and opened it by breaking the hinges and locks, making an entry for the Franks, who rushed in.

You would have heard the whole city shaken with a terrible roar. While some rejoiced in the completion of such a task, others wept at the unlooked-for destruction of their prospects. Neither the victors nor the vanquished showed any moderation or self-control. Bohemund ordered his standard, easily recognized by the Turks, to be placed on top of a certain mountain, in full view of the citadel, which was still resisting, to make the city aware of his presence. Wailing and shrieking filled the city; while throngs pressed through the narrow streets, the brutal, bloody shouts of the victors, eager to kill, resounded. As they recalled the sufferings they had endured during the siege, they thought that the blows that they were giving could not match the starvations, more bitter than death, that they had suffered. The same punishment inflicted upon the hordes of pagans was justly meted out to the treacherous Armenians and Syrians, who, with the aid of the Turks, had eagerly and diligently pursued the destruction of our men, and our men were, in turn, unwilling to spare them painful punishment. And yet I say that they would have spared many of them, had they known how to make a distinction between the native pagans and those of our own faith. In the confusion of the moment and of the action (it was night, and eagerness to capture the town and impatience with delay incited everyone), perhaps nothing permitted distinguishing foreigners by their clothing or beards. A terrible neglect covered the thinness of the weary cheeks of our men, who, continually prepared for battle, worn out by continual traveling, had stopped shaving their beards in the Franks' manner. The Bishop of Puy noticed this, and to prevent mutual slaughter in case they confronted each other in battle (each thinking the other a Turk because of the beard), ordered them to shave often, and to hang on their necks crosses made of silver or of some other material, so that no one, mistaken for a foreigner, would be struck down by a comrade. In the morning, those who had remained in the tents heard the tumult in the city, and came out. They saw Bohemund's standard fixed on the lofty mountain, in front of the walls of the citadel, which had not yet been captured. They quickly ran towards the gates of the city and broke in, cut down the Turks and Saracens whom they found there, while those, however, who had fled into the citadel escaped death. Some of the Turks, having learned that the Franks had taken control of the city, escaped through other gates of the city. Within the city, however, no one was spared because of sex; young children were killed, and, since those weak with age were not spared, there can be no doubt about the ferocity with which those who were young enough to be fit for battle were killed.

Meanwhile, fearing capture by the Frankish forces, and wishing to purchase his life by running away, Cassian, who was in charge of the city of Antioch, together with several of his leaders, took refuge not far from Antioch, in an area occupied by Tancred. Exhausting their horses by the speed of their flight, unable to proceed any further, they turned aside and stopped at a small house. When the inhabitants of the mountains, Armenians and Syrians, found their greatest enemy hidden, at the mercy of fortune, in a poor hut, they recognized him at once, decapitated him, and brought the severed head as a gift to Bohemund, expecting that they would obtain their freedom from him in exchange for the unusual gift. His baldric and the scabbard of the sword they took from him were estimated to be worth 60 besants. These events occurred on Thursday, the fifth of June. Then you would have seen the city overflowing with bodies and with intolerable stench. Markets, public places, the porches and vestibules of homes, which once were adorned with beautifully polished marble surfaces, were now completely stained with gore. Infinite numbers of corpses heaped up everywhere, a horrible spectacle, and the savagery of the foul air, horribly infected both the eyes and the ears. The narrow streets were strewn with deep piles of stinking bodies, and since there was no way to carry off so many dead, and there was no escape from the smells, the constant sight and stink made men used to the horror. Thus habit led to audacity, and no one feared to walk down the streets filled with bodies.

Therefore Kherboga, the mayor of the palace or rather the leader of the troops of the king of the Persians, whom they were accustomed to call Sogdianus,[168] the name of a previous king of the Persians (as the Romans are accustomed to call their leaders Caesars), while he was still within the kingdom of Persia, in the province called Khorasan (some say that this land derives its name by corruption from the name of the land around the Caucasus), was summoned by frequent messengers from Cassianus, the ruler of the city of Antioch, to bring help to him in his beleaguered position. Cassianus promised that, if he drove off the Franks, he would either turn over to him the liberated city, or provide him with a gift equal to his great labor. When the general, enticed by this promise, had put together a huge army, and had asked for and received permission to kill the Christians from the chief pontiff of their heresy (for even they have their pope, in the likeness of ours), he quickly set off to relieve the siege of Antioch. The prefect of Jerusalem (whom they call in their barbaric language "emir") also immediately increased the invading forces with his own army, which was, in turn, augmented by the considerable forces of the King of Damascus. The pagans recruited by the infidel prince, in addition to the Turks, Saracens, Arabs, and Persians (who are already familiar to historians), bore new names: they were the Publicans, the Kurds, the Azimites, and the Agulani, together with innumerable others, who were by no means human, but monsters. Three thousand of those who were called Agulani were said to be present, and they were afraid neither of swords, lances, arrows, nor any kind of arms, because they and their horses were covered with armor everywhere. In battles the only weapons they used were their swords. Kherboga therefore, with the great arrogance of the pagans, strove to drive the Franks from Antioch. As the prince approached the city, the son of the dead Cassian, Sensadolus by name, met him, and, with great sadness, said to him, "Since your strength is widely renowned, and the victories of you and your people are everywhere judged to be incomparable, certainly my hope for your aid will not be disappointed, O most victorious of men. No one denies the worth of your judgements; because of the brilliance of your deeds, your power is worshipped everywhere; therefore I need not be ashamed of lamenting my misfortune in your presence. I know for certain that I am not begging in vain for the things for which I ask. Your excellency remembers that you received ambassadors

---

[168] Sultan.

from my father when Antioch was being besieged, and that, while you were deciding to come to his aid, you heard that the city had been captured by the Franks. Now my father is dead, and I am besieged in the citadel of the city, undoubtedly awaiting the same fate that overtook my father. If they have invaded Antioch, and have done the same to many cities and towns of Armenia and Syria, they undoubtedly intend to do the same thing to you and to others of our race. May your excellency carry out with all your force what you have undertaken against these vicious men, so that the usurpations intended by these most wretched of men may be thwarted. For me, in this crisis, you remain the last hope." In response to these laments, Kherboga replied, "If you want my help in these present dangers, turn over to me the city which you are defending and for which you are pleading, and after I have put my men in charge of the citadel, then you will find out what I shall do on your behalf." Sensadolus replied, "If you kill the Franks for me, and bring me their severed heads, I shall let you into the city; then I shall swear allegiance to you and as your liege rule the citadel." Corboran said to him, "You will not behave like that towards me, but will hand over the city immediately." What more? The demand of the infidel ruler prevailed, and the young man surrendered control of the citadel to him who wrested it from him, but who would not long enjoy his power.

On the third day after the Franks had broken into Antioch, the vanguard of the Turks had appeared before the walls of the city, while the rest of their vast army set up their tents at the Pharfar bridge. First they attacked the tower closest to the bridge, and after they had captured it with very great effort, they killed everyone they found within in it, sparing only the commander of the tower, whom our men found, after a later battle against them, chained in irons. The next day the army hurried towards the city, chose a spot between two rivers for their tents, and remained there for two days. After capturing the fort whose commander, as I said, was put in chains, Kherboga summoned one of his officers, whom he knew to be wise and trustworthy, and gave him the following orders, "Go and defend the fort for me, with the fidelity that you owe me, and which I expect of you." He replied, "I shall have difficulty carrying out your command in this matter, but I shall carry it out on the condition that, if the Franks are victorious, you permit me to surrender the citadel to the victors." Kherboga replied, "I trust your discretion and your faithfulness in this matter, and shall firmly support whatever you choose to do." After the fort had been provisioned, the ill-fated prince returned to his camp, where some of his Turks, having stripped a poor foot-soldier of his arms, brought them to Kherboga to make sport of us. The sword was filthy with rust, the bow was black as soot, the dull lance was covered with the smoke of many years. Joking, they said to him, "Here are the weapons with which the Frankish army will defeat us." Smiling, Kherboga said to them, "Will they depopulate the East with these shining, powerful arms? Will the far reaches of the Caucasus submit to these men? Will the unarmed Franks be able to take away from us the lands which the Amazons once held, and which our ancestors once claimed?" He spoke, called a scribe, and said, "Write as quickly as possible the same letters on different pieces of parchment, so that they may be sent throughout the provinces of Persia, to our pope, to the lord and king of our Persians, to the governors and to our military peers in the different areas." This is the tenor of what he wrote:

> To the magnificent lord and king of the Persians, to the blessed pope, and to all of those sworn to fight a holy war against the Christians, Kherboga, prince of his army, wishes health and victory. Fathers and lords, I am grateful that the supreme divinity continually provides us with good fortune, and offers us victory everywhere over the enemies of the people. We are sending you three weapons which we have taken from the Franks, so that you may see with what equipment those who wish to drive us from our country fight. I would like you to know that I am besieging the Franks, who intend to destroy us, in the very city, Antioch, which they have just captured. I am in possession of the lofty citadel in the heart of the city. Since I can either put to death those who are shut up there, or place them in abject captivity, I do not want you meanwhile to be tortured with worry out of concern for us, but I want you to know that we are completely in control. Therefore give yourselves up to pleasures: in greater security than that to which you are accustomed, eat the finest foods; lie with multitudes of wives and concubines to propagate the race, so that the increasing number of sons may oppose the Christians, whose number now grows. I swear by the high Thunderer, that I, protected by the blessed Mahomet, will not appear before the eyes of your majesty until I have subdued the royal city, that is, Antioch, as well as neighboring Syria, the Greeks and the Epirites, whom they call the Bulgars, and I have conquered the Apulians and Calabrians as an additional ornament to your glory. Farewell.

Kherboga's mother, who lived in the city of Aleppo, came to him at this time, and sadly offered him counsel: "I would like to know whether what is said of you is true." Her son replied, "What is that?" She said, "They say that you are going to fight the Franks." He replied, "Absolutely true." She said, "Son, best of men, I dare to appeal to your native nobility not to fight them, lest you mar your reputation. Since the brilliance of your arms gleams as far as the furthest reaches of the Indian Ocean, and remote Thule resounds with your praise, why would you soil your weapons with the blood of poor men, whom it does not pay to attack, and from whose defeat you can gain no glory? Since you can compel distant kings to tremble, why harm wretched foreigners? My son, I say that you rightly despise them as individuals, but you should know for a fact that the authority of the Christian religion is superior. Therefore I beg you not to attempt something that you will later regret having undertaken." When he heard what she had to say, he looked at her with anger in his eyes and said, "Why do you weave these old wives' tales? You are raving, I suggest, insanely pouring forth words without understanding. All the men in their army do not amount even to the number of noble leaders from the cities who are fighting under my command. And do you, in your insanity, think that Christian presumption will obscure my power?" She said, "Oh most dearly beloved son, I place little value on the names of the people about whom we are speaking, but I beg you not to shun their leader, Christ. Perhaps they themselves do not have the power to fight you, but victory is certain for their God, if he wishes to prevail. He customarily defends his own men, though they be weak and ignorant, purely for his own glory, and watches over and protects them, whose shepherd, or rather redeemer, he says he is. Do you think that he who has looked after the empires of his faith, who has thus far granted them victory over us, is incapable at this very moment of easily overturning our efforts? For it was said to him by the Father, as though to a God about to rise again from the dead, 'Arise God, and judge the earth, for you will inherit it among the nations of men.'[169] Therefore, if he judges the earth, he sees and sets apart some from the mass doomed to destruction, while others he condemns, and he takes as his inheritance not all nations, but only a portion of the whole. May your foresight hear, my son, how severely he punishes those whom he permits to be ignorant of him. The prophet David says, 'Pour forth thy wrath against the nations that have not known thee, and against the kingdoms that have not cried out thy name.'[170] You do not condemn these Franks because they are strangers and you are gentiles; you do not reject them because their arms are humble or because they are impoverished; but rather you hate in them the name of Christ. Certainly He who is despised in them will fight for them, if necessary, with overflowing anger. If he has promised them with prophetic mouth that 'the name of God will be praised from east to west,'[171] for he is said to be exalted not over the Jews, but over all nations, and by the mouth of God himself it was said that the people who had not been his people were now his people, and those who had not been loved were now loved,[172] and what had been among the Jews was transferred to all nations by the grace of adoption, and among the rest of them the face of the God of the Jews was provided, then who except a madman would dare attack the sons of God? I predict that if you fight them, you will bring upon yourself great discomfort and shame. You will undergo certain military defeat, enrich the Christians with booty taken from you, and you yourself will run off in ignominious flight. Even if death does not wait for you in this battle, you may be certain that your life will end within a year. Their God does not take immediate vengeance when a crime is done, but defers the punishment until the crime itself has come to full fruition. For this reason, my son, I fear that you may be increasing the horror of your death by delaying it." Stunned by his mother's miraculous eloquence, pale and weakened by the announcement of his impending death, Kherboga replied, "And you, I would like to know how you came by this knowledge, how you have discovered that the Christian people will use their strength against us, that they are about to triumph in battle over us, that they will despoil us, and that I shall die a sudden death within the year." She said, "Son, we know that nearly one hundred years have gone by since it was discovered in certain secret books of a pagan sect that the Christian people would rise up against us in

---

[169] Psalm 81.8.
[170] Psalm 78.6.
[171] Psalm 92.3.
[172] Rom. 9.25

battle and subjugate us entirely, setting up their kingdom where we now exercise dominion, so that pagans would be subject to those of the true faith. But our knowledge was not clear in this respect: we did not know whether it would come about now or after a long time. I then diligently studied astronomy, examining innumerable possibilities, until, checking them against each other, I learned that we would inevitably be conquered by Christian men. For this reason I grieve for you with all my heart, because I have no doubt that I shall soon be deprived of you." And he replied, "Mother, I would like you to explain some things about which I am uncertain." She said, "Ask, so that you will not be in doubt. Whatever I know you will know immediately." He said, "Tell me whether Bohemund and Tancred should be considered gods or men, and tell me whether they will bring victory in battle to the Franks." She replied, "Son, Bohemund and Tancred are like us, subject to mortality, but because they fight for their faith, they have merited glorious renown, for God helps them. They declare that God is the Father, whose son, made into a human being, they worship in the same manner, and they believe that both are the same in the unity of the holy Spirit." He replied, "Since you testify, O mother, that they are not Gods, but merely human beings like us, no more doubt remains, and we may try our strength in battle."

Therefore, understanding that her son, intent on fighting with the Franks, was unwilling to heed her advice, the mother collected whatever supplies she could gather and, spurned by her son, retired to the above-mentioned city of Aleppo. And so, three days later, Kherboga took up arms, and a large group of Turks approached the city with him on the side where the fort they had recently captured and fortified was located. Our men, however, judging that they could resist them, set up lines of defense against them, but the number of Turks was so great that our men did not have the force or boldness to resist. Therefore they were compelled to retreat into the city, but, as they were entering the gate in crowded flight, the entrance proved too narrow, and many were crushed to death. It was the fifth day of the week, and some outside the city were attacking the gate, while others continued to battle the inhabitants inside the city until evening.

But because Christ knew once and knows now whom he has chosen, some men who, so to speak, were not of the kind by means of whom salvation would come to Israel,[173] when they saw that they were surrounded by the Turkish army,

and that the day's battle was scarcely ended when night came, they grew fearful and panic-stricken, aware only of their imminent death. Petrified, each saw his own life hanging before him, and in their frightened minds the men saw Turks already before them, about to strike them with deadly spears. Each lost faith in his own ability to fight, and therefore turned his mind to flight. Those who gave up hope in God made a filthy descent into the foul sewers, a worthy place for those who were giving such a bad example to the troops. The crawling cowards made their way to the sea, with the skin from their hands and feet torn

---

173 I Mac. 5.62.

away, and their bones stripped of flesh by the sharp rocks. Like Paul the doctor, who escaped from Damascus by means of a wall,[174] they showed that the sewers were fitting for them.[175]

Among those who retreated were a certain William of Normandy, nobly born, and his brother Alberic, sent to school early, who became a cleric, and then, out of a passion for fighting, dropped away from the church and foully, like an apostate, became a knight. I would name the towns from which they came, were I not constrained by my close friendship with some members of their family to limit my remarks, thereby protecting them from shame. A certain Guido Trossellus, well known for his power and influence in cities across the Seine, and who was considered remarkable by the whole race of Franks, was the standard-bearer for the escape. There were other deserters from the holy army also, who, when they came back to their native land, were held in contempt and denounced as infamous everywhere. Some of them we do not know; others we know very well, but we prefer not to humiliate them.

They came to the port which is called the gate of Saint Simeon, where they found boats and sailors, and they asked the sailors, "Why are you waiting here, unhappy men? You should know that all those to whom you customarily bring food are about to die, for the city and those within it are besieged by an army of Turks, and we scarcely escaped from their onslaught with our naked bodies." Stung by the dire news, they hesitated, stunned for a long time, and then placed all their hope in flight.

They got into the ships and sought the depths of the sea.[176]

Almost immediately afterwards, as their prows began to move through the waves, the Turks arrived, killed everyone they found there, burned the ships they found riding at anchor, and despoiled the bodies of those whom they had killed. After those base men, fleeing from divine assistance, had escaped through the foul places we have mentioned, those who had chosen to remain were no longer able to withstand the enemies' weapons or onslaughts. Therefore they built a wall between themselves and their enemies, which they patrolled night and day. The suffering of our men was so great there that they were compelled to eat the foulest food, the flesh of horses and donkeys.

One day, when the leaders of the army were standing before the citadel they were besieging, and were gravely worried about the misery they were suffering, a priest presented himself before them, and said, "Leaders and elders, I shall relate a vision of your excellence which, if you give it credence, may offer you some consolation, as I hope. While I was asleep one night in the church of the blessed mother of God, the Lord Jesus Christ, together with his most blessed mother and

---

174 Acts 9.25; II Cor. 11.33.   176 One dactylic hexameter.
175 Sixteen dactylic hexameters.

the blessed leader of the apostles, Peter, appeared standing before me and said, 'Do you know who I am?' 'Not at all,' I said. He spoke, and lo in a cloud above his head a cross appeared, like those one sees in paintings. Again questioning me, the image of the Savior repeated, 'Now do you know whom you see?' I said, 'O lord, I can recognize your identity only because I see above your neck the figure of the cross, which customarily represents your image wherever it is painted.' He said, 'You are not wrong. I am he.' Aware of how much we have suffered, I threw myself immediately at his feet and urgently begged him to relieve the suffering of those who were fighting for our faith. 'I have seen what you have endured,' he said, 'and I shall not now hesitate to bring you help. At my instigation you vowed to undertake this expedition; you have captured the city of Nicea with my support; under my leadership you have won many victories; having brought you this far, I have grieved for the sufferings you endured in besieging the city of Antioch, and which you are suffering even now within the city itself. However, after I raised you up with so much help and with so many victories, and I granted you victory in the city, preserving you safe and unharmed, you have behaved badly towards Christians, and have entered into filthy relations with pagan women; you have raised a foul clamor to heaven.' At this point the Virgin of unconquerable piety, always the intercessor with God for the human race, and Peter, the heavenly gatekeeper, and the patron bishop of Antioch, threw themselves at the feet of the most merciful Lord, praying and asking that He grant relief to his people. The miraculous Peter himself said, 'Your majesty remembers with what shameful things the pagans desecrated my home in this city, insulting your divinity by filling your shrines with disgraceful actions and with murder. Since you at last showed pity and expelled them, bringing joy to the heavenly kingdom, will you now relent and permit their pride to regain its former position against you yourself?' Moved by these words, God said to me, 'Go and tell my people to return with all their hearts to me, and I shall eagerly restore myself to them; within five days I shall provide the greatest help. Let them recite litanies, and let each man sing this response from *Ecclesiastes*: Our enemies have joined against me, and they rejoice in their strength; destroy their strength, O Lord, and scatter them.' "[177] The priest then added, "If you have any doubt about what I have said, I shall submit, in the name of truth, to whatever trial you wish, gladly undergoing trial by fire or by being thrown from a cliff. If I am harmed in the test, you may add to my injuries the worst punishment you can imagine." The Bishop of Puy, always attentive to church law, ordered the bible and the Cross brought forward, so that the reliability of his words might be tested by oath.

When this had been done, the leaders, after consultation, mutually pledged that neither death nor life would compel them to abandon the defense they had

---

[177] Scatter them that they may know that no other than you, our Lord, fights for us. Scatter them by your power, and destroy them, our protector, Lord. (Eccl. 36.1).

undertaken, no matter how difficult the circumstances. Therefore first Bohemund, then the Count of Saint Gilles, Hugh the Great, Robert of Normandy, Duke Godfrey, and the Count of Flanders, swore with equal vigor that they would never abandon the undertaking. But Tancred swore on this condition, that as long as he could rely on the support of forty knights he would not only refuse to retreat from the siege under which they presently labored, but he would not turn from the path to Jerusalem, unless death intervened. The news of these transactions fortified the hearts of the multitude.

Before Antioch was captured, a vision of the apostle Andrew appeared to one of the soldiers, whose name was Peter, and the vision said, "What are you doing?" Stunned, he did not reply, but asked who he was. He revealed that he was the apostle Andrew. "You should know, my son, that when the army of the Franks enters the city which God will open for them, you will go to the church of the blessed Peter, my brother and fellow apostle, and there in a certain place you will find the lance with which it is said the side of our Savior Jesus Christ was pierced." Saying no more, he departed. Peter wanted no one to know about the vision, nor did he think that it was anything more than one of those deceptive dreams to which we are all regularly subjected. But during his conversation with the apostle he had the presence of mind to ask him, "Lord, if I tell to our people what you have told me to do, what reliable evidence can I offer to overcome their doubts and to convince them to believe me?" In response, the glorious apostle took him and carried him in spirit to the basilica of his blessed brother, to the place in which the lance rested. After the city had been captured, when the people of God were subjected to the tribulations which we have described, the same memorable apostle who had undertaken to preserve in every way the elaborate beauty of the home of his famous brother again appeared to the man Peter, and said, "Why have you delayed carrying out my command? Since you see your people undergoing terrible hardships, attacked by the Turks, about to fall into the depths of despair, you should tell them what you learned from me, since they certainly should know that wherever they bear this same lance, they will have certain victory." After this second warning from the apostle, Peter began to relate to our people what he had seen in the vision. However, the people rejected his words, thinking them false, since they were surrounded on all sides by misfortunes, and could in no way conceive of any hope for their condition. Firmly relying on the authority of what the apostle had said, Peter insisted that the apostle had appeared to him and had said to him twice in a vision, "Hurry, do not delay telling the imperilled army of God, as quickly as possible, to set aside their fears and cling to their firm belief in God, who will help them. Within five days the Lord will reveal things that will joyfully relieve their hearts. If they go into battle carrying this sign before them, their opposition will quickly be defeated and will submit to them." Peter's steady persuasiveness began to have an effect, and the Christians began to urge each other to have some hope, and they began to feel some relief. They said, "We should not be so stupid as to believe that God, who has thus far given us so many victories, would now permit us, besieged while defending the true faith, having placed our trust in Him, with our souls eagerly groaning for him, to be cut down by Turkish swords. Instead, we should certainly believe that, after our long suffering, He will shine the light of pity on us, and will cast fear of Himself upon the peoples who have not sought Him out."

Then the Turks who were guarding the citadel made a sudden attack on our men, trapping three of our knights at a fortification facing the citadel. Then the pagans stormed out of the citadel against our men with such force that they were unable to resist. Two of the men under attack were wounded and escaped, while the third continued to defend himself vigorously against the enemy, killing two of them on the top of the ramparts, having broken the shafts of their spears, while the Turks themselves had shattered three spears in their hands. The name of this knight was Hugh, nicknamed "the Madman," and he was one of the servants of a certain Godfrey of Mount-Scabieuse.

Famed Bohemund, however, scarcely able to persuade some men to attack the citadel (for of those who hid in their homes, some suffered from lack of bread, while others were frightened by the ferocity and number of the pagans), driven by great anger, ordered that the part of the city around the palace of the now dead Cassian be burned. When they saw what was happening, they fled the conflagration, some towards the citadel, some towards the gate guarded by the Count of Saint-Gilles, and some towards Godfrey; each fled towards the people to whom he most closely connected. Soon the suffering was increased by a very powerful storm, and the power of the wind was such that almost no one could walk upright. Meanwhile, when Bohemund saw that the city would be entirely destroyed by the conflagration, he was seized with anxiety about the fate of the church of blessed Peter and of the Holy Mother, and other churches as well. From the third hour until midnight the raging flames turned two thousand churches and homes into dust. In the middle of the night, the force of the raging fire abated.

Meanwhile those in the citadel cruelly attacked our men, who turned back into the city, worn out by hunger; they struck our men with steady effort, and by day and by night the two sides were separated only by the length of their swords and spears. When our men saw that they were caught in a non-stop battle, and had no opportunity at all to eat or drink, even if they had had a great supply of food, they built a wall out of cement and stone, and quickly surrounded it with many machines, so that they would have a feeling of greater security. In the citadel, a group of Turks remained who would, almost continually, come out to harass our men in battle, while other Turks remained in the field, facing the fortification. On the following night, a kind of fire appeared in the western sky, falling between the enemy camps. To both sides the sight of the falling fire seemed miraculous. In the morning, the Turks left the place in which the celestial fire had fallen as quickly as possible, and set themselves up in front of the gate that Bohemund was guarding. The portent which had appeared clearly before them announced the destruction that was obviously approaching them, had they understood it. The inhabitants of the citadel, who made frequent, relentless sorties against our army, their bows always stretched, inflicted wounds and death upon our men. The Turks who surrounded the city outside, and who occupied all the territory near the walls, vigilantly blocked every entrance to the city, so that the Christians were unable to leave or to enter, except at night, and even then only secretly. The enemy had assembled here in such great numbers and with such wealth, that everywhere one looked there were only men and tents, expensive furnishings, the brilliance of variegated costumes, flocks of cattle and sheep to be eaten, and women dressed as though they were, so to speak, temples. To add to this list of luxury, young women came with quivers full of arrows, looking like a new form of the ancient Diana; they seemed to have been brought here not to fight, but rather to reproduce. When the battle was over, those who were present asserted that new-born babies, born by women brought for this purpose on the expedition, were found thrown into the grass by these women, who, in their urgent flight from the Franks, could not endure the burden, and, more concerned for themselves than for the babies, heartlessly cast them away.

In the way in which we have described, then, with Turks everywhere preventing our men from getting out, and therefore unable to procure provisions from outside, the dangers of famine took hold of nearly the entire army, and the extraordinary lack of food particularly weakened the courage of the poor people. Since the Franks, at the time that they were besieging Antioch, had prevented the inhabitants from increasing their dwindling supply of food, when they captured the city they found very little to eat. After they had used up everything they could find, a mere piece of bread cost a bezant. The scarcity of produce and of spices resulted in great hardship, and many died, their bellies bloated with starvation. About wine I shall say nothing, since no one had any at all, and he who had nothing to eat would certainly drink fruit juice. Since there was no proper meat to eat, no one finally refused to eat the flesh of horses, and the small amount of donkey meat, sought for throughout the marketplaces and purchased at exorbitant prices, was a bitter resource for many Crusaders. A chicken sold for fifteen sous, an egg for two sous, and a nut for a penny. If many men assemble in a place where food is scarce, everything becomes expensive. They ate a mixture of figs, thistles, and grape leaves; fruit could no longer be found on the trees; out of the leaves they made a substitute for vegetables. Wealthy men ate the flesh of horses, camels, cows, and deer, but the poor prepared the dried skins of these animals, cut them into slices, boiled them and then ate them.

Among the ancient stories of besieged cities, where might we find people who, exiles from their native land, enduring such suffering, were able to persevere as steadfastly as these men? Even the ten-year siege of Troy was often interrupted by mutually beneficial truces, during which men might recover their strength, and the earth and the sea might offer them sustenance. And even if any besieged men had suffered similar dangers, certainly they suffered to preserve their own freedom, and the defense of one's own life and country is considered more important than all other things. The Crusaders, however, were driven from their native soil by no desire for personal gain, but by the intention of working for God. To deliver the church from harm, they endured the hardships of famine, rough sleeping places, long watches during the night, cold, rain, and the torment of ceaseless fear, which exceeded that endured by anyone whose sufferings have ever been recorded. What must be recognized as even more of a miracle is the fact that these men, at home in their own native lands, could scarcely endure setting up their tents as part of the king's army for three days, even when they were not forced to venture beyond the borders of their own regions. In my opinion, none of those who risked such danger could remember all of the anxieties of mind and agonies of body they had been compelled to endure. For twenty-six straight days this punishment continued.

At that time, Count Stephen of Blois, formerly a man of great discretion and wisdom, who had been chosen as leader by the entire army, said that he was suffering from a painful illness, and, before the army had broken into Antioch, Stephen made his way to a certain small town, which was called Alexandriola.[178] When the city had been captured and was again under siege, and he learned that the Christian leaders were in dire straits, Stephen, either unable or unwilling, delayed sending them aid, although they were awaiting his help. When he heard that an army of Turks had set up camp before the city walls, he rode shrewdly to the mountains and observed the amount the enemy had brought. When he saw the fields covered with innumerable tents, in understandably human fashion he retreated, judging that no mortal power could help those shut up in the city. A man of the utmost probity, energetic, pre-eminent in his love of truth, thinking himself unable to bring help to them, certain that they would die, as all the evidence indicated, he decided to protect himself, thinking that he would incur no shame by saving himself for a opportune moment. And I certainly think that his flight (if, however, it should be called a flight, since the count was certainly ill), after which the dishonorable act was rectified by martyrdom, was superior to the return of those who, persevering in their pursuit of foul pleasure, descended into the depths of criminal behavior. Who could claim that Count Stephen and Hugh the Great, who had always been honorable, because they had seemed to retreat for this reason, were comparable to those who had steadfastly behaved badly? The results of the action for which they are blamed were so splendid, that surely one might praise them for what they did, while the behavior of the others embarrasses all good men. Let us look carefully at those who take pride in having been present at the capture of Jerusalem; we shall see that none permitted himself to be second to anyone else in committing crimes, betrayals, and perjuries. These two, however, were known for the nobility of their previous and subsequent behavior. The others, because they had seen Jerusalem and the Holy Sepulchre, thought that they could safely commit any crime, offering their own example as a reproach to holy men who had retreated, without considering how much they

---

[178] Iskenderum.

themselves should be blamed for the many stinking crimes they had committed. But laying these matters aside, let us continue in the direction in which we set out.

When he left Alexandriola, his own town, the count went to the town called Philomena.[179] The capture of Antioch had been made known to the tyrannical emperor, who had quickly set out in that direction with many troops, thinking that he would undoubtedly be given the town by the Franks. When he had met the greedy emperor, who asked him about the condition of the Christian army and of the betrayed town, the count told him that the town had been captured, but he also told him that the citadel was held by the Turks. "Alas," he said, "a second siege destroys the joy of winning the city, for those who had at first besieged the Turks are now, in a wretched reversal, surrounded by Turks. I do not know what happened between them after I left." This is what the count said in secret to the prince. When the emperor heard this, he became discouraged, and summoned Bohemund's brother Guido, a man conspicuous for his martial spirit, together with some others, and described the situation to them, although he exaggerated what the count had told him. "What do you think should be done? The Franks are surrounded by a terrible Turkish siege, and perhaps have already fallen before their swords, or have been led away to different regions under the yoke of perpetual slavery. Since we do not have the ability or occasion to provide them with aid, particularly since, if we went forward, we would have to fear being killed by the Turks we might encounter, we should turn back, if this is in accord with your judgement." Having said this, the traitor was undoubtedly pleased with himself, because he had heard that those whom he hated no less than the Turks had been killed.

But Guido, having heard of the danger in which his brother and the Franks found themselves, together with the entire Norman household, began to howl with grief, launching complaints self-righteously even against God himself; they said, "All powerful God, whose judgement never errs, who never permits the unjust to triumph over the just, why have you betrayed those who, out of love for you, have given themselves over to daily torment and death, who have left their relatives, wives, sons, the greatest honors, their native land, and why have you exposed them, without the aid of your protection, to be cut down by the swords of abominable men? If it becomes known that you have permitted profane hands to deliver them to a horrible death, whom will you find willing to obey your commands, since everyone will judge you unable to defend your own people? But so be it. It may be that you want them to die for you, and that you will crown them with glory and honor, yet even if you bestow land one hundred fold on these people, you will have brought about eternal shame among nations for the people of your own faith. You have plunged the entire Christian world into the depths of despair and incredulity, and you have provoked the worst men to

---

[179] Aksehir.

display relentless aggression against your people. From this day forth no man will expect anything great from you, since those who believed themselves dearer to you than all other mortals have been subjected to such an unworthy fate. Therefore, O most gracious one, from now on why should they call upon you, when your own people will expect such a death?" Thus they expressed their terrible grief and desperate anguish, so that for several days none of the astonished bishops, abbots, clerics or laymen in the entire army led by the tyrant dared to call upon God. Guido, remembering his love for his noble brother, going over in his mind the splendid qualities of the man, expressed his inmost anguish with many a groan.

Ready to retreat, the emperor, fearing that, with the Frankish bulwark broken, the Turks might now more freely move against him, gave orders to his troops, "Go," he said, "and promulgate an imperial edict throughout this region. Lay waste the Bulgar's land, so that, when the Turks attack to depopulate our lands, they will find no useful supplies." Willingly or not, the Christians who had been eager to rejoin us were compelled to return with the emperor. The knights hastened to carry out the tyrant's orders, while the conscripted foot-soldiers followed the army. In their attempt to follow the swift cavalry, they fell into inextricable problems because of their weakness. Therefore, wearied by the effort, they continually dropped away, falling in their tracks, worn out by exhaustion. When the tyrant returned to the city of Constantinople, the troops returned, by way of Greece, to the lands from which they had come. Let this book end here.

Book Six

When we read in the authentic histories of the holy Fathers about the wars waged under God's direction, and when we see that such things were accomplished by inconsequential people of such little faith (we do not place in this class the blessed Joshua, David, Samuel, but we are speaking of the despicable vanity of the Jewish people, with the exception of those whose radiance is now celebrated by the church of God), then we might think, if reason did not intervene, that such wretched men, serving God for their bellies only, were more pleasing to God than those whose whole spirit was devoted to him. For them, whose only virtue perhaps was that they were not idolaters, everything went well; they were frequently victorious, and had an abundance of everything. But for these Christians, victories came about only with great difficulty, at great cost; they had little wealth, and they lived in continual and great need, leading the lives not of knights but of piously impoverished monks. All of this is explained, however, by the grace of reason, when we recall that "God torments with whips every child whom he loves,"[180] and to those whom he deprives of the things of this world out of the rigor of his teaching, he gives spiritual gifts, out of the affection of his sweet love.

Therefore, after Peter had told what the blessed Andrew had revealed in a dream to him about the Lord's lance, the Christian people were filled with joy, and, in anticipation of the marvelous event, emerged out of the depths of despair. Led by this man,[181] everyone rushed to the designated place, and a hole was dug beside the altar of the Lord in the church of the blessed Peter. After thirteen men had dug up the earth from dawn to dusk, Peter himself found the Lance. What they saw before them corresponded in every way with the dream-vision which had been reported to them; they all began to rejoice, and their boldness against the enemy matched their joy. They bore off the lance with great exultation, and from that day forth they confidently went about planning to wage war. Then the leaders of the Christian army met in council, considered together what action was needed, and decided that the wisest thing to do before fighting was to meet first with the Turks, to urge them not to occupy Christian territory, not to drive the servants of Christ out of their lands, and not to kill them, but instead to remain within their own territories, content with their own lands. Peter the Hermit, who had helped to initiate the undertaking, was summoned, together with a man named Herluin, an interpreter proficient in both languages, and they were both sent to the pagan prince, with instructions about what to say. When they reached the tent of the pagan, and stood in the terrible presence of the diabolical man, they delivered a speech like this: "You should understand that

---

180 Hebrews 12.6.   181 Or "miracle" in B.

our leaders are shocked to find that you have profanely and wickedly undertaken to usurp a land firmly and freely possessed since ancient times by Christians. Since you have undoubtedly learned by our relentless victories against you that Christ's power has not declined, and you have found that your forces have little power against Christ, our leaders think that you, having been beaten so many times, will in no way dare to resume the madness of war against God. Therefore we unanimously judge that, in your wisdom, you have come here for no other reason than to learn the teaching of our faith from the Christian bishops who have come with us. For we are absolutely certain that you will hardly be able to ensure your safety if you try to wage war against the Catholic belief. Therefore, aware of your ignorance, we ask that you desist from this presumption, for we know that God gave the blessed apostle Peter authority over the city, and he who was its first bishop intends to restore the worship of God, which he was the first to bring here, using us, sinners that we are, as his instruments. Our princes, in their extreme generosity, will permit you to carry off everything which you have brought here, nor, if you retreat peacefully, will any of us do you any harm whatever."

But Kherboga was deeply stung by the words of Peter, and when the arrogant Turks who accompanied him raged when they heard these things, he said: "We shall demonstrate that we have every right to the land which you say has belonged to your Christianity since ancient times, particularly since we took it, by means of our remarkable strength, from a nation scarcely better than women. Moreover, we think that you are mad to come from the ends of the earth, threatening with all your might to drive us from our homes, when you have insufficient supplies, too few arms, and too few men. Not only do we refuse to accept the name of Christians, but we spit upon it in disgust. To respond briefly to the message you have brought: return, you who form this delegation, to your leaders swiftly and tell them that if they are willing to become like us and renounce the Christ upon whom you seem to rely, we shall give them not only this land, but land of greater wealth and size. After granting them castles and cities, we shall allow none of them to remain foot-soldiers, but shall make them all knights; and, when we have shared the same ceremonial rites, each side will rejoice in mutual and close friendship. But if they shall decide not to accept this proposal, they will undoubtedly die horribly, or endure the exile of eternal imprisonment, as slaves to us and to our descendants." He spoke, and the delegation quickly returned and told the leaders of the Christian army everything that had taken place.

The army was still in dire straits, suffering, on the one hand, from extreme hunger, and, on the other hand, tormented by fear of the pagans who surrounded them. Finally, placing their faith in divine assistance, they observed a three-day fast, instituted by the splendid Bishop of Puy. In every church they poured forth suppliant litanies, purifying themselves by sincere confession of sins; when the bishop had granted them absolution, they faithfully took communion of the body and blood of the Lord. Each gave alms according to his ability, and all prayed that divine offerings might be made for them. Finally, having derived some comfort from these activities, they prepared to fight, drawing up six lines of battle inside the city.

The first line of battle, which would bear the brunt of the Turkish attack, was led by Hugh, who truly was, as his cognomen indicated, great; he and his men were supported by the entire contingent of Franks, led by the Count of Flanders. I have heard about this royal man that, before the battle began, his quartermaster paid a remarkable amount of money for a camel's foot, since he was unable to find anything better for him to eat at that point. The unusual quality of this food had so weakened this man of God that he was scarcely able to remain on his horse, and when someone suggested that he not go into battle, but remain with those besieging the citadel, he quickly replied, "No! I certainly shall go; I only hope that I find a blessed death there with those who are to die today!"

The noble Duke Godfrey and his men formed the second line. Count Robert of Normandy and his men made up the third line, and the fourth was led by the splendid Bishop of Puy, carrying with him the recently found Lance of the Savior. This line was composed of the bishop's men and those of Raymond, Count of Saint-Gilles, who remained within the city, blockading the citadel, so that the inhabitants might not escape. Tancred and his men made up the fifth line, and Bohemund with his army made up the sixth.

Bishops, priests, clerics, monks, dressed in their ecclesiastical garb, marched forward, holding their crosses before them, eager to aid the soldiers with their tearful prayers, themselves awaiting the gift of martyrdom, if they should happen to be cut down. Others looked out from the ramparts of the walls, to watch the outcome of the battle, holding the sign of the Lord's cross in their hands, faithfully making the sign of the cross over the army as it marched forth. In the order I have given, they marched out the gate in front of the temple which our people call the Mahometry, walking so slowly that even a weak old woman would not have asked for a slower pace. God Almighty, with what heartfelt groans were you invoked; while their frail, frightened bodies were being overcome by long hunger, how rapidly did the grief of their wretched hearts reach your ears, O most high one! With what anguish were their minds still lingering in their racked bodies! When weakness was compelling them to despair of victory, God alone remained steadfast in the minds of all in their suffering for You. Their hearts were shattered by long anguish; desiccated by famine, their eyes were too dry to weep; since the exterior man was almost without material substance, spiritual desires struggled violently. Good God, what could you have denied to such devotion when you saw them, or rather made them burn in such agony? When I consider how they maintained a military fierceness on their faces, while their inmost hearts were preparing to undergo martyrdom, I seriously think that no army ever equalled their constancy. Indeed I truly should have said that they raised a shout to heaven; but then I say that they, who performed not with physical strength but with unusual daring of soul, made the sacred trumpets sound.

Meanwhile Kherboga saw them leaving the city, moving slowly; he laughed at the small size of the group, and said, "Let them leave, the better that they may, when they have fled from battle, be shut out of the city." But when the entire army had passed through the gates, and Kherboga noticed that the Frankish forces were mighty in order and in number, then, at last, he trembled. As he made preparations to flee, he immediately ordered the master of his palace to let it be known throughout the army, as soon as he saw flames coming from the nearest tents, that the French troops had won the victory. Meanwhile Kherboga began to retreat, little by little, heading for the mountains, while our men were pursuing him relentlessly. Then the Turks, uselessly clever, split their forces into two parts, one of which moved along the shore of the sea, while the other waited in place for the Franks to reach them, thinking that in this manner they might surround our men. When our men perceived this, they turned audaciously towards the Turkish troops, separating themselves from their fellows; because of this excessive boldness, they were the only group of our army that suffered a loss, with only a few knights and scarcely any foot-soldiers escaping alive. The instigator of this foray, together with some others, was Clairambaut of Vandeuil, who, although reputable in his own lands, did nothing useful in the East. Meanwhile, to face the Turks at the edge of the sea, a seventh group was formed out of the two armies led by Duke Godfrey and the Count of Normandy, and a certain Count Renaud was placed in charge. That day the battle was very bitter, and many of our men were slaughtered by the arrows of the enemy. The cavalry of the enemy extended from the river Pharphar to the mountains, a length of two miles. Squadrons of pagans attacked from both sides, and struck with arrows and javelins the group of Franks whom our men had placed in the vanguard as the strongest and most likely to resist the Turkish attacks. In charge of them was magnificent Hugh, regal in mind, no less brave than his ancestors, who proudly called out to his men, "Endure, and wait courageously for the second and third discharge of missiles, because they will then flee more quickly than speech."

And lo, innumerable forces began to come down from the mountains, and their horses and standards shone brightly; our men, however, were stunned even more now, fearing that these men were bringing reinforcements for the Turks, until they discovered that this was aid, now visible, sent by Christ. After the battle, they thought that these glorious leaders were, in particular, the martyrs George, Mercurius, and Demetrius. These things were seen by many of our men, and when they told what they had seen to others, their words were taken in good faith as true.[182] And if celestial help appeared long ago to the Maccabees fighting for circumcision and the meat of swine, how much more did those who poured out their blood for Christ, purifying the churches and propagating the faith, deserve such help. Therefore, when the first line of the enemy at the shore were driven back by our men, unable to bear our attack, they set fire to the grass, thereby

---

[182] Miraculous intervention at this point is reported also in the *Gesta Francorum* (Bréhier, 154), and in a letter published by Hagenmayer (*Epistulae et Chartae* 167), but neither Raymond nor Fulcher mentions it.

giving the agreed-upon signal to retreat to those who were guarding the tents during the battle. In response to the signal, they snatched anything of any value, and fled. But the Franks, when they saw where the pagans' greater forces were, raced to their tents. Duke Godfrey, the Count of Normandy, and Hugh the Great joined forces to attack those who were riding along the shore. These three, together with their men, with the image of the son of God crucified for their sake before their eyes, eagerly plunged into the thick of the melee. When our men saw this, they too drove forward vigorously. The enemy, screaming like madmen, rushed to meet them. For it was their custom when they entered battle to make constant, terrible noise with the metal shafts they used as spears, as well as with cymbals and with their own horrifying voices, so that horses and men could scarcely check their terror of such sound. But their efforts were entirely in vain; our men immediately overcame the enemy; once the battle had been joined, they subdued the enemy in the first attack, encouraging those who had for a long time been considering flight to carry out their plan. And even so, our men pursued them through the middle of their encampment. They were not carried away by the desire for the booty lying about, but instead preferred to feed only on the blood of the enemies of Christ, pursuing them to the bridge over the Pharphar, and to the fortress of Tancred. The glorious spoils covered the ground of the enemy encampment; the tents, though filled with gold, silver, and many kinds of equipment, stood there abandoned; herds of sheep, cows, goats, horses, mules, asses were spread about everywhere; there also was a great supply of wheat, wine, and grain. But, when the Syrian and Armenian colonists, who were scattered throughout the region, learned that the Franks had won an unexpected victory, they rushed into the mountains to face the fleeing Turks, killing those whom they found. Our own men, joyfully shouting praises to Christ for his help, entered the city with the honor of a heavenly victory. The Turk in charge of the citadel, however, seeing the leader of his own army fleeing with our men in hot pursuit, became frightened. Judging that he could no longer defend the citadel, he immediately asked for the standard of one of our leaders. The Count of Saint-Gilles, who was close to the spot where the request was made, quickly ordered that his own standard be offered to the man who made the request, who promptly affixed it to the tower. But the Lombards, striving to obtain the favor of their leader Bohemund (for they relied upon his favor), cried out to the man in charge of the citadel, "This is not Bohemund's standard." He asked to whom did it belong, and when he was told that it belonged to the Count of Saint Gilles, he took it down and gave it back to the count. Having asked for and received Bohemund's standard, he also accepted the promise that those who were with him might, if any wished to accept our religion, remain with Bohemund. Those who did not, might freely leave. With this agreement, the citadel was surrendered to Bohemund, who then chose men to guard it. After a few days, the man who surrendered the citadel received baptism, together with the other pagans who decided to take communion in the name of Christ. Those who chose to remain pagan were free to do so, and they were brought by Bohemund himself to Saracen territory.

On August 28, on the eve of their passion, Peter and Paul waged this battle, out of compassion for their wretched city, unable to tolerate the expulsion of the new citizens, who had driven out the pagans who had contaminated the holy temple of God. And it was right that they took pity on the city which they had both instructed by their preaching. In the churches stables for horses had been set up, and in part of the great basilica of Saint Peter they had erected a house of their Mahomet. While the defeated enemy was retreating in different directions, the mountains and the valleys, the fields and the forests, the roads and pathless places overflowed with the dead and the dying, and with innumerable wounded men. The objects of God's sudden compassion, however, were relieved of the pain of daily hunger; where an egg might have cost two sous, one might now come away with a whole cow for less than twelve cents. To sum up briefly, where hunger had raged like a disease, there was now so much meat and other food that great abundance seemed everywhere to pour in a sudden eruption from the earth, and God seemed to have opened the cataracts of heaven.[183] There were so many tents that, after all of our people had plundered one, they were so wealthy and sated with the weight of their booty, that almost no one wanted to take any more. If a poor man took something that he wanted, no wealthier man tried to take it from him by force, but each permitted the other to take what he wanted without a fight.

Then our leaders, Duke Godfrey, the Count of Saint-Gilles, Bohemund, the Count of Normandy and Robert of Flanders, and all the others, consulted with each other, and sent Hugh the Great and Baldwin, the Count of Mons, together with some others of great repute, to the emperor, so that he might receive Antioch from them, according to their agreement. They departed, but afterwards were slow to return to those who had sent them. For, in a certain place, the Turks attacked them; those who had horses nearby escaped; those who were not close enough to their horses were carried away as captives, or were slain by the sword. We are not at all certain yet about the unfortunate fate that befell the Count of Mons. According to some people, this provided Hugh the Great with a reason to delay his return; although capable in other matters, he showed himself less concerned in obtaining those things which are thought to be fitting for such a great man. A man highly fastidious about honor, he was afraid of being less well off among men to whom he was superior or in no way way inferior, but who were either more tenacious or more eager to acquire things. However, no one should complain about the return of a man who later died with the deserved repute of a martyr and fine soldier.

Finally, a short time later, they began again to consider how to get to Jerusalem, a task for which they had suffered so much, and how the people who so greatly wanted to arrive might be governed until they got there. The leaders took into consideration the fact that there would be very little water during the heat of summer, and therefore decided that the journey would be put off until the

[183] Malach. 3.10.

calends of November. Meanwhile, after everyone had agreed to this plan, the nobles of the army visited the various cities and towns they had captured, and sent heralds among the conquered people, to tell them that if anyone of them were in need, he could join them and receive remuneration for his services. Among them was a knight, exceptionally skilled with weapons, among the leading followers of the Count of Saint-Gilles, named Raymond Pelet, to whom many knights and foot-soldiers had affiliated themselves. His generosity and energy had attracted many men, and he set out with a large army into Saracen territory, and the first place they reached was a fortress called Talamina. The inhabitants, since they were Syrians, immediately surrendered to him. After staying in this town eight days, he heard that not far away there was a town filled with a large group of Saracens. He quickly launched an assault to enter the town; God led the penetration, and the town was captured. Those inhabitants who agreed to become Christian were spared; those who refused were killed. Having finished this business, they gave thanks to God and returned to Talamina. On the third day they again went out, this time to attack a village called Marrah, a fine city, well fortified, where people of many different nations had assembled. Close to the previously mentioned fortress, it attracted Saracens and Turks from nearby towns and cities, especially from Aleph. A force of pagans ready to fight approached our men, who judged themselves able to fight in the usual manner, but who were quickly deceived by the pagan's trickery. The enemy, advancing in great numbers, did great harm to our men. All that day each side in turn advanced and retreated. Our men suffered from the intense heat, and, their insides parched with unusual thirst, weary and unable to find relief, they decided to pitch their tents near the city. When the inhabitants understood that our men were faltering somewhat (it was the Syrians who first began to talk of flight more seriously), they became more aggressive in response to their enemies' fears, and no longer were afraid to attack. Struck down in this attack, many of our men piously delivered their souls to God; they died on the fifth of July. The remaining Franks returned to Talamina, remaining there with their leader Raymond for several days. Those who had remained at Antioch enjoyed peace and prosperity.

For reasons hidden from us, God confounded their rest with a cloud. He who had led them, and piously nourished both their internal and external needs, a man admired by God and by the world, Adhemar, Bishop of Puy, fell ill; the Omnipotent in his generous compassion permitted him to wipe away the sweat of his pious labor in a sabbatical of eternal rest. He died on the holy day of Saint-Peter-in-Chains,[184] and he had earned absolution by him to whom the keys to the Kingdom and the powers of absolution belonged, and it was fitting that Peter greet him at the gates of the celestial realm. A great sadness and bitter grief arose throughout the entire army of Christ; when each person, of whatever rank, sex, and age, recalled how many benefits he had received from this most

---

[184] August 1, 1098.

compassionate of men, and understood that the bishop was past help, he grieved inconsolably. At his funeral the princes themselves let out heartfelt groans fit for the death of the entire army. Before he was even buried, such offerings of money were made at the litter on which his corpse was carried by the people over whom he had ruled like a father, that I think no one had ever made such offerings in such a short time at the altars of any nations. These offerings were immediately distributed to the poor, for the benefit of his soul. While he was alive, he showed great care for the souls of the poor, always teaching the rich to love the needy, to help them in their need, insisting that they were the guardians of the poor. He said: "He will be judged mercilessly who has shown no mercy. If you do not show compassion for your inferiors, who are also by nature your brothers, and if you do not share with them equally those things that were created by God for you and them, which are now unfairly seized from them by you, you will undoubtedly shut the gate of divine mercy for yourselves. Give them, I say, out of gratitude for these things, some of your goods, certain that even as they cannot survive in this world without you, so you cannot live eternally without them." Of these and similar matters the remarkable man often reminded them.

Then Raymond, Count of Saint Gilles, entered the territory of the Saracens, and led his army to a city called Albara, which he attacked and quickly captured, putting to death all the Saracen men and women he found there. Once in control of the city, he filled it with Christian colonists, and, on the advice of wise men, ordered that a bishop be ordained for the city, who would gradually teach the natives Christian doctrine, and who would carry out in their temples, once they had been purified, the services of devotion, and the mysteries of rebirth. They chose a man of an appropriate age, who was known for his learning, and they brought him to Antioch to be ordained. After he had been ordained a bishop, he did not neglect to carry out the journey to Jerusalem, but he assigned the task of guarding the city to someone who volunteered for the task, and set out with the others. A brave man, with little income, he who remained behind set out to protect the citadel with the few people he could afford to hire. Because there were very few Saracens in the city, those pagans who remained submitted to his authority, and in exchange for their lives gave him part of their earned income.

Antioch was now flourishing with prosperity, and the holiday of All Saints was approaching, at the end of which the expedition was scheduled to begin again. Mindful of this, the leaders assembled at Antioch, and began to consult with each other about how they might best expedite the journey for which they had come. Before the army of the Lord made a move, Bohemund brought up the matter of turning the city over to him, according to the agreement which had been made. But the Count of Saint Gilles refused to assent, since he respected the oath he had given to the emperor. The bishops, who acted as intermediaries between them, met frequently in the church of the blessed Peter. Bohemund said that after the city had been betrayed by Pyrrus, parts of the city had been granted to him generously by the leaders themselves. The Count of Saint Gilles replied that he had given an oath to restore the city to the ruler of Constantinople, unless their agreement was broken by the emperor, and that all this was done on the advice of Bohemund. Meanwhile, the bishops, who were trying to bring the disagreement to an end, summoned Duke Godfrey, the counts of Flanders and Normandy, and other leaders, listened to what each had to say, and then met separately to sift the arguments and to come to a correct decision. However, after having heard the arguments, they remained undecided, and when they returned to the assembled leaders, afraid to alienate such men, they postponed making a decision. When the count saw that this was done deliberately, he said: "To prevent the present disagreement from generating discord among those faithful to Christ, and thereby delaying the day on which the tomb of the Savior will be set free, and to prevent us from being tainted with the charge of greed, I agree to the decision of my peers, the princes now present, as long as it does not contradict what you know, brothers and leaders, I unwillingly promised to the prince of Constantinople." Bohemund immediately agreed to the count's proposal, and they put aside their quarrel, placed their right hands in the hands of the bishops as a sign of good faith, and swore solemnly that the army of God in no way would be disturbed by their disagreements. After consulting with the others, Bohemund then fortified his fortress with men and food from the mountains. The Count of Saint Gilles also consulted with his men, and fortified at great expense the palace of Cassian, which the pagans called the Emir, as well as the tower which guarded the gate of the bridge which led to the port of Saint Simon.

The city of Antioch is incomparably beautiful, second to none in the majesty of its buildings; it is pleasantly situated, with an unequalled climate, and with fertile vines and rich fields. To the east it is surrounded by four high mountains; to the west its walls are washed by a river renowned in the Bible,[185] the Pharphar, whose waves are dense with fish. At the top of one of the mountains a remarkable, impregnable fortification stands; below it stands the city itself, filled with past glory and fiercely proud of the noble monuments of its ancient splendor, with 360 churches within its confines. The pontiff of the city, by right of apostolic succession honored with the title of patriarch, was in charge of 153 bishops. The city was surrounded by a double wall, one of which was of normal height, the other, however, remarkably broad and high, built out of massive stones, surrounded by four hundred and fifty towers. They say that it was rebuilt from that ancient Antioch in testimony of whose power many monuments have survived, and that such lofty citadels and such a variety of buildings were erected by the efforts of 50 subject kings and their subjects.[186] This is false, since Pompeius Trogus correctly said that it was founded by King Seleucus, who named it after his father, and it was built up by him and by the kings who succeeded him, even as he founded Laodicea, named after his mother, and Seleucia, which he named

---

[185] IV Kings 5.12.

[186] At this point manuscript I adds: "Jerome says, in the fifth book of his explication of Isaiah, that Antioch was the city of Reblata, in which King Nabugodonosor tore out the eyes of King Sedechia, and killed his sons."

after himself. All sorts of siege engines were of no avail against this city, and had Pyrrus not betrayed it to the besiegers, or rather had God not aided those whom he wished, French bravery would have endured famine and other suffering in vain. Our men had besieged the city for eight months and one day. Then they were themselves besieged for three weeks by an uncountable horde of pagans; after they finally defeated them, the Christians remained there five months and eight days, until the people were urged by their leaders again to take up the journey to Jerusalem.

But because it seems to me that I shall not have another chance to report what happened to the Pyrrus whom I mentioned earlier, I should do it now. Having received the sacraments, he accepted Christianity, taking, as his baptismal name, Bohemund. He helped us out at the siege of Jerusalem, and, when it was captured, returned to Antioch. There he sent out a messenger to announce that any Christian in the city or in the vicinity of the city might come with him to a far-off land, where he had considerable land, and he offered to make everyone rich. He inspired a large group of people with this hope, and he is said to have led this deceived group off to what he called his own land. When he had reached his own encampments, he betrayed some of the knights who had accompanied him by killing them, and he exiled others. Had word of the betrayal not reached the others, who were lodged outside of the encampment because of their great numbers, and who therefore managed to hide or to escape wretchedly, the freedom of all of them would have perished by the sword or in slavery. There Pyrrus deserted Christianity and returned to the filth of his old lechery and paganism. Nor was this unfitting, for the name Pyrrus in Greek is Rufus[187] in Latin, and the mark of treachery is branded on red-haired people; he is shown by no means to have been deprived of his lineage.

Towards the end of November, Count Raymond of Saint-Gilles moved his army out of Antioch; after passing the cities of Rugia and Albara, on the fourth day, which was the last day of November, he reached the city of Marrah.[188] A large group of Saracens, Turks, and Arabs had come together in that city, and the count prepared to attack with all his forces on the day after he arrived. Bohemund and his army quickly followed the count, and set up his camp next to him on a Sunday. The next day they attacked the walls so vigorously that their ladders clung to the walls, and they stepped on the walls themselves as they went up. The inhabitants resisted with such energy that nothing could be gained by our men that day. Then the Count of Saint-Gilles, seeing that his men were toiling in vain, ordered that a very tall, strong wooden fort be built, placed on four wheels, with room at at the top for a large group of soldiers. This armed group then moved the war-machine with great force against the walls of the city, near one of the towers. In response, the inhabitants quickly built a ballistic machine, with which they tried to bombard our fort with huge stones, threatening to destroy both our machine and men. They also hurled Greek fire at the machine, trying to set the

187 Latin for "red."   188 Ma'arrat-an-Nu'man.

scaffolding afire, but God thwarted their plan. The machine stood high over the city wall, and, in the midst of the clash, the sound of trumpets ringing stirred the combatants. Meanwhile, some of our soldiers who were in the upper part of the machine, including William of Montpellier and some others, were hurling huge stones against those who were defending the walls. As a result, many shields were pierced, and the shields and their owners, both now useless, fell from the wall. Others, with iron hooks at the tips of their spears, tried to hook the Saracen defenders on the walls, to pull them off. The battle went back and forth, and was hardly over by evening. In the rear, priests, clerics, and monks, dressed in sacred attire, each according to his rank, earnestly prayed that God intervene by reducing the strength of the pagans, and by increasing the strength of those who fought for the true faith. On the other side of the siege machine, other knights were climbing ladders that had been set in place, while the wildly energetic pagans tried to push them off the walls. A certain Goufier, impatient with their resistance, was the first to climb the wall, together with a very small group of men. The inhabitants fiercely attacked these brave men, with spears and arrows, and some of them became frightened at this resistance, and jumped from the wall. Those who remained stood up to the enemies' missiles, spurning flight, returning blow for blow, while those who remained below continued to mine the wall. Soon the inhabitants saw that they were doomed by the mining of the wall, and, intent only on the safety of flight, climbed back down into the city. This happened on a Sunday, while the sun was already setting in the West, when December had reached its eleventh day. Bohemund quickly sent an interpreter to the Saracen leaders, offering to conduct them, together with their own knights, children, and wives, and with all the goods and supplies they could gather, to a palace near the gate of the city, promising to protect their lives, and to defend their people and possessions. Having taken the city in this manner, they took possession of everything they found in the caves and in the homes. When night had ended and daylight began to appear, a crowd of our people raced through the city, killing every pagan they found. No gate of the city, no matter how small, was without a pile of dead Saracens, and the narrow streets were impassable, because pagan bodies obstructed the public ways. Bohemund himself attacked those whom he had commanded to shut themselves up in the palace mentioned before, and took what they had from them. Some he killed, others he ordered to be brought to Antioch and sold. The Franks remained there for a whole month and four days, and the people suffered from great hunger. Some of our men, entirely without resources, finding nothing in nearby areas to satisfy their needs, desecrated the bellies of dead Saracens, daring to probe their internal organs, because they had heard that pagans in serious danger would try to preserve their gold and silver by eating them. Others, they say, cut pieces of flesh from the corpses, cooked them and ate them, but this was done rarely and in secret, so that no one could be sure whether they actually did this.

Meanwhile, Bohemund had not forgotten the quarrel that had taken place between him and the Count of Saint-Gilles, but returned angrily to Antioch when the count refused to yield to him. The count quickly sent men to Duke Godfrey, to the Count of Flanders, to the Count of Normandy, and to Bohemund, summoning them to a conference in Rugia (a city I mentioned above). They hurried to the meeting to arrange for an agreement, so that the journey to Jerusalem might be delayed no longer. Angry and proud, Bohemund resisted reconciliation unless the count agreed to what Bohemund wanted, granting him the part of Antioch over which he had control. The count, however, was adamant, insisting that he had given his word to the emperor. Therefore, divided against each other by bitterness of mind, the man from Saint-Gilles, Bohemund, and the duke returned to Antioch. The Count of Saint-Gilles, however, placed his knights in charge of the palace and castle that looked down upon the gate at the bridge, and went off to Marrah, which he had recently captured. However, the count was not entirely unreasonable; considering that everyone would suffer because of his obstinacy, which would delay the liberation of the Tomb of the Lord, the noble man went barefooted out of Marrah on the thirteenth of January, and reached Capharda,[189] where he stayed three days. There he was joined by the Count of Normandy, who gave up his resistance.

The King of Caesarea had often sent ambassadors to the Count of Saint-Gilles, to persuade him to enter into a pact with him, promising that he would offer aid to the Christians everywhere in his kingdom, permitting them to purchase food, clothing, horses, and whatever else they needed. Pleased with this offer, our men chose to set up their tents near the city, where the Pharphar river flowed near the city walls. But the king of the city, not overjoyed at the prospect of such an army so close to him, took the move badly, and forbade them to purchase supplies unless they quickly moved further away. The next day he sent two of his people together with our own men, to show them a passage of shallows across the river, and to lead them to where they might capture some booty. Our men were led to a valley below the encampment, where they found many animals, and they took about five thousand of them; they also found abundant wheat and other supplies, so that God's cavalry was ready again for action. The fort was also surrendered to the count, giving him a considerable amount of gold as well as horses. They also promised that they would not harm our men. After remaining there five days, our men left, and reached another fort which was held by Arabs. When they had set up their tents, the leader of the town came out and made an agreement with the count. After hastily packing their tents, the Christians moved on to a beautiful, prosperous town called Kephalia,[190] situated in a valley. When the inhabitants heard that the Franks were coming, they fled from the city, leaving homes filled with food, and gardens overflowing with produce; all that was in their minds was to save their lives. Our men left this city after three days; they climbed tall, jaggedly rocky mountains, then descended into a valley no less fertile than the valley in which Kephalia was situated, where they stayed for fifteen days, rejoicing

[189] Kafartab. [190] Rafaniya.

in the abundance, and resting. The Franks then found out that there was a nearby fort, to which many pagans had come. Our men quickly laid siege to it, and were about to win the town, when the inhabitants offered a plentiful supply of cattle to them, together with some flattering words, tricking them into delaying the siege for a while. The next morning, our men moved their tents closer to the city, preparing to undertake the siege. When the pagans perceived what was happening, they fled quickly, leaving the town deserted. The Christian army entered, and found plentiful supplies of grain, wine, wheat, oil, and other useful items. They celebrated the holiday of the Purification of the Blessed Mary there, and received the delegates sent by the king of the city of Camela, who promised to give the count horses, gold and silver, and to do no harm to the Christians, but to show them appropriate respect. The King of Tripoli[191] asked the count if he wished to enter into an agreement with him, in exchange for ten horses, four mules, and a large amount of gold. The count said that he would not consider a peaceful settlement with him, unless the king became Christian. Then they left the fertile valley, which I mentioned above, and reached a place well fortified by nature, high on a rock, called Archas, on the thirteenth of February, on the second day of the week. They set up their tents near the fortress, which was filled with an innumerable multitude of pagans, Turks, Saracens, and Arabs, whose numbers increased the original strength of the locations. At this point, fourteen knights from the Christian army fighting at Tripoli, which was near to this fortress, happened to come along, for no other reason, I think, than to find food. The fourteen of them came upon nearly sixty Turks, who were accompanied by others, leading more than fifteen hundred men and animals whom they had captured. Those who were carrying out the Lord's promise that two would make ten thousand flee before them, and one would make a thousand flee, called to their pious minds the sign of the cross and, with the aid of God, attacked them with unbelievable bravery, killing six men and capturing as many horses. From the retinue of the Count of Saint-Gilles, Raymond, to whom we have given the additional name of Pelet, who deserves to be mentioned often in this little book, a man remarkable for sternness as well as for eagerness in battle, together with another man whose surname I do not know, who performed the duties of a vicount,[192] sought out the city of Tortosa. At their first attack, which they launched with great ferocity, they terrified the inhabitants. Like a swarm of flies, a remarkably large crowd of pagans flocked to the fort. The following night, our men set up their tents at one end of the city, and lit many beacon fires, giving the impression that the entire Frankish army was there. Desperately afraid, the pagans judged that they could not protect their lives with their shields, and decided that the only way to escape death was to flee on foot. During the night they slipped away silently, leaving the city filled with wealthy treasure, and empty of inhabitants. Thus they piously fulfilled Scripture, which says that, "Skin for skin,

---

[191] Abou Ali Ibn Ammar.   [192] Raymond, Viscount of Torena.

yea, all that a man hath he will give for his life."[193] This city, situated on the sea, has a fine port in one of its suburbs. The next day our men prepared to attack the city in full strength, but when they assembled to fight, they found that the city was empty. After entering, they remained there only until they set off to besiege the city of Archas, which I mentioned above. However, there was another city nearby, which was called Maraclea. He who was in charge of it, whom they called the emir,

> immediately prepared to enter into an agreement, and soon accepted our men and their banners in the city.

Meanwhile Duke Godfrey, Bohemund and the Count of Flanders had reached Laodicia.[194] But Bohemund, impatient at being separated from his beloved Antioch, left his companions and returned to her. With equal desire, the others set out to besiege a city called Gibel.[195] Rumor reached Count Raymond of Saint-Gilles that a huge force of pagans had assembled to wage war against him. He quickly called all the leaders of his army together, and asked them what should be done. The group replied that there was nothing to be done in these circumstances, except to call for help from their companions on the Lord's journey. He accepted and quickly carried out this plan. When the leaders, that is Duke Godfrey and Robert of Flanders, found out that their companions were in trouble, they made an agreement with the ruler of the city of Gibel, who gave them magnificent gifts of horses and gold, and they gave up the siege of the city, and went off to bring help to the count. Their expectation of waging war was disappointed, however, and they all decided to go back to the siege of the fort at Archas. They gave themselves to the project energetically, and a short time later undertook an expedition against the inhabitants of Tripoli, whom they found ready for battle, with an army of Turks, Saracens, and Arabs lined up in front of the walls of the city. Our men attacked them vigorously and compelled them to take refuge in flight. The result was not merely a carnage of the nobles of the city, but a wholesale slaughter, to the point that the waves of the river that ran through the city were dyed red with their blood, and the sewers were stained with this foulness. From that point on a day of no commerce[196] arose in the minds of the pagans, and the hearts of those who survived were so riddled with fear that none of them, for any reason whatsover, dared to go beyond the walls of the city. On the next day, our men went beyond the valley of Sem, an area which had been reached by those mentioned above on the third day after the capture of Kephalia. They found that it was rich in supplies, and stayed there fifteen days. They happily returned with what they had found there: cows, asses, sheep, with many

---

[193] Job 2.4
[194] Latakia.
[195] Djebali.
[196] Among the Romans, *iustitium* was a day on which no business could be undertaken due to natural disaster

other kinds of animals, including three thousand camels. They continued to lay siege to the fort of Archas for three months less one day, and celebrated Easter there on April 10. While they were engaged in the siege, the fleet which usually brought them provisions reached a nearby port, bringing a large amount of grain, wine, meat, cheese, barley, and oil, which provided the Lord's army with abundant supplies. Although they had to suffer no privation in this place, it seems to me foolish to have undertaken for such a long time such a useless task for such a trivial result.

After the death of the noble Bishop of Puy, who had managed, by a combination of love for his flock and discipline, to bind them together in harmony and unity, arguments and rude, arrogant behavior began to arise among the leaders; in particular, the middle and lower ranks began to behave badly, so that one might have thought that the Old Testament statement, "There was no longer a king in Israel, but each man did what seemed right in his own eyes,"[197] was being fulfilled. The bishops and others who remained, after the death of that glorious man who had been assigned the office of father and leader, did not have the same concern for them, particularly because they knew that that had not been granted the same powers that had been given to the Bishop of Puy. Therefore, since they had no single ruler, and every man thought himself the equal of every other man, justice diminished among them, and the will of the mob often prevailed. Therefore it happened that, after the discovery of the Lance, which the late bishop had accepted devoutly, a shameful and faithless rumor began to circulate; some said that the discovery had been staged, and that he had exhibited not the Lord's Lance, but merely a lance. Many people from the lower ranks began to grumble, and, by relentlessly lying, they corrupted those who had believed truly and had venerated the lance. They demanded proof of the discovery; they asked that the discoverer be tested by divine judgement. The man was compelled to pledge his word to those who were in doubt; he was compelled to offer what they forced from him, merely to deal with their lack of faith. Two pyres were constructed, in accordance with his orders, scarcely a cubit apart; many of the people, avid for novelty, heaped up a mass of kindling material, and when they had crowded together on both sides of the fire, only a narrow path remained between the flames. He then delivered a pitiful prayer, as was fitting, to merciful God, who is the Truth, without whose permission he knew he could do nothing about the situation, and walked briskly across the dark path of the flames, and then returned by the same path. A large crowd of western soldiers, in their war-gear, was present at this spectacle, awaiting, with different expectations, the outcome of this unusually daring undertaking. When he had returned, as I said, a huge crowd welcomed him as he came forth from the flames, and when they saw that he had escaped from the fire safe and sound, they snatched at his body and at his clothes, as though they were relics, and in the tumult of tearing and pushing, they killed

197 Judges 17.6.

him. Having barely escaped from the flames with his life, frightened by the danger from which he would not have escaped without God's help, trapped by people clutching at him from all sides, exhausted by the terror he had undergone, he could hardly have avoided being suffocated. When the man died, the common people, unreliable and fickle in their judgement, were disturbed by an even worse form of confusion, arguing about the outcome of the trial by fire. Some said that he had come out of the flames burned, others that he had escaped unharmed, and they reproached those who had killed him for no reason. However, whatever popular opinion may have been, we know that the glorious bishop embraced the sacred Lance with veneration, to the point that, in accordance with his directions, the body of the bishop was buried in the place where the Lance was found. So much for this matter.

While our men were unsuccessfully engaged in the lengthy siege of the citadel of Archas, set atop a high mountain, and the army had pitched their tents in a distant valley, Anselm of Ribemont, a rich and powerful lord, exceedingly generous and remarkably capable at leading an army, saw how difficult the siege had become, and, without delay, advised our men to use machines for launching stones. They had already begun to undermine a lofty tower, digging a long tunnel which they shored up with planks and posts; they dug and scraped steadily every day with great energy, and women and the wives of the nobles, even on holidays, in flowing robes or tunics, carried off the material that had been dug up. When those inside the citadel discovered what our men were trying to do, they put up great resistance to those carrying out the digging, doing them great harm. When he saw that undermining the tower could not be accomplished, Anselm undertook the task of urging our men to use the ballistic machines. When the machines were set in place, and had fired many stones at the tower, the besieged put in place a similar machine at the same spot. After it had been set in place, the machine hurled massive rocks down, doing great damage to the entire Frankish army; Anselm himself was the first, or among the first, to be struck down. He, who had always behaved faithfully and steadfastly as a member of the Lord's army, had shown other signs of his wisdom and strong faith; one particular example, which is most pleasing to men of letters, is brilliantly evident in the set of two letters he composed to Manassas, the Archbishop of Rheims, a man of pious memory, who died about two years ago,[198] in which Anselm related everything which our men did at the siege of Nicea, how they traveled through Romania and Armenia, how they attacked, captured, and defended what they had captured at Antioch, and how at the same time they had fought against the King of Aleppo, against the King of Damascus, and against the King of Jerusalem, whom he called the adulterer. As testimony of his devoted love towards the noble martyr, on the day of

---

[198] Manassas II of Châtillon died in 1106. Anselm's letters have survived and appear in *Epistulae et chartae ad historiam primi belli sacri spectantes*, ed. Heinrich Hagenmeyer, Innsbruck, 1901, pp. 144–146 and 156–160.

the anniversary of the passion of the blessed Quintinus,[199] he held a celebration, surrounded by a crowd of clergy whom he had assembled to honor the saint, and he offered a fine ceremony for the celebrants. On the same day Anselm himself, together with many others, underwent a joyous martyrdom, earning the kingdom of heaven as their reward for a holy death.

[199] October 31.

Book Seven

That the Eastern Church was restored by the labor of the Western faithful offers no small stimulus for our faith. We see the most pious battles fought solely for God, an army burning with a passion for martyrdom, without a king, without a prince, driven only by a dedication to their own salvation. We read of how the Gauls went off into the distant East, eager for battle, and they searched the secret places of Delphic Apollo, and we know that the treasures taken from the sacred shrines were thrown into the swamps of Toulouse. We know that all these troops were summoned together by the princes in those days; we have heard that, in this instance, not a single man was compelled against his will, by any master, to go on the journey. Here, weeping, confessing their sins, abandoning their possessions, spurning their wives and fleeing from their children, they took up arms. Foremost in the minds of all of them was the desire for a blessed death, for the love of God. Here, I say, I wish to weigh God's wonders: He who once strengthened the minds of the martyrs to undergo torture out of a love for invisible things, again in our own times, in an entirely unexpected way, which would have been considered absurd had anyone said it, placed in the hearts of our men such contempt for the things of this world, even in the hearts of the most bloodthirsty and greedy men. He accomplished so much with so few men, that one must refrain from praising those who did it, since it is clearly God who was responsible. This is clearly demonstrated by the fact that men who have won many victories often grow insolent, and princes rise up against each other, or they become stained with sin, and the Gentiles find them reduced, I might say, almost to the level of animals. However, if they were to grow aware of themselves, and were motivated by penitence, they would immediately be restored to their proper fortunes and pious successes. Let us rejoice then in the battles they won, undertaken purely out of spiritual desire, granted by a divine power, which had never before appeared, but was made manifest in modern times; and let us not admire the fleshly wars of Israel, which were waged merely to fill the belly.

The King of Tripoli ceaselessly petitioned our princes to remove themselves from the town, and make an alliance with him. In response, the leaders of the army, that is, Duke Godfrey, Raymond the Count of Saint-Gilles, Robert, Count of Flanders and Robert, Count of Normandy, took into account the fact that the land was abundant with new produce, that beans, sowed earlier, ripened by the middle of March, and that barley could be harvested before the middle of April, and they also considered the general condition of the land, and the great quantities of supplies, and they decided to resume the journey to Jerusalem. They abandoned the siege of the town and reached Tripoli on the sixth day of the week, on May 13, and they remained there three days. The King of Tripoli made an agreement with our leaders, and immediately freed more than 300 captives whom he held in chains. At their departure, as a sign of his gratitude, he gave them 15,000 besants, as well as fifteen costly horses. In addition, he gave our men a very good price on horses, donkeys, and other goods that would prove useful for the army, as a result of which the Lord's expedition was now fully restored to fighting condition. After this agreement had been made, he also added that if the Crusaders won the war which he had been told they were preparing strenuously to wage against the Emperor of Babylon, and if they captured Jerusalem, then he would immediately convert to Christianity and hand himself and his land over to them. When they left this city, on the second day of May, they traveled over a rough, narrow road all day and all night, and they finally reached a fort named Betholon.[200] Then they traveled on to a city located on the sea, called Zabari,[201] at whose river, called the Braim,[202] they quickly and opportunely relieved the great thirst from which they had been suffering. On the evening of the Ascension of the Lord they ascended a mountain along a very narrow road, in great fear that the narrowness of the path might prevent them from evading any enemies they might meet at the end of the road. But God's providence prevented anyone from daring to attack them. Our soldiers formed a vanguard that kept the road free from hostile attack. At length they reached a city by the sea, which was called Baruth; then they went on to Sarepta,[203] once inhabited by the Sidonians, and made famous by Elijah's feeding of the widow;[204] from there they went to Sur,[205] and then to Acre, once the capital of Palestine. Continuing on, they came to a castle called Caiphas, finally reaching the renowned Caesarea of Palestine, where they remained for three days after the end of May, celebrating Pentecost. Then they went on to Ramathan,[206] famed as the birthplace of Samuel, which some wiser men, more knowledgeable about topography, claim to be Ramothgalaad, in the struggle for which the wicked Ahab was defeated by Benadab, the king of the Syrians.[207] When they heard that the Franks were coming, the inhabitants fled. This city, even if it were not notable for any ancient monuments, would still seem to me to overshadow all other cities because of the presence of the brilliant martyr George, whose tomb they claim is there. After the inhabitants left, a large supply of every kind of food was found there, which offered, for many days, ample provisions for our army. The leaders, after consulting with and obtaining the approval of the clerics and bishops who were able to be present, decided to choose a bishop for this city. They tithed themselves, enriching him with gold and silver; they also supplied him with horses and other animals, so that he and his household might live without the pain of indigence, and in accordance with his rank. Amid general rejoicing, the bishop[208] settled in the city which had been entrusted to him, to guard the people, to build a cathedral as soon as possible,

---

200 Botron.
201 Jubail.
202 Nahir-Ibrahim.
203 Saida.
204 I Kings 17.9.

205 Tyre.
206 Ramla.
207 I Kings 1.
208 Robert, a Norman cleric.

and to install officials who would look after the church, ready to obey the leaders who had vehemently sought this out of love and worship of the martyr.

Finally they reached the place which had provoked so many hardships for them, which had brought upon them so much thirst and hunger for such a long time, which had stripped them, kept them sleepless, cold, and ceaselessly frightened, the most intensely pleasurable place, which had been the goal of the wretchedness they had undergone, and which had lured them to seek death and wounds. To this place, I say, desired by so many thousands of thousands, which they had greeted with such sadness and jubilation, they finally came, to Jerusalem. As one reads that the sojourners ate and worshiped the Body of the Lord,[209] so it may be said of these men that they adored Jerusalem and took it by storm. On Tuesday, the sixth of June, the siege was begun with remarkable energy, by a remarkable combination of forces. From the north, Count Robert of Normandy laid siege to it, near the church of the blessed Saint Stephen, who, because he said that he had seen the Son of man standing at the right hand of God, was covered with a rain of stones by the Jews. From the west, Duke Godfrey, the Count of Flanders, and Tancred attacked. From the south, the Count of Saint-Gilles laid siege, on the mount of Zion, near the church of the blessed Mary, mother of God, where the Lord is said to have sat at dinner with his disciples, the day before his Passion. On the third day after they had arrived at the city, Raymond, whose deeds on the Lord's expedition were well known, this man, I say, whom they called Pelet, together with another man who had the same name, and several others, marched some distance from the place of siege, to see if he could find any of the enemy wandering into our ambushes, as they often did. Suddenly a band of nearly 200 Arabs fell upon them; as soon as Raymond saw them, he attacked as fiercely as a lion, and, in spite of their boldness, with the aid of God, they were subdued. After killing many of them, and capturing thirty horses, they brought the victory back to the army, which took pleasure in their glorious deed. At dawn, on the second day of the next week, the outer, smaller wall of the city was attacked with such force and with such teamwork that both the city and its outskirts would have immediately fallen to the Franks, if they had not lacked ladders. After the outer wall was broken, and a broad passage opened through its rubble, the ladder they did have was extended towards the battlements of the main wall. Some of our knights climbed it quickly and began to fight at long range. And when the arrows ran out, they fought with lances and swords; both the defenders of the city and the besiegers battled hand-to-hand with steel. Many of our men fell, but more of their men.

One should know that while Antioch was under siege, Jerusalem was held by the Turks, under the authority of the King of Persia. Moreover, the Emperor of Babylon, as I mentioned previously, had sent ambassadors to our army, for the sole purpose of determining the condition of our enterprise. When they saw the terrible need that afflicted the Christian army, and when they discovered that the

[209] Psalm 21.30.

nobles had become foot-soldiers because of a lack of horses, they considered us valueless in a struggle against the Turks, whom they hated intensely. The King of Persia had taken a great part of the Babylonian empire, which was very large, for his people were wiser and more energetic in military matters. When the Babylonian prince heard, however, that the Franks – that is, God working through the Franks – had taken Antioch, and had defeated Kherboga himself, together with the pride of Persia, before the walls of Antioch, he quickly gathered his courage, bore arms against the Turks, and laid siege to them in Jerusalem, which they occupied. Then, I don't know whether by force or by some agreement, they entered the town, and placed many Turks, whether to guard it or to take charge of it I don't know, in the tower bearing the name of David, which we think more correctly should be called the tower of Zion. In any case, during the siege they harmed none of us, merely watching peacefully over their assigned tower. As a result, our men fought only with the Saracens.

They were unable to buy bread during the siege, and for nearly ten days food was difficult to find anywhere, until God brought help, and our fleet reached the port of Jaffa. In addition, the army also suffered from thirst, and they not only were worn out by this great discomfort, but they had to drive their horses and pack animals a great distance, six miles, to find water, all the while fearful that the enemy might attack them. The fountain of Siloah, famous for having cured the blind man in the Gospel,[210] which rises from springs on mount Zion, supplied them with water, which was sold to them at the highest prices. After messengers had announced that the fleet had arrived at Jaffa, the leaders held a meeting and decided to send a group of knights to the harbor to guard the ships and the men in them. Early in the morning, at the crack of dawn, Raymond, of whom we have spoken often, together with two other nobles, took 100 knights from the army of his lord, the Count of Saint-Gilles, and set out for the port, with his customary decisiveness. Thirty of the knights separated from the main group and came upon approximately 700 Turks, Arabs, and Saracens, whom the King of Babylon had sent to watch our comings and goings. Although greatly outnumbered, our men forcefully attacked their troops, but the strength and ferocity of the enemy was so great that we were threatened on all sides with imminent death. They killed one of the two leaders, whose name was Achard, as well as some of the most respected among the poor and the foot-soldiers. As they were surrounding our men, pressing them with arms on all sides, so that they were about to despair utterly, one man came to the above-mentioned Raymond and told him of the plight of his peers. "Why do you and your men remain here? See how your men, who recently separated from you, are now fiercely surrounded by an swarm of Saracens and Arabs. Unless you bring them help very quickly, you will undoubtedly soon find them dead, if they have not already perished. Therefore fly, hurry, I say, so that you may not be too late." Together with all of his nobles, Raymond

[210] John 9.7.

quickly set off to look at the place where the fighting was going on. In preparing for combat he placed his faith not in arms, not in strength, but in faith in the Saviour. When the Gentile troops saw the Christian army, they swiftly broke up into two groups. Calling upon the Most High for support, our men attacked with such force that each man knocked the opponent charging at him to the ground. Judging themselves unable to withstand the onslaught of the Christians, the pagans stopped, and, driven by fear, fled swiftly. Our men followed them quickly, pursuing them for four miles. After having killed many of them, they brought back 103 horses as trophies of victory. They refrained from killing only one man, whom they brought back with them, and from whom they learned everything that was going on among their enemies, including what the prince of Babylon was planning against us.

Meanwhile the army was suffering from a terrible thirst, which compelled them to sew together the hides of cattle and oxen, in which they carried water from six miles away. They used the water carried in such bags, which were putrid with recent sweat, and multiplied the great suffering caused by hunger, to make barley bread for the army. How many jaws and throats of noble men were eaten away by the roughness of this bread. How terribly were their fine stomachs revolted by the bitterness of the putrid liquid. Good God, we think that they must have suffered so, these men who remembered their high social position in their native land, where they had been accustomed to great ease and pleasure, and now could find no hope or solace in any external comfort, as they burned in the terrible heat.[211] Here is what I and I alone think: never had so many noble men exposed their own bodies to so much suffering for a purely spiritual benefit. Although the hearts of the pilgrims burned for the dear, distant pledges of their affections, for their sweet wives and for the dignity of their possessions, nevertheless they remained steadfastly in place there, and did not cease to pursue the battle for Christ.

The Saracens were always waiting in ambush around the springs and rivers, eager to kill our men wherever they found them, strip their bodies, and, if they happened to gain booty and horses, to hide them in caves and caverns. Terrible hunger and thirst raged through the army surrounding the city, and the very great rage of the enemy prowling here and there thundered against them as well. But the leaders of the sacred army, seeing that so many men of such different capacities could scarcely endure such pain any longer, urged the use of machines by means of which the city might be made more vulnerable, so that, after all they had gone through, they might finally stand before the monuments of the passion and burial of the Saviour. In addition to the many other instruments, like battering rams with which they might tear down the walls, or catapults to topple the towers and walls, they ordered two wooden castles to be built, which we usually call "falas." Duke Godfrey was the first to build his castle, together with other

---

[211] Guibert has elided the assertion in the *Gesta Francorum* that the Arabs had poisoned the wells, substituting instead these remarks sympathetic to the class from which he sprung.

machines; and Raymond, Count of Saint-Gilles, who permitted himself to be second to no one, also built his own. When they saw the machines being built, the castles being constructed, the missile-launchers and equipment being moving up to the towers, the Saracens began, with unusual speed, to extend and to repair their walls and towers. Working all night long, they surprised our men by the speed with which they accomplished things. Moreoever, the wood from which our men had built the castles and other machines was brought from a distant region. When the leaders of the army of the Lord perceived which side of the city was most vulnerable, on a certain Sunday night they brought the castle, together with some other machines, to that place. At dawn they set up the machines on the eastern side, and on Monday, Tuesday, and Wednesday they established them firmly in place. The Count of Saint-Gilles, however, set up his machine on the southern side. As they burned with eagerness for the siege, their hearts were burning with intolerable thirst, and a silver coin could not purchase enough water to quench a man's thirst. Finally, on the fourth and fifth day, gathering all their forces, they started to attack the walled city. But before the attack took place, the bishops and priests directed the people who were their subjects to sing litanies, and to undertake fasts, to pray, and to give alms. The bishops remembered what had once happened at Jericho, that the walls of the perfidious city had fallen when the Israelites' trumpets sounded, and they marched seven times around the city, carrying the sacred ark, and the walls of the faithless city fell down.[212] They too circled Jerusalem in their bare feet, their spirits and bodies contrite, as they tearfully cried out the names of the saints. Both the leaders and the people came together in this time of necessity, to implore divine assistance. When this was accomplished with great humility, on the sixth day of the week, after they had attacked the city with great forcefulness, and their common effort had proved to be of no avail, such a great torpor fell upon the whole army that their strength vanished, and the steady misfortunes undermined the determination of the most courageous men. As God is my witness, I have heard, from men renowned for their truthfulness, who were present in the divine army, that after their unsuccessful assault upon the walls of the city, you would have seen the best of the knights who had returned from the walls striking their hands, shouting angrily, lamenting that God had deserted them. And I also learned, from sources no less reliable, that Robert, Count of Normandy, and the other Robert, Prince of Flanders, met and shared their mutual grief, weeping copiously, and declaring themselves the most wretched of men, since the Lord Jesus had judged them unworthy of worshipping His Cross, and of seeing, or rather of adoring, His tomb. But as the hour drew near at which Jesus, who for the second time delivered the people from the prison of Egypt, is believed to have ascended the Cross, Duke Godfrey and his brother, Count Eustace, who had not stopped battling from their castle, steadily struck the lower walls with battering rams, while at the

---

212 Joshua 6.20.

same time attacking the Saracens, who were fighting to protect their lives and country, with stones, with various other kinds of missiles, and even with the points of their swords.

Meanwhile, Lietaud, one of the knights, who will be known for generations to come for his daring and for his deeds, was the first to leap onto the walls of the city, startling the Gentiles who surrounded him, and robbing them of their confidence. When he had mounted the wall, several of the young Franks whose pious boldness had made them preeminent rushed forward, unwilling to seem inferior to him who had preceded them, and they climbed to the top of the wall. I would insert their names on this page, were I not aware of the fact that, after they returned, they became infamous for criminal acts; therefore, according to the judgement of men who love the name of God, my silence is not unjust. Very soon, when the Saracens saw the Franks breaching the walls, they quickly fled over the walls and through the city. While they were retreating, our entire army rushed in, some through the breaches made by the battering rams, others by jumping from the tops of their machines. Their struggle to enter resulted in harmful speed; with each man wanting to be perceived as the first, they got in each other's way. Moreover, near the entrance to the gates to the city, the Saracens had built secret covered pits, which injured many of our men, not to speak of the difficulties caused by the narrowness of the entrance as our men rushed in. The Franks chased the fleeing pagans fiercely, killing everyone they came upon, more in slaughter than in battle, through the streets, squares, and crossroads, until they reached what was called the Temple of Solomon. So much human blood flowed that a wave of damp gore almost covered the ankles of the advancing men. That was the nature of their success that day.

Raymond, the Count of Saint-Gilles, moved his army from the southern flank and had a very large machine on wheels brought to the wall, but between the machine, which was called the Castle, and the wall, was a very deep pit. The princes soon conferred about how to accomplish the breaching of the wall quickly, and ordered a messenger to announce throughout the army that anyone who carried three stones into the ditch would certainly receive a penny. In the space of scarcely three days the moat was filled in, since night did not prevent them from carrying out their project. When the moat had been filled in by this means, they pushed the machine against the walls. However, those who had taken on the defense of the inner city resisted us, not out of bravery I say, but out of obstinate madness, hurling what they call Greek fire at our men, and damaging the wheels of the machine with stones. The Franks, however, with remarkable skill, often managed to evade their blows and efforts. Meanwhile, at the eastern side of the city, the tumult of battle alone made the aforementioned count think that the Franks had broken into the city, and were racing though it, spreading death. "Why," he said to his men, "do we delay? Don't you see that the Franks have taken the city, and are now triumphantly seizing great booty?" The count, together with his men, then swiftly invaded the city. When he learned that some of the Franks had spread through the city's palaces, some into the Temple of the

Lord, and that many were fighting at the altars of the Temple of Solomon, as it was formerly called, in order to retain power in the captured city he spoke with the emir (as they called him) in charge of the tower of David, which was called Zion, demanding that he hand over the tower with which he had been entrusted. Thus the satrap, after a pact had been agreed upon between them, opened for him the gate through which the pilgrims used to pass when they entered Jerusalem, and where they were cruelly and unfairly compelled to pay tribute, which was called *musellae*. When the Provencals, that is, the army of the Count of Saint-Gilles, and all the others had entered the city, a general slaughter of the pagans took place. No one was spared because of tender years, beauty, dignity, or strength: one inescapable death awaited them all. Those who had retreated to the Temple of Solomon continued to battle against us throughout the day, but our men, enraged at the feeble arrogance of these desperate men, attacked them with united force, and by means of their combined efforts penetrated to the depths of the temple, where they inflicted such slaughter on the wretches within the temple that the blood of the innumerable crowd of those who were killed nearly submerged their boots. An innumerable crowd, of mingled sexes and ages, had poured into this Temple; the Franks granted some of them a few moments of life, so that they might remove from the Temple the bodies of the fallen, of whom a foul pile lay scattered here and there. After they had removed the bodies, they were themselves put to the sword. Those who had climbed to the top of the Temple, a large crowd of the common people, received the standards of Tancred and Gaston as a sign that peace had been granted to them in the meantime. However, whether Gaston, a famous and very wealthy man, was a Gascon or a Basque, I don't exactly remember, but I am certain that he was one or the other.[213] The army then ran amok, and the entire city was looted. Palaces and other buildings lay open, and silver, gold, and silken garments were seized as booty. They found many horses and mules, and in the houses they found great abundance of every kind of food. This was right and proper for the army of God, that the finest things that offered themselves to each man, no matter how poor, became his by right, without doubt or challenge, no matter the social class of the man who first came upon them. And then, putting these things aside, they ran, equally joyful and sad, towards that which they had thirsted for so fervently.

They approached the sepulchre of the Lord and thanked Him for what they had sought, the liberation of the Blessed Places; He had performed such great deeds with them as his instruments, that neither those who had performed them nor any other men could properly evaluate these great deeds. They kept in mind how much anguish they had endured to achieve this, and how they had accomplished what they could not have hoped for, and when they considered that they themselves had done deeds which had been unknown for centuries, no man could understand how blessed were the tears which they poured forth.

---

213 The author of the *Gesta Francorum* gives his name as Gaston Bearn.

Omnipotent God, what deep emotion, what joy, what grief they felt, after un-heard-of sufferings, never experienced by any army, like the tortures of child-birth, when, like new-born children, they saw that they had attained the fresh joys of the long-desired vision. Therefore they were sad, and after they had joyfully wept tears sweeter than any bread, they rejoiced, and with overflowing emotions they embraced the most pious Jesus, the cause of their excruciating daily labors, as though he had been hanging on the cross, or had been held until that moment in the shelter of the tomb from time immemorial. Magnificent gifts of gold and silver were offered there, but sincere devotion was more valuable than any gift.

At last the next day shone forth, and the Franks, sorry that they had permitted those who had climbed to the top of the Temple (to whom Tancred and Gaston had given their own standards, as we said earlier) to remain alive, invaded the heights of the temple and cut the Saracens to pieces, killing the women together with the men. Some of them, preferring suicide, threw themselves from the top of the Temple. Tancred, however, because he and Gaston had given their pledges of security, was much disturbed by this killing. Then our men ordered some of the Saracens to carry off the dead, because the foul stench of the bodies was oppressive, and the city was filled with so many corpses that the Franks were unable to move without stepping on dead bodies. Therefore the pagans, when they had carried the bodies from the city, in front of the main gates piled up mountains of corpses, and burned them in a huge pile. We merely read about, and have never seen, such a killing of Gentiles anywhere; God repaid them who had inflicted such pain and death upon the pilgrims – who had suffered for such a long time in that land – by exacting a retribution equal to their hideous crimes. For no one except God himself can calculate how much suffering, how many labors, how much destruction all of those who sought the Holy Places endured at the hands of the arrogant Gentiles. God certainly must have grieved more over their suffering than over the delivery of his Cross and Tomb into profane hands. But before we turn our stylus to other matters, it should be made clear that the Temple of Solomon, to which we referred earlier, is not the structure which Solomon himself built, which the Lord had predicted would not continue to stand, "one stone upon another," and which was destroyed, but an imitation of it, built by I don't know whom, as tribute to the noble ancient House. It certainly was a place of very great beauty, built out of gold and silver, of immeasurable price, and of incredible variety, with walls and gates plated with layers of precious metals. Count Raymond then had the prefect who had been in charge of the citadel, to whom he had sent his banners, brought out of the citadel that night, together with his entire retinue, and given safe conduct to Ascalon.

Then, when the holy places had been liberated, the entire Christian army was ordered to give alms and offerings, so that their souls might be properly receptive to the divine grace that they needed to choose the man who would rule the holy city as its king. On the eighth day after the taking of the city, they made an offer to the Count of Saint-Gilles, because of his excellence, but he, although mindful of his high position, refused to take on such an onerous task, for good reason (he was an old man, who had only one eye, but was famous for his remarkable feats of arms and for his energy). Finally, they approached Duke Godfrey, and, at the urgent insistence of everyone, the labor rather than the honor of this task was imposed upon him, for he would have to battle unremittingly against the great strength of the Gentiles, and to show good will towards the neighboring Christians. Slender, relatively tall, eloquent, and even-tempered, he had made himself known for his strength in battle on the Lord's expedition. According to reliable, accurate testimony, the following story is told about a remarkable deed he did, when he met at Antioch, on the bridge over the Pharphar, a Turk, wearing no cuirass, but riding a horse. Godfrey struck his guts so forcefully with his sword that the trunk of his body fell to the earth, while the legs remained seated as the horse moved on. The men of Lotharingia customarily had remarkably long as well as sharp swords.

We think that another of his deeds, no less glorious, and worthy to be told, should be included. They had taken Nicea, and since things had gone well at Nicea, they hurried off to besiege Antioch; on the way, from time to time, when the chance to relax their usual caution occurred, they hunted beasts in the nearby forests (the fields in this region were not as tall and thick as in our country). On one occasion, a bear of enormous size came out of the bushes; when the army caught sight of him, they set out in pursuit. Frightened by the shouting crowd, the bear immediately sought out the woods from which it had emerged. While many men were surrounding it, one wretch happened to reach the beast's lair. Leaping forward, the bear attacked the rash man, pinned him in his arms,

and with his teeth swiftly seized the leg of the man lying there.[214]

Then the duke, separated from his men, went to help him; when the wretched man, weeping with pain and fear, saw him, he called upon the man's noble nature, and urged him to help him. Nor did the duke, whose nature consisted almost entirely of virtue, delay helping him, but he swiftly drew his sword from its scabbard and forcefully struck the head of the beast. More annoyed than wounded, because of the hardness of its bones, the beast attacked the duke, removing its teeth from the leg of the unfortunate man whom he had first attacked so fiercely. The man quickly departed, without troubling himself about the duke's difficulty, but saving himself, leaving the man and the beast to resolve their conflict between them. The beast, angry at the blow he had received,

leapt up, seized the duke with his claws, threw him down, and pinned him under his terrible limbs. With his raging mouth he bit the duke's leg,[215]

---

214 Part of a dactylic hexameter couplet.
215 Three elegiac lines.

but the noble-minded man

> remained steadfast in spite of his fall, and tightly held onto the sword he had drawn.[216]

As he lay there, and the beast continued to gnaw at the hip he had seized, the duke, fully aware of his predicament, placed his sword between the head and arm of the beast, gathered all of his strength, and drove the point of the blade into the depths of the beast's body. When he felt the metal gliding through his viscera, the beast finally relaxed the jaws that had sunk into the duke's flesh. When the duke saw that he had been released from the beast's mouth, and noticed that the beast was not moving from its place, he pushed with both feet, but in the act of pushing he received an almost mortal wound in his leg from the sword that was stuck in the breast of the beast above him. He fell down in worse shape than when he had been held by the beast, and now, weakened from loss of blood, after some time he was found by his men. The duke was now sorry, although too late, for having gone out by himself, since this adventure was costly for his own warriors, and for the entire sacred army. Until the siege of Antioch was over, he had to be carried on a litter, and since he could not look after himself or others, he quickly lost almost 15,000 men of those who had belonged to him, but who abandoned him when he became disabled.

Since we have dealt with the bear, we would also like to mention a deed performed by his brother Baldwin, who is now still the ruler of Jerusalem, since no other more fitting place for the story may occur. He suffered a similarly severe wound in battle, in the course of saving one of his foot-soldiers, who had supported him bravely. Foresight led the doctor whom he summoned to resist covering the wound with medicinal poultices, because he knew that the wound was very deep, and while the skin could be made smooth, the wound would fester deep within his body. He proposed to conduct a remarkable experiment. He asked the king to order one of the Saracens whom they held prisoner to be wounded in the same place and in the same manner that Baldwin himself had been (for it was forbidden for him to ask for a Christian), and to have him killed thereafter, so that he might look more freely into the corpse, and determine from this inspection something about the king's own internal wounds. The prince's piety recoiled in horror at this suggestion, and he recalled the example of ancient Constantine, declaring that he would not be the cause of the death of any man, no matter how insignificant, for such insignificant salvation, when it is ever doubtful. The doctor then said to him, "If you have decided that no man's life can be spent for your own well-being, then at least give the order to bring forward a bear, an animal useless except for show, and have it hung up by its front paws, then struck with an iron blade, so that I may then examine his entrails, and I shall be able to measure how far it went in, and thereby determine the depth of

---

[216] Two dactylic hexameters.

your own wound." The king answered him, "The beast will be brought immediately, since it is necessary: consider it a done deed." When the doctor had finished his experiment at the animal's expense, he found, as we mentioned above, that harm would come to the king if the wound were quickly covered, unless the pus was removed and the interior part of the wound would heal. To have said these things about the piety of the kings is sufficient; they would have been deservedly famous had the choice of a bishop, and the bishopric itself, not been defective.

Up to this point the careful Muse has proceeded through brambles, along a narrow path. A cloud obscures the traveller's path, and the dawning of the late star scarcely grows warm. Let the plague of blood have run only thus far; let there be no further time for slaughter and hunger. If Fortune has sometimes smiled on our efforts, the rapacious air of destruction has soon followed. When the walls of Nicea fell, and the city of Antioch was captured, what good was produced? The good that resulted from the sufferings, for each holy martyr, when death was conquered. For if grievous things had to be suffered, bearing poverty and death at the same time, the grief brought about future joys. I shall use the voice of the writer of the Psalms, "I was glad when they said to me, let us go into the house of the Lord;"[217] our feet shall tread the halls of Solyme, walking there joyfully. Franks, take these rewards of labor; do not grieve for the unhappiness you endured. Take pleasure in the sight of the Sepulchre you had long hoped for, and in the restoration of the tear-stained Cross, and all suffering will leave your hearts. This city, often made the spoil of kings, was given over to utter ruin. O city made blessed by this capture, from now on you should rule, drawing to you Christian kingdoms. You will see the glories of the earth come here, to show filial gratitude to you. Not Ezra nor Judas Machabee did as much, after your sufferings; Hadrian, whence Elia gets its name, was not able, in reviving you, to give so much. This world fights for you and yours; concern for you involves almost the entire age. Once Judea, when it was at its strongest, could match this glory. Why are knights sung of in battle? I ask that you be the ruin of Persia and not of yourself. Attack the prince of Babylon, and whatever stands in the way of Jerusalem, so that good men may visit the Cross of Jesus, bowing their pious heads at the Tomb. I shall cry out that our times have learned what no future annals will teach.[218]

While temporal activities, which are thought to be the concern of the royal administration, were being taken care of, internal ecclesiastical concerns were not to be neglected, and as soon as a king was set up, they dealt with replacing the patriarch. At that time there was a cleric, of what rank I am not sure, named Arnulf. He had some skill at logic, significant knowledge of grammatical learning, and for some time had taught, in the subject mentioned above, the daughter of the King of England, a nun. The Count of the Normans, through his sister, had promised him as much as a bishop's honors, if any of his bishops happened to

---

217 Psalm 121.1.
218 Forty-eight iambic trimeters.

die. Meanwhile, when the journey to Jerusalem was proposed, the Bishop of Bayeux, whose name was Odo, and who was very wealthy, vowed to undertake the journey. Since he was the brother of William the elder, King of England, and, in addition to the office of bishop, among the English he held the county of Kent, with the expectation of great wealth, he seemed ready to dare new enterprises, to the extent of plotting to take over the kingdom from his brother. When the king found out about his intentions, he put him in prison, where he remained until the day the king died. At this time the bishop regained his freedom and office, and, as I said earlier, when the pilgrimage was proclaimed, Odo, accompanied by a large retinue and immense resources, set out on the journey. Arnulf enrolled himself in his retinue, and when death overtook this bishop, within the borders of Romania if I am not mistaken, Odo bequeathed, out of the fortune which he left behind, a legacy to him, which consisted of almost all of his most precious possessions. Since he possessed a considerable amount of literary knowledge, as well as native eloquence, and his increased wealth made him more well known, he began to drive our men on with many speeches, and to increase his fame in this way. The fact that learned men were in short supply made him even more illustrious, and since a man's voice is of more concern than the life he has led, he was called to the patriarchy of Jerusalem. For some time, then, he presented himself as the bishop, though in name only; he fulfilled his new office by sermonizing. Finally, after a short time, when news of his election reached the Apostlic See, after the death of the Bishop of Puy, Pope Paschal decreed that Daimbert, the Archbishop of Pisa, should administer pastoral care to the Lord's army. After Jerusalem had been captured and the king had taken office, Daimbert arrived with a large fleet; a short while later he examined the process by which Arnulf had been chosen, and decided that, in accordance with canon law, it should be challenged. After a thorough investigation of the man's origin, he was found to be the son of a priest and therefore one who should not only be barred from sacred office, but, according to a decision by the council of Toledo, he should be ordered to become an eternal slave of that church whose dignity had been affronted by his engendering. When he had been deposed, then, in spite of his strenuous efforts to defend himself, the leaders wanted to mitigate the shame that he felt at being rejected, and so they asked him whom they should choose. In accordance with his depraved nature, which envied both his peers and juniors, he said, "Choose the Pisan himself, who is carrying out his assignment." The leaders agreed with his words, seized the archbishop in the church where he was sitting, almost without asking his consent, and escorted him themselves to the cathedral to take up the see. A short time later, after the death of the glorious King Godfrey, during the reign of his brother Baldwin, who had previously ruled over Edessa, they accused Daimbert of treason. Convicted of the crime, he who had resigned his metropolitan see was deprived of the office of patriarch. When another election was held to determine who would be bishop, Arnulf shrewdly nominated one of his peers, whom he knew to be submissive, a simple, illiterate man, named Ebremar, who would offer no resistance to Arnold's power. He, however, behaved in a religious fashion, and I think that he did not carry out Arnulf's wishes in every way. As a result, he soon was accused at the Apostolic See, but the accusation failed miserably. As a result, Arnulf, together with those who had been his accomplices in the accusation against Ebremar, incurred the wrath of the king, who deprived him of the guardianship of the Sepulchre, and drove him from the city. Reinstated by the leaders of the Apostolic See, the bishop returned to Jerusalem, to the great shame of his persecutors. This is quite enough to have said about the election and deposition of that would-be patriarch. The election, which was null and void in the minds of all right-thinking men, took place on the day of the festival of Saint-Peter-in-chains, but since he had no help from a pious life, it dissolved. The city was captured by the Franks on the fifteenth day of July, on the sixth day of the week, almost at the hour when Christ was put on the cross.

A short time later, only a few days in fact, ambassadors[219] arrived from the city of Naplouse,[220] which, unless I am mistaken, in ancient times was called Emmaus. They invited Tancred and Count Eustachius, the brother of the duke who was now king, both of whom were brave, noteworthy men, to set out for the above mentioned city, bringing with them a large army, to take control of it. They set out, bringing many men with them, including a great number of footsoldiers, and reached the outskirts of the city. The residents of the town, of their own free will, then opened the fortifications and surrendered to them. Other messengers came to King Godfrey, bearing the news that the Emperor of Babylon was getting large numbers of troops ready to wage war against him. The king, made fiercer by what he had just been told, dispatched messengers to his brother Eustace and to Tancred, instructing and urging them to return to Jerusalem as soon as possible. The king also indicated that the battle would take place at Ascalon. When these most fearless men heard what had happened, they hastily set off through the mountains, where they found none of the Saracens they thought would be up in arms against them; then they reached Caesarea in Palestine. From there they retraced their steps, proceeding to Ram, the town mentioned above, made famous by the memory of Saint George, and situated on the shore of the sea, where they met up with many Arabs, who were the vanguard of the army they were to face. Our men joined forces against them, attacked them, and by their united efforts overwhelmed the enemy, who were compelled to flee. Many were captured alive, and they revealed the enemies' plans for the battle about to take place: where the army was going to assemble; what was its size; and where they planned to stand and fight. After he had gathered this information, Tancred sent messengers directly to Godfrey, King of Jerusalem, to tell him what he had learned. He sent other messengers to Arnulf, the man known as the patriarch, and to the other leaders, saying, "You should know that a great battle awaits you, and since it is certainly about to take place, come quickly to Ascalon, supported by as many fine troops as you can quickly and carefully gather." The

---

[219] Guibert multiplies the single *nuntius* of the *Gesta Francorum* into *legati*.
[220] Sichem, then Flavia Neapolis, then Nabulus.

king, than whom no one was wiser in his faith in God, by the authority invested in him proceeded to rouse the entire army of God to perform this task, and designated Ascalon as the place to which they should proceed to face the enemy. He himself, together with the man called the patriarch, and Robert, Count of Flanders, left the city on the third day of the week.

But the Count of Saint-Gilles and the Count of Normandy informed the king that they were unwilling to proceed until they learned whether the battle was certain to take place; they said that meanwhile they would return to Jerusalem, offering to come quickly if needed. The king departed, and when he saw the enemy from afar, quickly sent news of what he had found back to those who were in Jerusalem. He summoned a certain bishop,[221] and sent him to the city, to entreat everyone to delay no longer, but, at this moment of need, to join him. On Wednesday the leaders gathered together the Lord's expeditionary forces and moved their camp outside the city. The bishop who had brought the king's words to those who had remained in Jerusalem was captured by Saracens, as he was making his way back to the king. It is not clear whether he died or was led away captive. Peter the Hermit, the official in charge of work that to this point was pious, together with clerics, both Greek and Latin, remained in the city, organizing processions, supervising prayers, preaching sermons, urging the giving of alms, so that God might deign to add this supreme victory to the victories of his people. The ecclesiastics who could be present, dressed in their sacred vestments, as though they were going to perform sacred offices, marched to the Lord's Temple, where they led masses and delivered sermons that moved the men and women deeply, asking God to end their exile. But the man with the name of patriarch, together with the other bishops who were present, gathered with several of the leaders at the river which is known to be on this side of Ascalon. There, by the trickery of the Gentiles, many thousands of animals, including herds of cows, camels, and sheep, had been put in place. When the leaders learned that they had been placed there as booty to tempt our men, the order was circulated throughout the encampment that none of this booty was to be found in anyone's tent, unless he could show that it was necessary for his food that day.[222] Meanwhile, 300 Arabs rode into view, and our men pursued them so effectively that they captured two of them as they fled, and harassed the others by pursuing them to their encampment.

Later on the same day, the man performing the function of patriarch had the announcement made through the entire army that early the next day everyone would prepare for battle, and he threatened to excommunicate anyone who stopped during the battle to pillage; each man was to suppress his desire for booty until the end of the battle. He asked that they concentrate on killing the enemy, so that they might not be diverted from the task by desire for shameful

---

221 Arnulf of Martirano.
222 The *Gesta Francorum* reports the presence of the animals without attributing them to any Arabian design.

gain, thereby permitting greed to stand in the way of the victory they had in their grasp. Friday morning our army entered a very lovely valley, on a level with the nearby river, where they set up their separate battle lines. The duke, who was now king, the Count of Flanders, the Count of Normandy, the Count of Saint-Gilles, Eustace of Bologne, Tancred and Gaston together, in addition to others, both in single and in shared commands, stood before their units. Bowmen and lancers, who customarily march in front of the troops of foot-soldiers, were drawn up, and King Godfrey with his troops took up the left side, while the Count of Saint-Gilles took up a position near the sea, and the counts of Flanders and Normandy rode on the right side. Tancred and others marched along in the center. Our foot soldiers moved against the enemy's forces; the Gentiles prepared themselves for battle without moving. You would have seen them carrying on their shoulders vessels,

> which enabled them to hold the cool water in small sacks,[223]

from which they thought that they would drink while pursuing us as we fled. But God provided something other than the enemy race was imagining, for meanwhile, Robert, the Count of Normandy, saw shining from afar the spear of the leader of the army; it seemed to be covered with bright silver, and its top decorated with thick gold. Steadily spurring his swift horse on, he attacked the prince, who was carrying a spear as a standard, with great force, wounding him with a terrible blow. On the other side, the Count of Flanders loosened his horse's reins and plunged into the thick of the enemy. Tancred

> rushed among the tents with a great company, and the troops, along with their leaders, were revelling everywhere.[224]

The fields and plains became bloody with carnage. The enemy was unable to bear their losses, and soon fled in despair. Even as the number of pagans was great, so was the carnage great. If the waves of the sea were great, so the Lord shows himself much more marvelous in the deeps.[225] Then, so that it might be clear that the hand of God only, and not that of man, was waging war, you would have seen them flee blindly, with their eyes open, and in their attempt to avoid our weapons, they threw themselves on them. There was no place of refuge:

> tall trees offered no protection for many of them, nor were they able to escape our arrows. Swift blows created massive destruction.[226]

All those whom flight could not protect were dead or almost dead from the blows of our arrows and swords, which cut them down like cattle. The Count of Saint-Gilles, near the shore, from which he had launched his own army against

---

[223] One dactylic hexameter.
[224] Two dactylic hexameters.

[225] Psalm 92.4.
[226] Three dactylic hexameters.

the enemy, attacked them like a storm, with such vehemence that many of them, trying to escape from the blades, voluntarily plunged into the sea.

When the victory had been won, thanks to God's leadership, the prince of the Babylonian army, who, in their language, is called an emir, was confounded, and, unable to control his astonishment at what had happened to him, lamented at great length. He thought about the great amount of supplies that he had brought, and the superb, strong, fine-looking young men, the noble arms, the power of his allies, and, I should have said, all the knights; in addition, he saw that they had what would make the most sluggish of men secure, that is, they had fought in front of their own city's gates, to which they could surely retreat, and, what made it even safer, in their own land. And he looked upon the Franks, in every way inferior in military might, whose young men had been weakened by long hunger, whose swords were rusty, whose lances were darkened, whose few remaining troops were worn out, all of whose leaders were exhausted by bitter suffering, as they rode on horses racked with every kind of disease, and, to put it briefly, he marveled that these poor wretches, a band of exiles, had conquered the countless soldiers of his own nation, and that the glory of the entire East had been brought down by the least of men. Our victory was also aided by the fact that, when the cry for retreat spread through the enemy's army, the emir in charge of Ascalon, seeing the Babylonian prince turn to flee, ordered that all those who fled should be prevented from entering his city. The enemy was very much astonished that the Franks had chosen not to fight before the walls of Jerusalem, but had marched for nearly two days to meet them.

While the Franks were thanking God, as was right, for such a victory, Robert, the Count of Normandy, a man of remarkable generosity, even in his impoverished exile, bought for twenty silver marks, from the man who had captured it, the spear, which, as we have said, was covered with silver, and which had stood before the prince of Babylon as his standard. He then gave it, to stand at the Tomb of the Lord, as a symbol of such a victory, to Arnulf, who was called the Patriarch. They say that the sword which had belonged to this prince was bought by someone for sixty besants. In addition, a large fleet had followed the army to Ascalon so that, after the Franks had been defeated and made captives, they might buy them from the victors, and carry them off to be sold throughout the furthest kingdoms of the East. However, when they saw the Egyptians shamefully fleeing, they set sail instantly, and made their way into the interior by sea. Finally, after having slaughtered the Saracens, and the Egyptians as well, the Franks returned to the abandoned tents and collected booty beyond count. They brought out a horde of gold and silver, the wealth of the Assyrian nobility, and whatever precious household goods they had, as well as all kinds of animals, and a collection of various arms. They kept whatever could be used, and burned the rest. Then they returned to Jerusalem, with overwhelming joy, pouring out unnumbered tears of gratitude in memory of the passion and burial of the Lord. As a result of this fortunate turn of events, the Franks were now so prosperous that those who had begun the journey in poverty and without enough to sustain them on the pilgrimage, now returned from it laden with gold, silver, horses, and mules. They won this glorious battle on August 13.

Since we offered, at the beginning of this volume, examples from Scripture which we thought were relevant to such an enterprise, we may now be able to find something in the words of the prophet Zechariah that fits the siege of Jerusalem. He says, "The Lord, who stretches forth the heavens and lays the foundation of the earth, and forms the spirit of man within him, speaks." He stretches the skies who spread (the influence of) the church, as he propagated his seed from the East, according to Isaiah,[227] by means of the apostles, even as he had to gather the church through them from the West. He lays the foundations, since he permits the pagans to persevere in their heard-hearted falsehood. He places the spirit within man when he grants innate reason in the mind of every true believer. "Behold I shall make Jerusalem the lintel of intoxication unto all the people round about."[228] The lintel rises about the door; a house is entered through the door; drinking is harmful to the stomach. If we call the door faith in the Lord Jesus, through whom we come to the Father, then the Church of Jerusalem, because both the Law and the Word of the Lord came from it, we may correctly call the lintel, because it gave rise to these things. For Paul, after fourteen years, returned to it, to confer with Peter and the others about the Gospel, "lest he had run, or should run, in vain."[229] But this is the lintel of drunkenness unto all the people round about, since all nations were disgusted and nauseated by those things in which the traces of our faith resided. "But Judah will be in the siege against Jerusalem."[230] He says not only that it will be a terror to foreigners, but that Judah, that is, the faithful people, will besiege Jerusalem, acknowledging that it will be trodden by the nations. "In that day I shall place Jerusalem as a heavy rock upon all people."[231] If I may take the part for the whole, in accordance with the frequent practice of Scripture, Jerusalem becomes a heavy weight for all the people because it recently imposed upon all people who are called Christian the weight of a very great labor for her liberation. "All that lift up Jerusalem will be cut in pieces, and all the kingdoms of the earth will be gathered together against it."[232] Who are those who will lift it up, if not those who, after the times of nations have ended, lift it up from its own destruction? The Lord says, "Jerusalem will be trodden down by the Gentiles, until the times of the Gentiles be fulfilled."[233] They will be torn apart because no one can say or even imagine how great the labor, the suffering, the misery of hunger and thirst would be that they endured in the siege. And, to speak like Ezekiel, "Every head was made bald, and every shoulder was peeled;"[234] that is, perhaps, either by the steady attack of siege-machines, or by carrying heavy weights. But after Jerusalem has been raised, "All the kingdoms of the earth will gather against her," which should not

---

227 Isaiah 43.5.
228 Zechariah 12.2.
229 Galatians 2.2.
230 Zechariah 12.2.

231 Zechariah 12.3.
232 Zechariah 12.3.
233 Luke 21.24.
234 Ezekiel 29.18.

be taken allegorically, but, as the story that has just been told, was offered as something visible to heavenly eyes. For what kingdom of the East did not send its men to war, bringing every kind of siege-engine, which I did not mention earlier, and everything necessary to besiege a city? They brought, in addition to soldiers, merchants to buy the Franks, since they expected that the pagans would win because of the great size of their forces, and perhaps they had heard that the number was greater than Kherboga actually had. "On that day, God says, I will smite every horse with astonishment, and his rider with madness."[235] If the horse is taken to mean earthly honor, the rider of the horse is undoubtedly to be understood as he who is preeminent in honor. All honor is astonished because every power or kingdom, stupified by God's army, dares do nothing. Every prince went mad, because he did not know what to do, nor where to turn; deprived of force, each learned what the strength of God's army was. "And I will open my eyes upon the house of Judah, and I will smite every horse of the people with blindness."[236] If Judah is the confessor, I may certainly call them confessors who have never chosen to abandon the origin of their faith, that is, the Franks, upon whom the entire weight of the journey fell. God opened his eyes upon them when he showed the grace of his goodness to them by bringing about this outcome. He struck the horses of the people with blindness when he punished the arrogance of the Gentiles by showing them his displeasure. In Sacred Scripture the horse often stands for pride. For what greater blindness is there than to make war on the sons of God? What is more blameful than to fail to acknowledge God, to glory in one's own ignorance, and to war against the faithful? But why exercise the license of allegory, piecing words together, when historical truth prevents us from going astray in belief? Didn't we say earlier that the enemy was struck with blindness, and overcome with astonishment at the swords which threatened them? And I marvel that the horse was able to see well enough to move when its rider had clearly gone mad. "And the leaders of Judah shall say in their heart: The inhabitants of Jerusalem shall be confident in the Lord of hosts, their God."[237] Whom should I call the leaders of Judah, unless they be the leaders of that faithful army, who prayed that the inhabitants of Jerusalem be confident, when they ardently desired to restore the holy city by means of the strength of the Christian army, so that Christianity might grow, the Lord's memory be honored, and the Gentiles everywhere be attacked? But their strength is said to be in the Lord of armies, which can be seen today, when a small force of men assembles against all of the pagan kingdoms. Everything they did was foreseen by Him who rules the heavenly powers. At this point one should add, "Their God," since their thoughts were not directed to any but their own God, that is, the Christian God. "In that day will I make the governors of Judah like a fiery furnace among the wood, and like a torch of fire in a sheaf; and they shall devour all the people round about, on the right hand and on the left."[238] On this day, I say, of faith or

---

[235] Zechariah 12.4.
[236] Zechariah 12.4.

[237] Zechariah 12.5.
[238] Zechariah 12.6.

of divine prosperity, the leaders who govern the Christian people, either externally in arms, or internally by means of spiritual doctrine, will become the
furnace. That is, burning internally with heavenly love, they consume the wood
of sinners among the Gentiles, while externally, they consume the evil-doers in
battle as though they were straw. We have no doubt that God did not undertake
this merely to liberate one city, but to scatter the seeds that will grow long and far
against the madness of the Antichrist. They devour all the people round about,
on the left and on the right, for they bring all those on the right into the piety of
Christianity, while they destroy the wicked, those who are recognized as belonging to the left, and who are worthy of vengeful destruction. "And Jerusalem shall
be inhabited again in her own place, in Jerusalem."[239] If Jerusalem is the Church,
its place is the faith of Christ, therefore Jerusalem inhabits Jerusalem, since the
terrestial city is restored so that she may long for a vision of heavenly peace, since
she has a place, since she clings steadfastly to Christ. "The Lord also shall save the
tents of Judah, as in the beginning, that the glory of the house of David and the
glory of the inhabitants of Jerusalem do not magnify themselves against
Judah."[240] The Lord saves the tents of Judah in the beginning, since He, after
having accomplished miracles for our fathers, also granted glory to our own
times, so that modern men seem to have undergone pain and suffering greater
than that of the Jews of old, who, in the company of their wives and sons, and
with full bellies, were led by angels who made themselves visible to them. I say
that today's men are the ones whom he more truly saves, because he truly receives
as his children those whose bodies he has allowed to be slain, and whom he
punishes in the temporal world. He says, "That the glory of the house of David
may not glorify itself," that is, that the ancients, who excelled in their victories in
war, may refrain from excessive pride, when they think of how modern men have
done better than they. "The glory of the inhabitants of Jerusalem may magnify
itself against Judah," opposes to modern accomplishments the pride of those
who once reigned in Jerusalem and did famous things. By David, who was the
most powerful, he expresses whatever generates the greatest pride, as though he
were saying that although David had been the most celebrated in warfare, and
some of the kings who succeeded him sought glory, they could in no way equal
what our own men have done. The word "to dwell" (habitare) however, we say
means "to dominate," since it is the frequentive of the word "to have" (habeo,
habes). David raising himself up in glory against Judah and the glory of the
inhabitants of Jerusalem are mentioned because they are the material in which
those who wish to make little of our deeds take pride. "In that day shall the Lord
defend the inhabitants of Jerusalem."[241] And did he not today also protect that
meager band whom he guarded in the midst of countless pagans? They make
bold, armed attacks on the neighboring nations every day, who have all they can
do to protect themselves against their attacks, without presuming to go on the

239 Zechariah 12.6.   241 Zechariah 12.8.
240 Zechariah 12.7

attack themselves. "And he who has offended among them in that day shall be as David, and the house of David shall be as God, as the angel of the Lord before them."[242] Certainly David, whose punishment is not described in the present passage, is not to be considered seriously at fault. Therefore whoever of us shall offend is like David, for God does not permit his lechery or his pride to go unpunished, as the deeds related above indicate. And soon, in the course of their sinning, he inflicted upon them the punishment that they very much deserved, either hunger, or some other kind of torment. Therefore the house of David became like the house of God, because it was returned to spiritual grace by means of divine censure. Those like David, upon whom God imposes his paternal correction, may still be embraced by his spirit. In the sight of God he becomes like an angel, for when through imminent punishment man sees himself banished by God's authority from his own affections, he then burns more ardently to love God. When he understands that he is being punished like a child, he loves like an angel. The sight of God is the pious emotion of the inner man. "And it shall come to pass in that day that I will seek to destroy all the nations that come against Jerusalem." We generally seek for things that are not visible to us. Why would God seek unless to propose the things that should be done according to eternal providence? Therefore God seeks "to destroy all the nations that come against Jerusalem,"[243] and, "in that day," because in his fine judgement he foresees and ordains that those who resist the faith are struck with eternal damnation, or are destroyed or diminished according to the extent of their own weakness. Therefore he says, "Thou shalt break them like a potter's vessel,"[244] whom you shall rule "with a rod of iron."[245] But God does this by internal illumination, which is certainly what is meant by "day," but this is something which cannot be expressed in rational terms. "And I will pour upon the house of David, and upon the inhabitants of Jerusalem, the spirit of grace and of supplications."[246] I have said that the inhabitants of Jerusalem were the house of David, whom omnipotent God, although he has granted and still grants them many victories, subdued and continues to subdue with frequent misfortunes. While he does not permit them to despair at their continual misfortunes, nor does he allow them to grow prideful at their frequent good fortune, the sacred distributor necessarily pours the spirit of grace and prayers upon them, so that, while no prosperity, even the most satisfying, seems to smile upon them without soon being followed by adversity, the soul always filled with anxiety is compelled to place its hope in Him who aids them in every circumstance. Now, laying aside all mystery, we may think how this material Jerusalem was so often in doubt and fear, since she was, according to Ezekiel,[247] "set in the midst of the nations, with nations around her," a tiny city surrounded by countless nations. And while they steadily fear the attacks of barbarian nations, since they are not utterly stupid, they are never

---

242 Zechariah 12.8.
243 Zechariah 12.9.
244 Psalm 2.8.

245 Apocalypse 2.27; 19.15.
246 Zechariah 12.10.
247 5.5.

without the grace of the fear and love of God, these people who never lack matter for pious affection and prayers. Of course, with the arrows of adversity the Omnipotent is accustomed to compel his people to remember him; by stimulating the flesh he customarily inflames their minds, and while they fear destruction they are always ready to invoke the aid of God with their vows and prayers.

We have said many times, and do not hesitate to repeat, that this had never been accomplished in any age. If some one cites the sons of Israel and the miracles God performed for them, I shall offer something more miraculous: an open sea filled with Gentiles; a cloud of divine fear rising from a column among them; I shall point to the light of divine hope offered to those whom Christ inspired, himself a column of uprightness and strength, those who were comforted by the food of the word of God only, like divine manna, when they had no earthly hope. Those men spurned the heavenly food that they were offered, and looked back in their minds and with their voices to the Egypt they had left behind, but our men never looked back, but instead eagerly embraced whatever poverty and suffering came upon them. Certainly the steady, destructive starvation endured at Antioch was also accompanied by noble scenes. In the midst of every kind of poverty, than which nothing more painful had ever been endured by men, how bravely did those men who did not refrain from participating in this Christian drama perform. Those who were present report that while the city was under siege, and the besiegers and the inhabitants of the city were fighting hand-to-hand, it frequently happened that, when the men withdrew on both sides, and wisely and reasonably refrained from fighting, a contingent of boys, some from the city, and some from our own camp, marched out and met each other, to fight in a worthy manner. As we said at the beginning of this history, when the expedition to Jerusalem spread throughout the Western lands, fathers set out on the journey together with their little sons. When it happened that the parents of some of them died, the little boys continued to follow the army, and they grew accustomed to the hardships. Their ability to tolerate privation was in no way inferior to that of their elders. When they set up their battle lines, they appointed leaders from among themselves, and they called them Hugh the Great, Bohemund, the Count of Flanders, the Count of Normandy, with a different person playing each role. Whenever they saw that their subjects were suffering from lack of food, they went off to ask for food from the princes after whom they were named, and these princes gave them enough supplies to nourish them properly in their need. This remarkable army often challenged the city's children, using long reeds as spears, weaving shields out of twigs, and brandishing small arrows and missiles, according to what each could do. As their elders looked on, both from the city and from the encampment, the city children came out of the gates of the wall, and our children came from the tents, to face each other in the middle of the field. There one could see the shock of combat, the shouts on both sides, and the bloody blows, delivered without mortal danger. Often these preliminaries incited the hearts of the adults to go to battle. For when they watched the souls burn within those weak limbs, and they saw such frail muscles eagerly wielding arms, the adults groaned at the sight of children on both sides being wounded, and moved the children off the battle field, rushing forward themselves to renew their usual fighting. Thus the Lord's army was scarcely found at rest; every day some were practicing, while others were fighting.

There was another kind of man in this army, who was bare-footed, carried no arms, and was not permitted to have any money. Dirty, naked, and poor, he marched in front of everyone, feeding on the roots of herbs, and on the most wretched things that grow. A Norman, well-born, said to have been formerly a knight, but now a foot-soldier, he saw them wandering without a leader, and laid aside his arms and the clothing he wore, wishing to declare himself their king. He had himself called Tafur, a term taken from the barbarian language. Among the pagans they are called Tafur whom we call, to speak less literally, Trudennes, that is, men who kill time, that is, who pass their time wandering aimlessly here and there. It was the Tafur's custom, whenever the people he was leading arrived at a bridge to be crossed, or at a narrow pass to be traversed, to rush forward to observe very carefully, and if he saw that anyone of his men possessed two deniers, he would quickly separate him from the general group, order him to purchase arms, and assign him to the section of the army that bore weapons. However, those in whom he saw a love of the simple life, who had no impulse or desire to save money, he made members of his inner circle. Perhaps some might think that these men were not useful for the general good, and that he could have fed others what he was uselessly giving to them. But no one can describe how useful they were in carrying food, in collecting tribute, in hurling stones during the sieges of cities. They were better at carrying heavy burdens than the asses and mules, and they were as good at hurling projectiles as the machines and launchers. Moreover, when pieces of flesh were found among the pagan bodies at Marra, and elsewhere, during a terrible famine, a hideous rumor (based on something that had been done furtively and very rarely) circulated widely among the pagans, that there were some men in the Frankish army who eagerly fed upon the corpses of Saracens. To circulate this rumor among them even more vividly, the men carried the battered corpse of a Turk out in full view of the other Turks, set it afire, and roasted it as if the flesh was going to be eaten. When they learned what had happened, thinking that the charade was real, they grew even more afraid of the fearlessness of the Tafurs than of our other leaders. Like the ancient pagans, the Turks were tormented more by unburied bodies than any Christian seems to be concerned with his soul or fears damnation. To incite their wrath even more fiercely, at the siege of Antioch the Bishop of Puy promulgated an edict throughout the army, offering an immediate reward of twelve deniers for every decapitated Turkish head brought to him. When the bishop received the heads, he ordered them placed on long poles, before the walls of the city, where the enemy could see them. When they saw this, they squirmed in anguish. The bishop also did something there, after consulting with our leaders, that I should not pass over silently; when the inhabitants of the city understood that our men were struggling because of the scarcity of food, our men proceeded to yoke bulls to the plow, to dig up and seed the ground in sight of the city. By this means the inhabitants of the city understood that no cause could compel them to abandon the siege that they had undertaken, since they were in the process of growing food for the next year. These and other remarkable things were done on this expedition, which we think can be described in their entirety by no one. No one in any age has ever heard that any nation, without a king, without a prince, departed from its own lands and that, under God only, both the lowly and the great learned to carry the yoke, so that the servant did not serve a master, nor did the lord claim anything more than brotherhood from the servant. Thus, I say, we cannot offer examples from the past to match this, nor do we think that anything like this will occur in the future. Our argument is based most of all on the fact that, after the capture of Jerusalem, we saw so many Christian nations moving, so many people of great dignity, so many battalions of noble knights, such a great number of foot-soldiers setting out after those who had preceded them and opened the way, that we understood that in wealth and in number we might judge that this second movement was scarcely inferior to the first. For who could describe how great a crowd of nobles, burghers, and peasants, from Frankish lands alone (of the others I say nothing) accompanied Count Stephen, whom we mentioned earlier, and Hugh the Great, brother of King Philip, when, later on, they again undertook the journey to the tomb of the Lord? Not to speak of the Count of Burgundy, what shall I say of the Count of Poitou, who brought not only a large group of knights, but a crowd of young girls as well? When his renown had been established everywhere, he came to Constantinople and held a conference with the tyrant Alexis, the most abominable of men. This wretched traitor informed the Turks by letters of his arrival, before the count had left the royal city. "Lo," he said, "the fattest sheep from France are moving in your direction, led by a foolish shepherd." What more can I say? The count went beyond the borders of the tyrannical prince; suddenly before him stood an army of Turks, who scattered, preyed upon, and conquered the disorganized foreigners. There Hugh the Great, struck in the knee by an arrow, after a long illness died, and was buried at Tharsa in Cilicia. They say that these things were done in the province called Satyria.[248]

But Count Stephen, with certain bishops of our kingdom, among whom were Hugh of Soissons, William of Paris, fine, noble men, who were splendid, accomplished young rulers, and Enguerrand of Laon – would that he had been as preeminent in his religious belief as he was in appearance and eloquence – together with many dignitaries of all ranks, entered the city of Constantinople. The emperor summoned them into his presence and rewarded their leaders with large gifts. They consulted with him on whether they should follow the route of the previous army, or some other, and he truthfully told them that they did not have enough horsemen to take a route different from that of the first expedition.

[248] It is not clear what this province is. The RHC editor tentatively suggests "Isauria."

However, thinking that they could do new things and do them better than those who had preceded them, they declared that they would go on to other regions. They also asked the emperor to give orders that they might purchase supplies anywhere in Grecian territory. He agreed, understanding that, in their insolence, they were in effect bringing about their own ruin, which he foresaw clearly, as he happily agreed to their error. They went into Paphligonia, a province unknown not only to pilgrims, but scarcely mentioned in Scripture, where for some unknown reason they were persuaded to enter the desert. The emperor urged them not to take more than forty days worth of supplies, and discouraged them from bringing more by promising that they could purchase supplies freely anywhere for their entire journey through the land. Therefore, having marched into these solitary depths, the mob foolishly moved forward, without supplies, hoping that the opportunity they had been promised to make purchases would come about, and they began to suffer from terrible hunger, swelling up and dying, and the army, which was following behind them, began to be annoyed by the stench of corpses lying everywhere. At times, when the leaders of the starving multitude castigated those in the rear for not more swiftly following the knights in front of them, to avoid sudden attack by the Turks, these men, driven by the pain of hunger, hoped and prayed that the Turks would actually come. Now they had almost reached the borders of Armenia, and the men were exhausted, and the animals dying of starvation, when thousands of Turks suddenly attacked. But the Franks, who seemed to be in charge of the front line, in spite of their weariness, easily drove off the enemy forces. The next day, when the Turks saw that the Franks had moved out of the front line, and the Lombards, Ligurians, and Italians had taken their places, alas, the enemy sensed the sluggishness of those in the front line and attacked fiercely. Those who were in the vanguard and carried the standards turned their backs shamefully, and the entire army, already too weakened by hunger to flee, lay open to hideous slaughter. Those who fled did not return in the direction whence they had come, nor did they move in a single group, so that they might at least form an organized retreat. Instead each turned his steps in whatever direction appealed to him, clearly going to his death. This pursuit and bloodshed continued steadily for almost eight days. In the army there was an archbishop of Milan, who had brought with him the cope, that is, the chasuble and alb (I don't know if he brought anything else) of Saint Ambrose. It was adorned with gold and gems so precious that nowhere on earth could anyone find its equal. The Turks took it and carried it off, and thus the foolish clerk was punished for having been insane enough to bring so sacred an object to barbarian lands. Such a slaughter of Christians of both sexes took place, so much money, clothing, gold and silver was taken, that this one victory was enough to recompense the Turks for the losses inflicted upon them by the first expedition. Of the 200,000 – or more, as some argue – Christians who were there, hardly 7000 remained alive. Count Stephen, together with several other leaders, including Harpin of Bourges, a splendid man, and Count Stephen of Beyond-the Saone, finally reached Jerusalem. When they arrived, the army of the emperor of

Babylon was at the city of Ramla, fighting Baldwin, who was now the king. The above-mentioned Harpin urged the king to delay battle until he could collect as many men as possible. The king said, "If you are afraid, run back to Bourges." Having spoken, he rushed unwisely into battle, lost all of his troops, was driven from the city of Ramla, and escaped alone. Many of his men were captured, and we still do not know what happened to many of them. Harpin was led away captive, was finally released, returned to France, and become a monk. Nothing certain is know about Stephen of Chartres, but he is believed to have been killed, although we have no evidence. Presumably he was shut up in a tower within Ramla, together with many others, but we have not yet been able to determine from the sources whether he was delivered into captivity or death, although we are inclined to believe that he died, since he has never been found. After victory, the Turks customarily decapitated the dead bodies, to carry them as trophies of victory, and with the heads removed, it is difficult to recognize someone from his decapitated body. The same doubt exists today about the fate of other great men. Meanwhile, the king himself, who, as we said, was the only one to escape, was mourned by his people, not only because they were threatened with death themselves, but because his death had been announced mockingly by the pagans. He himself, however, making his way through terrifying mountains known to very few men, two days later, if I am not mistaken, finally reached Jerusalem, which was expecting great dangers with justifiable grief. When he had swiftly collected whatever knights he could, together with the best foot-soldiers, he prepared to fight against the temporarily triumphant pagans. Therefore, at the moment that they thought the king was dead, he suddenly appeared with new troops, and fought with greater authority than before, driving them into flight, and piling up new carnage with his sword.

Since we have not described the death of King Godfrey, Baldwin's brother, because other material took precedence in the narrative, it is fitting that we briefly tell how his life came to an end, and where he is buried. They say that a certain neighboring pagan prince sent him gifts dipped, as became clear, in deadly poisons. He carelessly made use of them, thinking that he who had sent them was a friend; he fell ill suddenly, and died very soon afterwards. Some people, however, reject this opinion, and say that he died a natural death. He was, however, buried in accordance with the eternal redemption that his faith and life testified he had deserved, next to the very place of the Lord's Passion, thereby obtaining the monument which he had liberated, and which he had defended from being trampled and destroyed by the pagans. His remarkable humility and modesty, worthy to be imitated by monks, added glory to his already exemplary reign, for he would never wear the royal crown in the city of Jerusalem, out of consideration for the fact that the general author of all men's salvation, our Lord Jesus Christ, provoked human laughter by wearing a crown of thorns. As we said earlier, he died, and, believing him to be no less temperate and wise than his brother, they brought Baldwin from Edessa, and set him up as king of the new sacred Christian colony. In the brilliant nature of these men they recognized and loved the peaceful and modest behavior, the relentless courage, the fearlessness in the face of death, which exceeded what might be expected of royal majesty, as well as the great self-control, and an extreme generosity that exceeded their resources. Baldwin's loyalty towards his people and disregard of himself can be inferred from one event: in an expedition he was conducting against the enemies, to save a certain foot-soldier, he put himself in great peril, received a serious wound, and narrowly escaped death.

Meanwhile, there was something which very much frightened the many people who surrounded them about attacking our small group, and it frightens them no less today. The study of the stars, in which Westerners have only the mildest interest, is know to burn more brightly, because of its steady use and constant study, among the Easterners, where it had its origin. The pagans admit that they had received a prophecy, and a long time before the present misfortune they had predicted that they would be subjugated by the Christian people, but they were unable, because of their limited skill, to determine at what time the prophecies would be fulfilled.

Approximately twelve years before our leaders had gone on the journey to Jerusalem, Robert of Flanders, the elder count, about whom we spoke in the first book of this work, went to Jerusalem, with much wealth, to pray. He remained in the city for some days, wishing to see the holy places, and his generosity enabled him to learn much – even about what went on among the pagans. One day, as I learned from those who had accompanied the count, nearly all the inhabitants of the city assembled at the temple of Solomon; they held a meeting throughout the entire day, and finally returned home in the evening. The count was then received as a guest by an old, wise man, who had led a virtuous life by Saracen standards, for which reason they usually called him, "the Servant of God." When they returned to his house, he asked him why they had sat so long in the temple, and what was the nature of the difficult issues they had been disputing. The man replied, "We have seen unusual signs in the comings and goings of the stars, from which we have inferred that men of the Christian belief would come to these regions and would conquer us by means of steady and frequent victories in battle. Whether this should happen in a later time or closer to our own time, is profoundly uncertain. From this astronomical portent, however, it is very clear that these men, whom celestial judgement has permitted to conquer our people, and to drive us from our native shores, will, at a later time, be conquered by us, and will be driven by military force from the lands which they usurped. This celestial sign is in accord with a thorough and regular reading of the ancient texts of our faith, which openly state what the celestial brightness has indicated in a veiled manner." The words of this noble man are in harmony with the words of Kherboga's mother, which were given earlier. Nor do we at all doubt that for the same reason that she discouraged her son from fighting against the Christians, those who burned with desire to destroy Jerusalem restrained themselves, lest they oppose what was clearly a fatal decree by entering a battle. If at first they seemed to attack us in many battles, now they fought less eagerly, since they understood that they were not fighting against us, but against God, who was exerting himself and fighting for us. However, if it seems unbelievable to anyone that someone might be able to learn the future through the art of astrology, this argument seems clear evidence to us: the emperor Heraclius, through this kind of study, foresaw that a circumcised race would rise up against the Roman empire, but he was unable through this method to foresee that it would not be the Jews, but the Saracens who would do this. Let us also consider the Magi who, when they discerned by a swift inspection of a star that a king would be born, and that he would be both God and man, also knew over whom he would rule, although they could not have known, by means of the method mentioned, had a divine light not pointed the way.

In this new battle of God against diabolical men, it will be worthwhile considering the many apparent resemblances between what happened and what happened to Gideon.[249] Although everyone considered the infinite number of our men sufficient for the undertaking, they were tested by the waters, that is, pleasures and delights. That is, those who loved following God did not yield to the tortures of hunger and thirst, nor to the fear of various forms of death. But those who placed God after the interest of their bodies weakly submitted themselves to desires, symbolized by bent knees. Those who drank by bringing their hands to their mouths are those who, like Diogenes, heedless of all pleasures, intent on serving God, satisfied nature in whatever way was available. Three hundred were proven under Gideon, so that externally and internally they carried the cross, which, by means of the letter Tau, signifies the three hundred who were honored for their perseverance. Why did many of our men depart like wretches from the Lord's army, if not because they were in the grip of great, steady hunger, and because, "Without bread and wine, Venus is cold."[250] Because their bodies were so weak, none of them had the ability to perform sexually, and even if they wanted to, no opportunity presented itself. Therefore those who were found to be wise held trumpets in their hands, because they offered divine speech, the only solace among so many hardships, in their works. They hold vessels because, continually preparing for battle, they restrained themselves from all the foulness of carnality. Within the vessels they hold lamps, because in the vessels of the bodies the brilliant treasures of pious intention shine more brightly than any light. That Gideon divided them into three parts may be interpreted in the following ways: Christ draws some of them to the crown when they pour out their own blood; others he brings to guard the sacred city, to preserve the promised land, and through these few men today, he resists the entire empire of the East; still others he permitted to return to their native land as testimony to such a victory, and to urge others to emulate their own pious exile. Therefore when the vessels are broken the lamps shine forth, because, when their bodies died, the spirits burning with divine love emigrated directly to God. The frightened enemies were defeated, because they rightly feared those men who, brave with the

[249] Judges 6, 7, 8.

[250] Terence, *Eunuch* 4.6.6.

spirit of eternity, embraced death more dearly than life. As the Apostle says,[251] "For the bodies of those beasts whose blood is brought into the sanctuary by the high priest are burned without the camp." Therefore God suffered beyond the gate. Thus they went out of the camp to him, that is, beyond the desires of the flesh, by carrying his shame, the mortification of the cross, in the midst of sinful desires.

The value of taking up this great task, along with the emotion of good will can be inferred from considering the one example that we have offered on this topic, which we think clearly demonstrates how much those who devoutly undertook the pilgrimage, after confession and sincere repentance, profitted, if it did such great good for those who were almost without penitence and confession, and if it even struck terror into the heart of the devil.

A man of knightly rank, living on the shore of the sea, lost his brother in the fighting. Hardly able to bear his death, he wore himself out in inconsolable grief, since the man who had killed him seemed so strong that the grieving man's hope of vengeance had been entirely extinguished. Worn out by intolerable grief, his mind dwelling at every moment and in every place upon his brother, the pain of his irreparable loss increased each day; without hope of solace, the poor man was tortured by the inescapable memory, until the difficulty of obtaining vengeance increased his distress so greatly that the devil, whose long experience had made him crafty, shrewder by nature than any mortal, on the lookout everywhere for occasions and motivations, smiled at the opportunity provided by his excessive grief. Therefore, on a certain day, worn out by putrifying internal anguish, gasping with the deepest weariness, he mounted his horse and brought it to drink at a river, where he saw the devil standing on the other side. He appeared in the guise of a man with crooked legs, whom he often used to see. He seemed to be a knight, holding a sparrow-hawk in his hand, wearing his usual orange-yellow tunic. After watching him from afar, and remembering the weakness and the look of the man whom he thought he had known, he was struck by the unexpected change, when the evil spirit, mindful of its ancient effrontery, spoke first: "I am not who you think I am: know that I am a Devil, sent to offer a remedy for the torment you undergo every day. My master, who compassionately deigns to help all those who suffer, if they submit to him, sent me to you. If you obey him, just as I say, your relief will not be delayed. For since he is generous, and possesses an infinite treasure of things to be distributed to those with a desire for riches, he gives lavish and incalculable gifts; to those in need he provides assistance beyond their wildest hopes. Therefore you, who bitterly bewail an old misfortune that remains ever new, if you have a complaint, share it, certain in the knowledge that you will receive far more than you might dare to ask for. In the case of your dead brother, you can certainly hasten to take vengeance; if you want increased wealth, you will be amazed to see your wish granted. Therefore ask for what you want, and your

[251] Hebrews 13.2.

ability will be equal to your wish." He had been watching this truly unusual creature, stunned that the devil was speaking, both attracted by the alluring offer and frightened by the enormity of the one making the offer. However, finally carried away by his desire for what he was being promised, he said that he would gratefully accept the Devil's offerings. "However," the Devil said, "if the fruits of my offerings appeal to you, and the freely given benevolence of my prince, who sent me to you, captivates you, when you have truly experienced the results of what I have said, both about avenging your brother and adding to your wealth, then my master requires that you offer him homage, by promising to transfer your allegiance from the Christian faith to cling indivisibly to him, and by abstaining from those things that he forbids. There are certain things that he wishes you to agree never to do: never enter a church, or accept baptism from a sacred font." He also forbad a third thing, which escaped the memory of the person who told me about this. The man replied to him: "I can adhere to these prohibitions easily and without delay, but I ask for a short delay on the subject of offering homage." Since he had the free use of his rational faculty, the man very much abhorred the execrable change of faith that was being demanded of him, but he thought that it was more tolerable to abstain from Christian practices than to lose the foundation of his belief. Finally, without delay, the opportunity for taking vengeance for his brother, following the suggestions of the Devil, was offered to him, in such a way that the fondest wishes of the man were far surpassed by his increasing good fortune. In this way, as the remedy grew more effective, the bitterness of his grief gradually diminished, but meanwhile he did not dare violate any of the Devil's prohibitions. The ancient enemy of mankind continued to appear to him regularly, not only, as he used to do, when he was alone, or in out of the way places, but in the midst of a crowd of people he would suddenly make an unexpected appearance, point out the benefits he had already received, offer him better ones in the future, and insistently urge him to transfer his faith to him. The man, however, extremely grateful for the generosity he had received, promised eternal obedience to the generosity of the prince, but in the matter of the homage which was often demanded of him, he continually begged for delays. Therefore, while he was being pressed insistently by these appearances, even invisible ones in the midst of large crowds, news of the journey to Jerusalem spread, by the will of God, throughout the Latin world. Whoever felt that he was caught in sin was directed thither, where God showed a new way to repent. Among them this man chose to set out, although he had not confessed the foul pact he had already almost entirely concluded with the Devil. Thus this man, eager to emulate God, although not in keeping with doctrine, in that he had not confessed his sins before beginning his good works, was accompanied by such an abundance of the grace of God on the journey, and his labor was so pleasing to God, even though his efforts were not performed out of pure piety, that while traveling on this expedition the grim overseer did not dare to harass him. Moreover, as though he had no memory of the pact he had made, he never in any way appeared to him in a vision. After the capture of Jerusalem, when he was staying in the city with the others, one night, while he was thought to be asleep, along with the other soldiers, he became concerned about the horses that belonged to him and to his companions, who were resting under the sky, as was the custom in that region, and he went to look at them. Seeing the figure of a man standing among them, and suspecting that he was a thief, he got up and asked, in a disturbed voice, who he was. In his usual manner, as though pious and humble, he replied to him: "Don't you know me?" And he, as though reminded of his old shame, replied with great severity: "I know you." After this initial exchange, the one offered no further questions, and the other added nothing to his reply. Although this apparition seems to have been idle, we know that it is of no idle significance to us, by God's dispensation; the Devil had not forgetfully passed him by, but had announced, by his appearance, what he wanted, and had indicated, by his silence, what he was unable to ask for. What more should I say? He went home, but on his way home the Devil never showed himself, or made any trouble. But a short time after he arrived home, he who provides wretched men with wicked counsel was aroused, so that the man had very few moments free from admonishments of this kind; men may put some distance between themselves and what they fear, and their rooms and walls may separate them from their anxieties, but neither the presence of other people, nor the locks on doors can protect them from their spiritual crimes, no matter where they go. One day, the man who had undergone excruciating, deadly suffering at the hands of the indivisible thief happened to meet a priest of Christ, distinguished for his learning, gentleness, and pious cheerfulness, whose name was Conon. When he had described, in the little time available (each was concerned with his journey), how much he had endured, the good man gave him whatever comfort he was able to give, extracted the promise that he would return, and sent him on his way. However the cruel beast did not remain silent, but persistently continued to offer enticements. The man soon grew weary of the burdensome and almost daily incursions, and returned to the doctor, made a clean confession, eagerly undertook penitence, and, once he had begun repentance, never again saw his tormentor. By this example we can understand how valuable the pilgrimage must have been for the pure in heart, since it offered so much defense and support for the impure.

It is also significant that for good reasons kings were excluded from participating in the grace to be earned from this journey, lest the visible royalty seem to arrogate to itself divine operations.[252] Therefore praise should be offered to the heavenly Lord, and utter silence to the human being. No leader assembled so many soldiers, or deserved so many triumphs. Regulus deserved praise for beat-

---

[252] Three times in the course of the last book of the *Gesta Dei* Guibert finds something positive in the absence of Western kings on the expedition to Jerusalem. Among the practical reasons for their absence: (1) Philip I and the Holy Roman Emperor were excommunicate at the time; (2) William Rufus was anticlerical and otherwise occupied; (3) the Italian rulers were absorbed with local problems.

ing the Phoenician rebels. Alexander, battling the Eastern kingdoms, worn out with great battles, managed to acquire the name of the Great. However, Count Stephen, who had been granted the leadership of the holy army, like a man who had recklessly usurped those things that properly belong to God alone, was rejected as though charged with cowardice. And Hugh the Great, in effect, a man of royal name, was put aside. Therefore, when the "shades of a great name"[253] were rejected, and the power which had supported them was removed, the little people remained, relying now on God's aid only. And when things were decided, not according to birth, but according to God's choice, the unexpected one wore the crown.[254] God, who makes miracles, did not want the glory of his name given to another, for he was the sole leader, he was the king, the chastiser, who brought things from their beginnings to their conclusions, who extended his kingdoms this far. Therefore he gathered into *his*, not *their* arms, the lambs whom he had made out of wolves, raised them, children filled with the joy of pious hope, to the protection of his bosom, and he carried them to what they had longed to see.

As we were about to put an end to the body of the present history, we discovered, with the aid of the author of the world, that a certain Fulker, a priest of Chartres, who had for a long time been the chaplain for Baldwin at Edessa, had spread word, in a manner different from ours, about a few other things that were unknown to us, and these were erroneous and in rough language. We decided to include some, though certainly not all, of this material in these pages. Since this same man produces swollen, foot-and-a-half-long words,[255] and pours forth the blaring colors of vapid rhetorical schemes, I prefer to snatch the bare limbs of the deeds themselves, with whatever sack-cloth of eloquence I have, rather than cover them with learned weavings. Unless I am in error, at the beginning of his little work he says that some of those who set out on the journey to Jerusalem arranged for boats and sailed across the sea that separates Apulia and Epirus, and, whether because they committed themselves to a sea that was unknown to them, or because the ships sank because overloaded, it is reported that the ship carrying nearly 600 men was dashed to pieces. After they were drowned in the roaring sea during a storm, and quickly washed up on shore by the force of the waves, signs of the cross which they all wore on their cloaks, tunics, and mantles were found on the skin of their shoulders. No one, that is, of the faithful, doubted that the sacred stigma could have been imprinted on their skin by God, to make their faith manifest, but the man who wrote it, if he is still alive, had to think carefully about whether it actually happened. For when the beginning of this journey was announced everywhere among the Christian people, and it was proclaimed throughout the Roman Empire in accordance with God's will, men of the lowest social class, and even worthless women, laid claim to this miracle in every way, in every part of their bodies. One man scratched his cheeks, drew a cross with the

---

[253] Lucan I.135.
[254] Eccl. 11.5.
[255] Horace, *Ars Poetica* 97.

flowing blood, and showed it to everyone. Another showed the spot in his eye, by means of which he had been blinded, as a sign that a heavenly announcement had urged him to undertake the journey. Another, either by using the juices of fresh fruits, or some other kind of dye, painted on some little piece of his body the shape of a cross. As they used to paint the area below the eyes with antimony, so they now painted themselves green or red, so that, by means of this fraudulent and deceitful exhibition, they might claim that God had showed himself in them. The reader will remember the abbot of whom I spoke above, who cut his forehead with iron, and who I said was made the Bishop of Caesarea in Palestine. I swear by God that I saw, when I was living in Beauvais, in the middle of the day, clouds approach each other somewhat obliquely, so that they scarcely seemed to form anything other then the shape of a crane or a stork, when suddenly many voices from everywhere in the city cried out that a cross had been sent to them in the sky. What I am about to say is ridiculous, but has been testified to by authors who are not ridiculous. A poor woman set out on the journey, when a goose, filled with I do not know what instructions, clearly exceeding the laws of her own dull nature, followed her. Lo, rumor, flying on Pegasean wings, filled the castles and cities with the news that even geese had been sent by God to liberate Jerusalem. Not only did they deny that this wretched woman was leading the goose, but they said that the goose led her. At Cambrai they assert that, with people standing on all sides, the woman walked through the middle of the church to the altar, and the goose followed behind, in her footsteps, with no one urging it on. Soon after, we have learned, the goose died in Lorraine; she certainly would have gone more directly to Jerusalem if, the day before she set out, she had made of herself a holiday meal for her mistress. We have attached this incident to the true history so that men may know that they have been warned against permitting Christian seriousness to be trivialized by belief in vulgar fables.

Finally, the same author claims that God appeared to Pyrrus, the man who betrayed Antioch, and commanded him in a vision to betray the city. This was easy to do for him who made himself audible to Cain and Hagar, and made an angel visible to an ass. Certainly all those who returned after the capture of the sacred city, and who sent to us letters about the things that happened, particularly Anselm of Ribemont, said no such thing. Anselm makes no mention of Pyrrus, but reveals that it was betrayed by three men. According to the letter, before the three leaders engaged in serious discussions about handing over the city, they offered us a false peace, promising that they would soon thereafter give up the city. The mutual confidence that resulted was so great that they sometimes welcomed Franks within the walls of the city, and their men often mingled with ours. But when our army became less watchful and too comfortable, the Turks set ambushes and killed some Franks, and themselves suffered losses. There our men lost an excellent young man, who had been the constable for the King of the Franks, and his name was Gualo.[256]

---

[256] Robert the Monk, RHC.HO III, p. 794, provides a longer passage on Gualo.

Fulcher denies the discovery of the Lord's Lance, claiming that the man who discovered it was exposed as false, and punished by death in the trial by fire which he undertook. Not only do recent testimonies contradict him on this event, but the most pious ancient writers stipulate that long ago, when they visited the Holy Places, before the Turks invaded the kingdoms of the East and of Syria, they used to worship and kiss this same lance in that city. Will the cleverness of the priest Fulcher, who, while our men were suffering from starvation at Antioch, was feasting at ease in Edessa, prevail over the inspired work of the wise men who died at the time that it was found? Baldwin, who ruled this Edessa after the previous Baldwin, in his letter to Archbishop Manassa said that it was found by means of the revelation of Saint Andrew, and that it instilled bravery and faithful confidence in our men to battle the attacking Turks. Was the worthy Bishop of Puy so foolish as to have carried a lance of questionable authenticity with such reverence when he went out to fight Kherboga? A certain memorable event occurred there: when Kherboga ordered the grass to be burned, the bishop saw that the dense smoke was pouring into the faces and eyes of the Franks as they rushed into battle, and he held the holy Lance in front of him, while, with his pious right hand, he made the image of the cross in the face of the rising smoke, tearfully imploring the aid of all-powerful Jesus; then, swifter than speech, his piety sent the round mass of foul smoke right back at those who had sent it. In addition, to speak about the death of the man who found the Lance, who is said to have died a few days after undergoing the trial by fire, I shall say how he died, although no one is certain whether he was harmed by the flames, if they tell me why he who had received the gift of tongues according to Gregory destroyed his limbs with his own teeth.

Furthermore, if I am not mistaken, he adds that, while they were maintaining the siege of Antioch, a brilliant red light, like a fire, shone in the night above the army, and it also unmistakably took the form of a cross. Some of the wise men there related the fire to future battles, and said that the appearance of a cross was a sign of certain salvation and victory to come. We do not call this an error, for many witnesses confirm this testimony. About this, I say, leaky Parmeno should be able to keep silent.[257] Something like this occurred at the beginning of the journey, which I happened to pass over earlier[258] when I spoke of the movements of the eclipses and shooting stars which were seen. One day during the summer, towards evening, such a great fire appeared in the Northern sky that many people rushed from their homes to find out who was the enemy destroying their lands with such flames. All these events we firmly believe to have been portents of the wars which were to come. And now, having put aside the things that we thought might be treated separately, let us return to the order of the narrative.

No one can express how courageously Jerusalem was defended by its inhabitants

---

[257] In Terence's *Eunuch* (I.ii.105), the slave Parmeno says he can keep silent about the truth, but must immediately speak (or leak) what is a lie.
[258] RHC IV 149F.

during the siege. You would have seen how they had learned to hurl stones at the ballistic machines, how to cover their walls with timber and mats, and how to hurl what they called Greek fire at the machines, since they knew that the greatest difficulty for the besiegers was the lack of material. But the Franks, known for their cleverness, quenched the raging fire by sprinkling vinegar on it; in addition, they struck with sharp scythes anything found hanging over the walls. The Saracens added iron hooks to their long spears, with which they struck our men who, dressed in cuirasses, were fighting from the tops of machines; drawing their swords, our men made sticks out of their spears. But what best showed the vehement commitment of the Saracens was the fact that when one of them was struck by one of our men, the shield of the man who had been struck was snatched up, quicker than speech, by another man, who took up the place from which the first had fallen, so that none of our men could have known that his blows had wounded any of them.

When the city was fortunately captured, Bohemund, who had won the right to rule, by means of the hunger, cold, and loss of blood suffered by the Franks, preferred to remain there, rather to go on to trouble about liberating the tomb of Jesus Christ. And while he was inappropriately fighting to win a house and small tower, he lost the fruit and joy of all of his previous labor. What good would it have done him to run, when he was unwilling to understand in which direction to go? However, since he had until this time performed so well for the army of the Lord, both in arms and in counsel, it is not inappropriate to weave a few words into the text at this point, to indicate how it came about that he went. When he sent a messenger to Baldwin at Edessa, asking him also to come with him to look at the tomb of the Savior, Baldwin held back from rushing off to besiege the city, not because he was greedy, but because he had to look after his own city. The city was filled with Christians, and often endured the attacks of the surrounding Gentiles. After the man had promised to go on the journey, both men gathered large numbers of knights and foot-soldiers, since they feared not only those, but nearly everyone in the surrounding territory, and they set off for Jerusalem. After they had pitched their tents together, and nearly 20,000 men had assembled, a terrible lack of food began to assail them, so that they had nothing to put on their bread, and no bread on which to put anything. The supplies of the provinces, drained by the constant, various sieges, and the extended and lengthy expeditions that had passed through them, were in no way sufficient to maintain so many animals and men. Therefore the multitude, driven by the wretched lack of food, again resorted to their earlier strategy of eating the flesh of asses and horses, and they not desist from this practice until they reached the longed-for city of Tiberias, famous for having fed 5000 men under the Lord's guidance. There for a little while their mad hunger was relieved by a plentiful supply of food, and then they went on at last to Jerusalem, where they found a huge number of stinking bodies, hacked to pieces, so that they could not breathe without the stench penetrating their noses and mouths. They were welcomed joyfully by King Godfrey, and they remained there because Christmas was approaching. They celebrated Christmas at Bethlehem, as the judgement of reason would dictate, not only because they had come together there with a mutual purpose, but also because of the unexpected victory granted in their own time, which aroused unbelievable celebration among the Franks. After they left, each for his own territory, Bohemund was attacked by a large Turkish force as he was entering a certain city, and led away as a captive to a distant region of Persia. When news of this event reached the illustrious Tancred, he hurried as quickly as he could to occupy Antioch, and to fortify Laodicea, since both were under Bohemund's control. Robert, the Count of Normandy, held Laodicea first, but when the city's inhabitants could no longer bear the taxes levied by this prodigal man, they drove the guards from the citadel, freed themselves from his authority, and, out of hatred for him, abjured the use of the coinage of Rouen. After some years in prison, Bohemund's release was finally obtained by a treaty and a ransom.

Since much has been said earlier, my praise of Godfrey's great knightly prowess can be brought to a conclusion by using the words of the Baldwin whom I just mentioned, the son of Count Hugo of Rethel.[259] When King Baldwin came to the throne he was put in charge of Edessa, but, alas, a band of Turks attacked him[260] and he was imprisoned by the pagans, and if he is alive, he is still there. This is what he said, although clothed in my words, about Godfrey: "It happened on the holiday of Saint-Denis. The king was returning from a city called Morocoria, and 120 Turks lay in ambush, while he was accompanied by only twenty knights. Fearlessly we awaited their attack, gripping our arms, while they, because they had attacked suddenly, thought that we would flee because we were so few. But we, made more audacious by the aid we had continually experienced from God, upon whom we relied spiritually, attacked the barbarians, and wreaked such havoc upon them, that we killed eighty men and captured ninety horses." Then he remembered, with a mocking smile, those who had fled from Antioch, and those who, after they had carried out their mission in Constantinople, had put off returning, and, to inspire the Franks who had remained in France, he added the following about his own fortune: "We have a vast fortune, and, not counting the treasures that belong to others, ten castles that belong to me alone, and an abbey pay me annually a total of 1500 marks. And if God favors my taking Aleppo, I shall soon have 100 castles under my command. Do not believe those who have retreated, claiming that we grow weary with hunger, but rather trust in my words."

When this king left his noble life for a more blessed future life, the inhabitants of Jerusalem, mindful of his temperance and mildness, and afraid of losing his nobility of lineage, sent ambassadors to his brother, the Duke of Edessa, to take control of the kingdom. He lived in splendor in his realm; whenever he went out he had a gold shield carried before him, which bore the image of an eagle, in the Greek manner. Like the pagans, he went about in a toga, let his beard grow, accepted bows from his worshippers, and ate on rugs laid on the ground. If he

---

259 1066–1118.   260 1104.

entered one of his towns or cities, two knights blew two trumpets before his chariot. Baldwin then yielded to the ambassadors and set off for Jerusalem. But when the neighboring pagans heard what he proposed to do, and saw him depart, they embarked in their ships, with a favoring wind, although in vain, since the duke was hurrying along the sandy banks of the sea, accompanied by a small group of men, while they rowed furiously, their prows plowing the waves, striving to intercept him, hurrying to bring their ship to the shore. But the duke,

with all of his mortal strength gone,[261]

in his great anguish called upon the Most High, promising that he would always obey Him and that he would rule the kingdom in accordance with Christian faith. And lo, the ships which had been moving as though they had wings now stood still as though stuck in mud, and the more each man struggled to sweep the sea with his oars, the more the hope was ridiculed by the steady backward movement of their boats. Thus the efforts of the unjust were confounded, and the duke remained deservedly free, seeing in this auspicious event a sign that heaven favored his assuming the purple. I have omitted mentioning the fact that Daimbert, the Bishop of Pisa, had already set out for Jerusalem, together with a group of his people, accompanied by the Bishop of Apulia, by Bohemund, and by this very duke.

After he accepted the kingdom, it is said that his first expeditions were undertaken against the Arabs. When he reached the slopes of Mount Sinai, he found a barbaric group of people, who resembled the Ethiopeans. He spared their lives because of their untamed behavior and ugliness. There, in the church which is called Saint Aaron, where God had given his oracles to our fathers, he prayed, and the army drank from the fountain of refutation, where, because Moses had drawn a distinction with his lips, and did not sanctify the Lord in the presence of the sons of Israel,[262] the Lord kept him from the promised land. Here the opinion of my priest has faltered, for it is is known that not Sinai, but the mountain Or, which forms the border of the ancient city of Petra in Arabia, was the place where Aaron lost his life, and water emerged from the depths of the rock which he struck.

In that holy city of Jerusalem, an ancient miracle renewed itself, and I call it ancient because the Latin world does not know when it begun. Our conjecture is that it began when, after the city had begun to be trampled by pagans, before our times, the Lord granted it both to those who lived there, and to those who happened to be there at that time. Every year, on the Sabbath of Easter, the lamp of the Lord's tomb seemed to be kindled by divine power; it was the custom in that city that the pagans went through everyone's house, extinguishing every fire, leaving only ashes in the hearths; the pagans made such a search, because they thought that the miracle was the product of the fraud, and not of the faith of the

---

[261] One dactylic hexameter.   [262] Numbers 20.2–13; 23.38.

faithful. When Vulcan had been turned out by this means from the city, at the hour at which our religion's law has determined that the Catholic people are to be present at the service of the solemn resurrection and baptism, you would have seen pagans moving throughout the basilica with their swords drawn, threatening to kill our people. You would also have seen those natives who worshipped our faith entrusting their profound grief to God, both those whose prayers had drawn them from the furthest reaches of the world, and those who had come because of the miracle, all to pray singlemindedly for the gift of light. Nor was there any unsuitable delay, but the passionate request was granted swiftly. I have heard from some old men who went there that the papyrus or wick (I don't know which of them was used) was once removed by a pagan's trick, and the metal remained empty, but, by means of a miracle from heaven, when light shone from the metal, he who wanted to defraud the heavenly powers learned that natural forces fight even against their own natures for their God.

In the year that Baldwin accepted the sceptre from his predecessor, it is said that the miracle was obtained with such difficulty that night was almost upon them before their prayers and tears were answered. The priest mentioned above delivered a sermon to the people, asking for sinners to confess; the king and the priest urged them to make peace among themselves, and they promised to remedy whatever was contrary to faith and to virtue. Meanwhile, because of the urgency of the matter, so many hideous crimes were confessed that day, that if penitence did not follow, it would have seemed correct for the sacred light to have been removed without delay; however, soon after the reproof, the lamp was lit. The next year, when the time came for the celestial flame to make the tomb glorious, all men lifted up their prayers from deep within. Greeks and Syrians, Armenians and Latins, each in his own language, called upon God and his saints. The king, the leaders, and the people, with penance and grief in their hearts, marched behind the priests; all men were racked with pain, because, since the day that the city was won by the Christians, things had happened there that they had never heard of happening under the pagans. Fulker of Charters, however, taking with him the chaplain of the patriarch Daimbert, went to the Mount of Olives, where the lamp of God used to appear when it did not come to Jerusalem. When they returned, bringing nothing to please the ears of the expectant Church, many sermons were delivered to the people, which gave no solace to those who were suffering, but rather cause for anguish. That day, when the miracle did not happen, everyone returned home; there was a double night, with bitter sadness tormenting their breasts. The next day they decided to make a procession, with appropriate mourning, to the Temple of the Lord. They went, without the joy of Easter, dressed no differently from the day before, when suddenly, behind them, the keepers of the temple proclaimed that the lamp of the sacred monument was lit. Why do I delay? On that day such grace shone, augmented abundantly by the delay, that the brilliance of God illuminated, although not simultaneously, but sequentially, approximately fifty lamps. Not only during the sacred mysteries, but even when the king, after services were over, ate in the palace, messengers came frequently to summon him to leave the table to see the lights newly lit. One cannot describe how much grief was changed to relief when, on that day, he agreed to what he never had consented to before, to be crowned king in that city, in the house of the Lord, in acknowledgement of the Lord's gift.

Then the Franks, who had redeemed the city with their blood, eager to see their parents, sons, and wives, and perhaps confident in their number and bravery, decided to return to their own sweet home by the same land route they had taken when they came. Although they thought that they would be able to pass freely through the land surrounding Nicea, which they had seized earlier, the Turks, who had been placed there by the emperor once the city had been turned over to him to impede the Franks when the occasion arose, put up strenuous resistance to them. Unless I am mistaken, my priest[263] says that they cut to pieces 100,000 men, but I fear that the man is wrong in offering such a number, because it is the case that he is eager to offer such guesses elsewhere. For example, he dares to estimate that those who set out for Jerusalem numbered 6,000,000.[264] I would be surprised if all the land this side of the Alps, indeed if all the kingdoms of the West, could supply so many men, since we know for a fact that at the first battle before the walls of Nicea scarcely 100,000 fully-equipped knights are reported to have been present. And if he was concerned with including all those who had gone on the journey, but who died, on land and on the sea, of sickness or hunger, in the various regions through which they passed, they still would not amount to such a great number of men. After the Franks, then, had suffered hideous carnage, most of those who had survived returned to Jerusalem, having lost what they owned. The generous king genuinely commiserated with them, gave them many gifts, and persuaded them to return to their homeland by sea.

But the Prince of Babylon, less concerned with the loss of Jerusalem than with the proximity of the Frankish settlement, set out to launch a heavy offensive against the new king, often striving to attack the port city of Acre. Count Robert of Normandy had besieged Acre when the army of the Lord was advancing to besiege Jerusalem, but Duke Godfrey had brought him away, in expectation of a more successful undertaking. The Babylonian then gathered a vast army and challenged the Christian king to battle. He gathered his small band, to whom the Lord said, "Fear not,"[265] and, setting his troops in order as well as he could, he attacked the impious ones. Killing them swiftly, like brute beasts, he scattered them, like a hurricane driving dust. A second time he sent his 9000 knights forward, supported by 20,000 Ethiopean common foot-soldiers. The pious king assembled against him scarcely 1000 knights and foot-soldiers, forming seven battalions out of them, and he sent them with great confidence directly at the thickest ranks of the enemy. When the prince saw far off a pagan knight, he rushed at him with such force that he drove his spear, together with its standard,

---

[263] Fulker.
[264] In RHC, p. 333, Fulker mentions 600,000.
[265] Luke 12.32.

into the man's breast, and when he pulled the spear from the wound, the standard remained in the man's breast. Frightened by the courage of the prince and his men, the enemy retreated at first, but their courage returned, because of the strength of their numbers, and they united to attack our men, compelling them to think of fleeing. They said that this misfortune had happened to them because, in their foolishness, they had not brought the cross of the Lord to this battle. They said that, guided by a Syrian or some Armenian, they found this cross, which, like the Lance, had lain buried somewhere. They drew a lesson from this incident, which was more a blemish of a victory in the process of being won than a defeat, and when the army of the Babylonian prince, as strong as the previous one, came forward to fight for the third time, the splendid king, together with what forces he could gather, deriving his confidence from God, went up against them. After he had drawn up his troops as well as he could, the clash of men was so great that, although the armies were unequal, both sides suffered severe losses, as 6000 pagan soldiers, and 100 Christians, lay dead. And because they had no prideful concern for banners with eagles and dragons, they raised aloft the sign of the humiliating Crucifixion, the Cross, and as praiseworthy conquerors drove their enemies to flight.

When they had been driven off, as was right, he assembled as much of a larger army as he could, and surrounded the extraordinary city of Palestinian Caesarea, with no concern for the number of men, but instead for their might. Siege engines were quickly built, many ballistic machines were drawn up around the walls, and a beam with a metal front, which was called a battering ram, was put in place. Towers were prepared and moved forward at different times, whose armed men not only rained down torrents of various kinds of missiles on the Saracens who were standing on the battlements of the walls, but who also struck and slew them with their swords. There you would have seen catapults with huge rocks not only striking the external walls, but delivering the weight of harsh blows to the city's lofty palaces. As they smashed the building and walls, they also used slingshots to scatter sticks burning with liquid lead, to set the town on fire. Meanwhile the battering-ram crashed against the walls; as it began to open a hole in the lower part of the wall, all the surrounding structures began to crack. Then, while the Franks struggled to enter, and eagerness to attack drove the Saracens to come forth, blood was shed on both sides. When one of our machines fell, killing many of our men, both sides became more courageous, for the Saracens, who do not like fighting in open combat, were remarkably competent when on the defensive. On the twentieth day of the siege, the king, supported by the best of his young knights, attacked the inhabitants fiercely, suddenly leaping from an assault tower, with one knight behind him, onto the wall, and driving the enemy into flight. The Franks swiftly followed the king, annihilating multitudes throughout the city, sparing no one, except the young women who could become slaves. Treasure was sought everywhere; they cut open not only chests, but the throats of the silent Saracens. When they were struck by a fist, their jaws yielded the besants that had been poured into them. They found pieces of gold in the wombs of the women who had used these areas for purposes other than the ones for which they were intended. A contingent of Franks was promptly left to guard the captive city, and shortly thereafter the king marched to Acre, wore it down with daily attacks, until it submitted to his authority. He is known to have captured many other cities, but since they were located in the middle of the insane pagans, he could not be sure that our colonists would be safe there. The series of battles and victories made the Saracens increasingly contemptible to the Christians; for example, here is something that we learned happened last year.

A certain knight,[266] whom the king had made prefect of the city of Tiberias, behaved insolently towards the king. Angry at the man's insolence, the king ordered him to leave the land he had been given. He hastened to leave, taking with him as his retinue two armed knights, and soon encountered a large troop of pagans. Putting his trust not in the number of his own men, but in God, he tore his shirt, which they call an undertunic, placed it as a banner on his spear, and commanded his companions to do the same. They did so, cried out loudly, spurred their horses forward, and charged headlong at their enemies. Frightened by the sudden attack, and thinking that a large army was following these men, they fled, leaving themselves mortally vulnerable to these three men. Many were killed, and more booty was taken than they could carry. Returning after this event, grateful to God, he was moved to prostrate himself before the king and he promised that he would faithfully obey him from that point on.

Once, when the king was suffering from a great lack of money, and did not have enough to pay the monthly stipend to his knights, divine mercy suddenly and miraculously granted aid. Things had become so difficult that the servants and knights were thinking of leaving, when the young men of Joppa, washing themselves, or rather enjoying a swim in the sea, on a certain day found in the swirling sand and water sacks filled with large amounts of gold, which the Venetians had lost here in a shipwreck. Brought to the king, they offered solace to everyone, an amazing miracle, both to the king, who had been close to despair, and to the new Christian community.

But since the charge has been spread about that the king repudiated his wife, here is what is said about it. His wife was descended from the finest pagans in the land, and in obedience to him, she followed her husband to Jerusalem, arriving by ship at the port of Saint-Simeon. There she was transferred to a faster ship, in an attempt to make the trip more quickly, but she was brought by unfavorable winds to a certain island inhabited by Barbars. The islanders seized her, killed a bishop of her retinue, together with some other officials, and, after holding her captive for some time, finally released her. When she reached her husband, the king, suspicious, and not unreasonably, of the Barbars' sexual incontinence, banished her from his bed, changed her mode of dress, and sent her to live with other nuns in the monastery of Anne, the blessed mother of the virgin mother of God.

---

[266] The *Gesta Francorum* gives his name: Gervais de Bazoches.

He himself was glad to live the celibate life, because, "his struggle was not against the flesh and blood, but against the rulers of the world."[267]

Around the time of Easter last year, the knight I mentioned earlier, whom we called the prefect of Tiberiad, and who had been victorious in that battle, was involved in another encounter, less fortunate for our men, in which he was captured, and brought alive by the pagans to a city belonging to them. During I don't know which one of their sacrilegious celebrations, they brought this knight out and urged him to renounce and to abjure his own belief. Splendidly obdurate, he rejected such criminal behavior, and was horrified even to hear such a suggestion. This praiseworthy man was immediately seized, tied, as they say, to a tree that stood in the middle of a field, and was torn by a hail of arrows from all sides. The crown was then sawed from his head, and the rest was made into the form of a cup, as though to hold drinks for the King of Damascus, by whose orders these acts had been done, to frighten our men. By dying to preserve the confession of his faith, this knight made himself a martyr who would be known for ages to come. His name was Gervais, of noble blood, from the castle of Basilcas[268] in Soissons.

These are the things that, by the grace of God, we have found out from entirely reliable men up to this day. If, in following the opinions of other men, we have said anything false, we have not done so with the intention of deceiving anyone. We are grateful to God, the Redeemer of this holy City, through the efforts of our people. For when the siege of the city began, He himself revealed, to an anchorite living in Bethania, as the story has been reliably told to us, that the city would be besieged furiously, but that it would be entered on Easter day, at the hour at which Christ was brought to the cross, to demonstrate that He again redeemed it from its afflictions by the suffering of his own limbs. This anchorite then called together some of our leaders, and told them these things, which were all proven true by the manner in which the city was actually captured. We thank God for having composed these deeds with his own spirit, through our mouth. For the rest, if anyone thinks that we have not laid things out as diligently as Julius Caesar and Hirtius Pansa[269] did in the history of the Gauls, Spaniards, Pharsalians, Alexandrians, and Numidians, he should carefully consider the fact that the same people who waged the wars wrote them down. As a result, nothing general or particular that happened is omitted from their accounts. They tell how many thousands of men there were, how many from each region, who the princes were, to whom power was delegated, who the leaders and princes were on the other side, what the cavalry, what the lightly armed troops did, how many shields were pierced by javelins, and, if I may use their own words, "after the consuls and their

---

267 Ephesians 6.12.
268 Bazoches.
269 Aulus Hirtius, a contemporary of Caesar, and a continuator of Caesar's *Commentaries*, was nominated for the consulship of 43 B.C., together with C. Vibius Pansa, with whom either Guibert or his sources seem to have confused him.

officers had sounded the retreat," how many men were missing and wounded at the end of the battle. Since another profession detains us who write this history, and our confidence is not strengthened by what we saw, we have decided, in reporting what we have heard, to exercise restraint. Observing the discipline of the Julian Quirites,[270] the officers of the legions, the troops of cavalry, the common soldiers, and the cohorts were compelled to rally around their banners, and if the locations were favorable, and in suitable places they set up their encampments, as though they were towns or cities, with moats and towers. Before they set up battle lines, they occupied the neighboring mountains, taking into account the irregularities of the terrain, and they had large numbers of servants, workers, and expensive baggage. Since almost nothing like these arrangements and activities existed among our men, their deeds were due, I shall not say to Frankish courage, but rather to their strength and their aroused faith. Let those who wish say that I have omitted more than I have written: I prefer being less to being more. If anyone knows other things that were done, let him write what he please. We thank God and such victors, who, when they had no grain, learned to feed upon roots that they dug up. If anyone is in doubt about the name of the Parthians, whom we have called Turks, or of the Caucasus, let him read Solin on *Wonders*, Trogus-Pompeius on the origin of the Parthians, and Jordanus the Goth on the Getae. May God stand watch as this pious work comes to an end.

[270] i.e., Caesar's soldiers.

Lightning Source UK Ltd.
Milton Keynes UK
27 January 2010

149187UK00002B/82/A